ARISA

2

Natsumi Ando

Translated and adapted by
Andria Cheng

Lettered by
North Market Street Graphics

KC
KODANSHA
COMICS

A Kodansha Comics Trade Paperback Original.

Published in the United States by Kodansha Comics, an imprint of Kodansha USA Publishing, LLC., New York.

Publication rights for this English edition arranged through Kodansha Ltd., Tokyo.

First published in Japan in 2009 by Kodansha Ltd., Tokyo.

ISBN 978-1-935-42916-6

Printed in the United States of America.

www.kodanshacomics.com

2 4 6 8 9 7 5 3 1

Translator/Adapter: Andria Cheng
Lettering: North Market Street Graphics

CONTENTS

HONORIFICS EXPLAINED

Throughout the Kodansha Comics books, you will find Japanese honorifics left intact in the translations. For those not familiar with how the Japanese use honorifics and, more important, how they differ from American honorifics, we present this brief overview.

Politeness has always been a critical facet of Japanese culture. Ever since the feudal era, when Japan was a highly stratified society, use of honorifics—which can be defined as polite speech that indicates relationship or status—has played an essential role in the Japanese language. When addressing someone in Japanese, an honorific usually takes the form of a suffix attached to one's name (example: "Asuna-san"), is used as a title at the end of one's name, or appears in place of the name itself (example: "Negi-sensei," or simply "Sensei!").

Honorifics can be expressions of respect or endearment. In the context of manga and anime, honorifics give insight into the nature of the relationship between characters. Many English translations leave out these important honorifics and therefore distort the feel of the original Japanese. Because Japanese honorifics contain nuances that English honorifics lack, it is our policy at Kodansha Comics not to translate them. Here, instead, is a guide to some of the honorifics you may encounter in Kodansha Comics books.

-san: This is the most common honorific and is equivalent to Mr., Miss, Ms., or Mrs. It is the all-purpose honorific and can be used in any situation where politeness is required.

-sama: This is one level higher than "-san" and is used to confer great respect.

-dono: This comes from the word "tono," which means "lord." It is an even higher level than "-sama" and confers utmost respect.

-kun: This suffix is used at the end of boys' names to express familiarity or endearment. It is also sometimes used by men among friends, or when addressing someone younger or of a lower station.

-chan: This is used to express endearment, mostly toward girls. It is also used for little boys, pets, and even among lovers. It gives a sense of childish cuteness.

Bozu: This is an informal way to refer to a boy, similar to the English terms "kid" and "squirt."

Sempai/ Senpai: This title suggests that the addressee is one's senior in a group or organization. It is most often used in a school setting, where underclassmen refer to their upperclassmen as "sempai." It can also be used in the workplace, such as when a newer employee addresses an employee who has seniority in the company.

Kohai: This is the opposite of "sempai" and is used toward underclassmen in school or newcomers in the workplace. It connotes that the addressee is of a lower station.

Sensei: Literally meaning "one who has come before," this title is used for teachers, doctors, or masters of any profession or art.

-[blank]: This is usually forgotten in these lists, but it is perhaps the most significant difference between Japanese and English. The lack of honorific means that the speaker has permission to address the person in a very intimate way. Usually, only family, spouses, or very close friends have this kind of permission. Known as *yobisute*, it can be gratifying when someone who has earned the intimacy starts to call one by one's name without an honorific. But when that intimacy hasn't been earned, it can be very insulting.

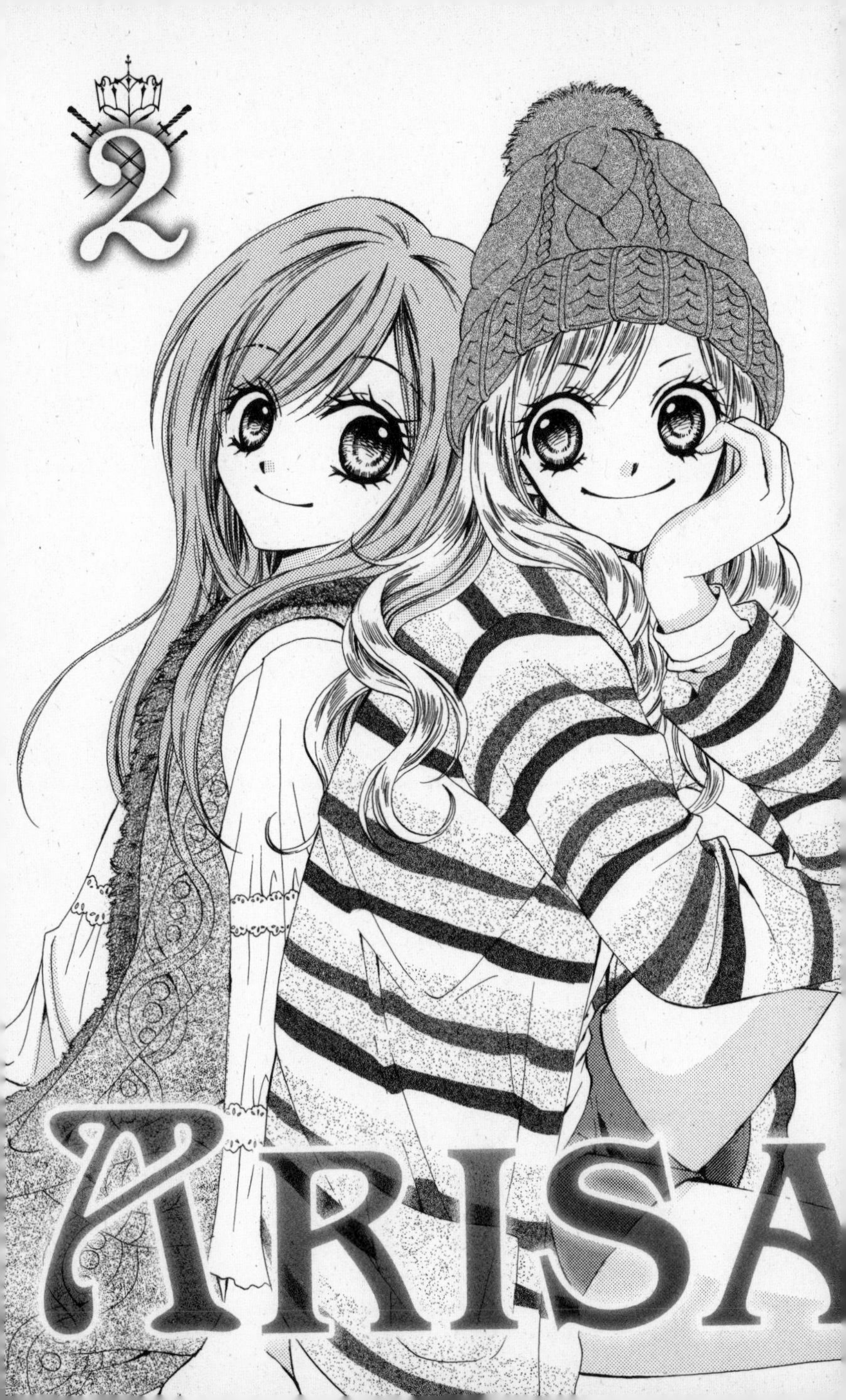
2
ARISA

Contents

ARISA

Secret King's Room

The story so far

Tsubasa and Arisa are twin sisters separated by their parents' divorce. They finally reunited after three years of being apart, but their happy time together came to a sudden end when Arisa jumped out her bedroom window right in front of Tsubasa, leaving behind a mysterious card...

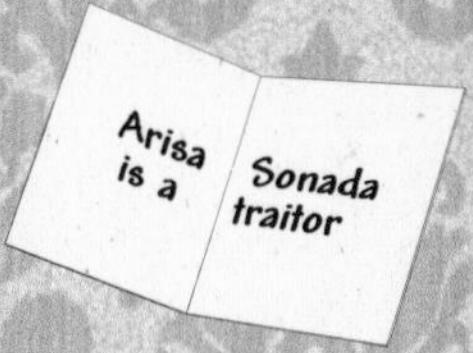

Arisa is a
Sonada traitor

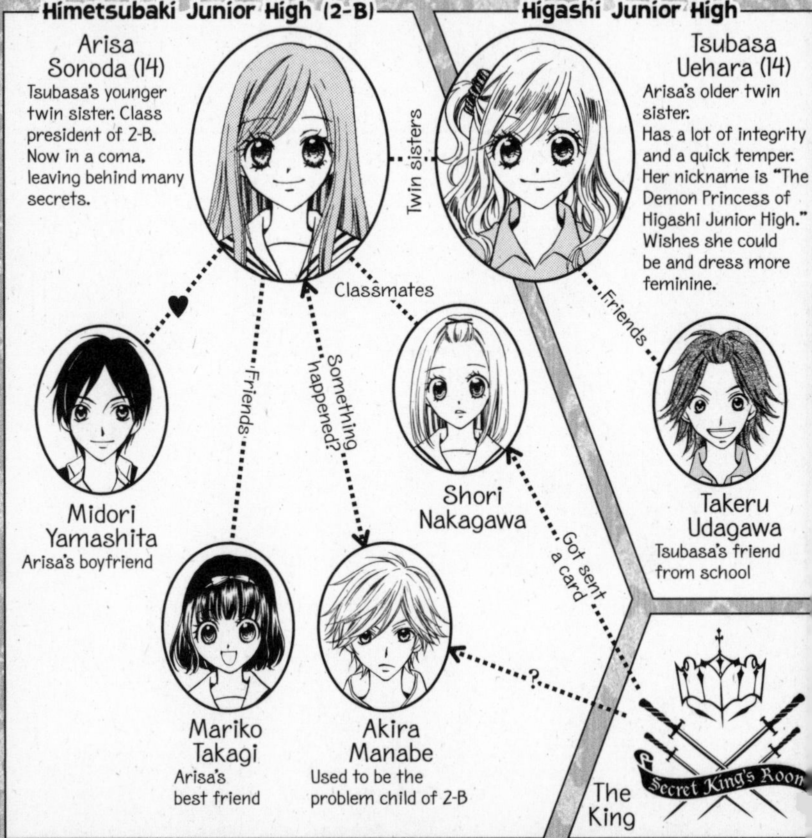

Himetsubaki Junior High (2-B)
Higashi Junior High
Arisa Sonoda (14)
Tsubasa's younger twin sister. Class president of 2-B. Now in a coma, leaving behind many secrets.
Twin sisters
Tsubasa Uehara (14)
Arisa's older twin sister.
Has a lot of integrity and a quick temper. Her nickname is "The Demon Princess of Higashi Junior High." Wishes she could be and dress more feminine.
Classmates
Friends
Midori Yamashita
Arisa's boyfriend
Friends
Something happened?
Shori Nakagawa
Takeru Udagawa
Tsubasa's friend from school
Got sent a card
?
Mariko Takagi
Arisa's best friend
Akira Manabe
Used to be the problem child of 2-B
Secret King's Roon
The King

In order to discover the secrets Arisa was hiding, Tsubasa pretended to be her and attended Himetsubaki Junior High. In Class 2-B, a mysterious internet presence called "The King" led strange incidents and bullying. Thinking it had something to do with Arisa's accident, Tsubasa investigated the identity of the King. Then, Akira Manabe confessed to her that he knew the King's true identity...

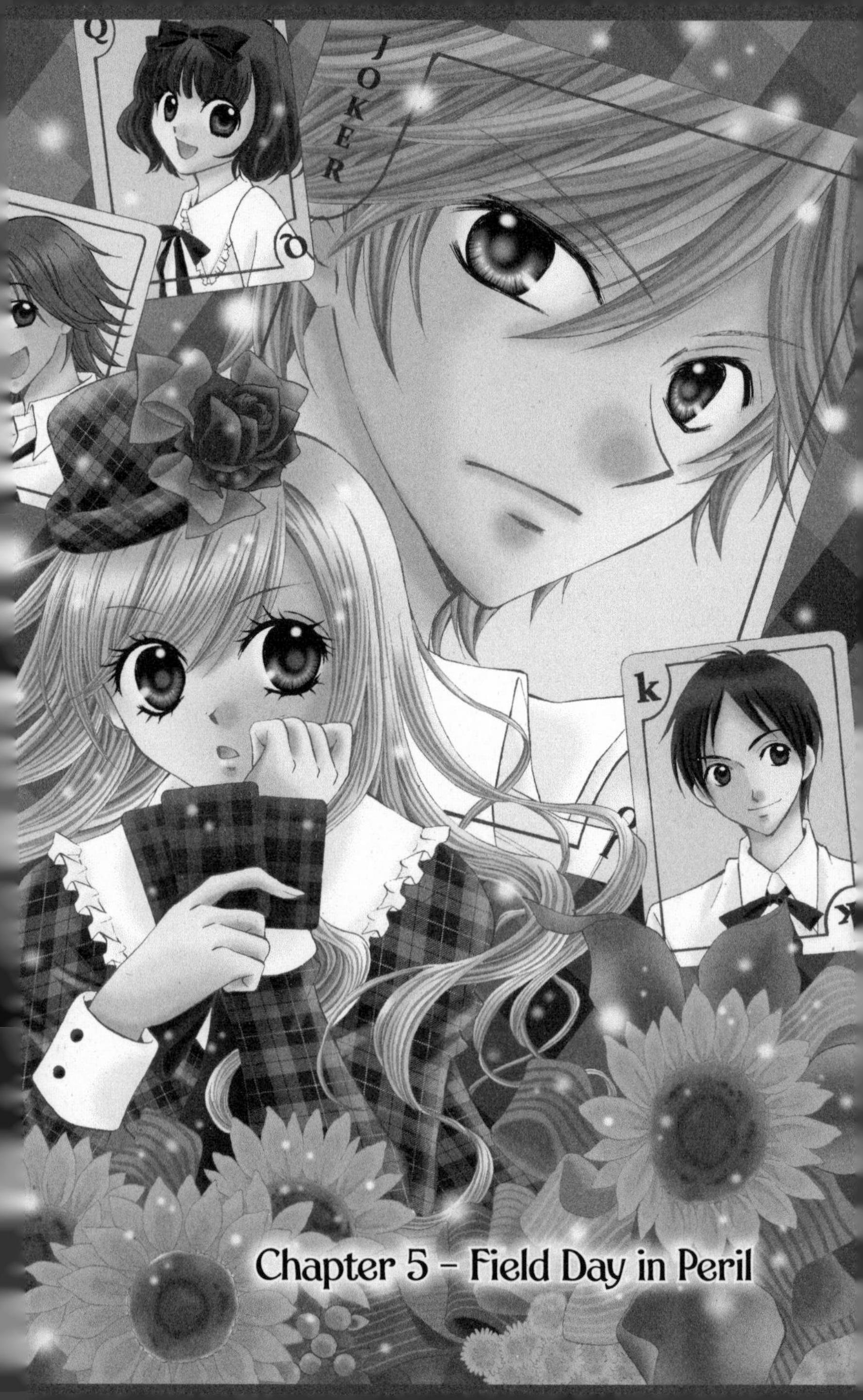
Q
JOKER
k

Chapter 5 - Field Day in Peril

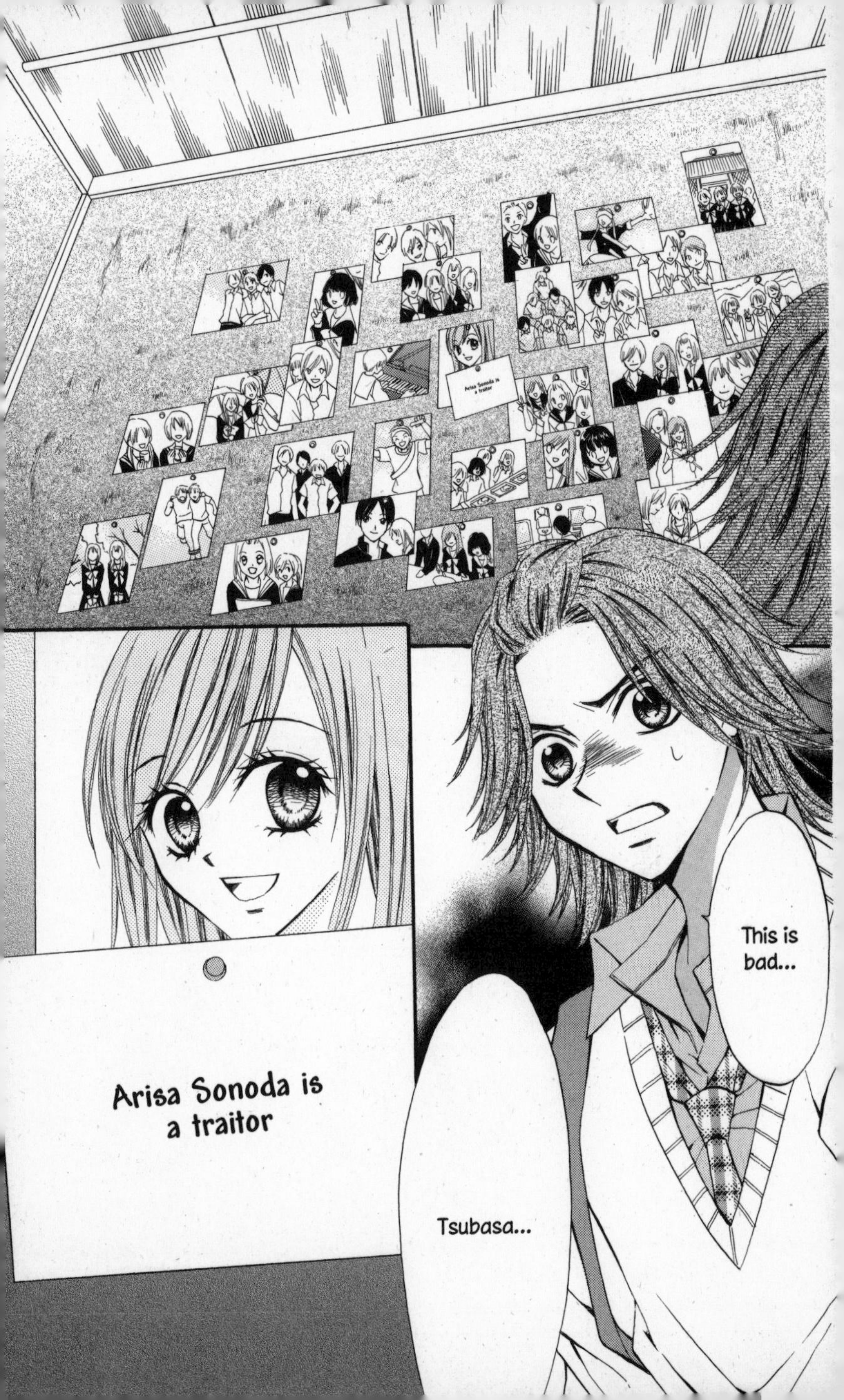
Arisa Sonoda is a traitor
This is bad...
Tsubasa...
Arisa Sonoda is a traitor

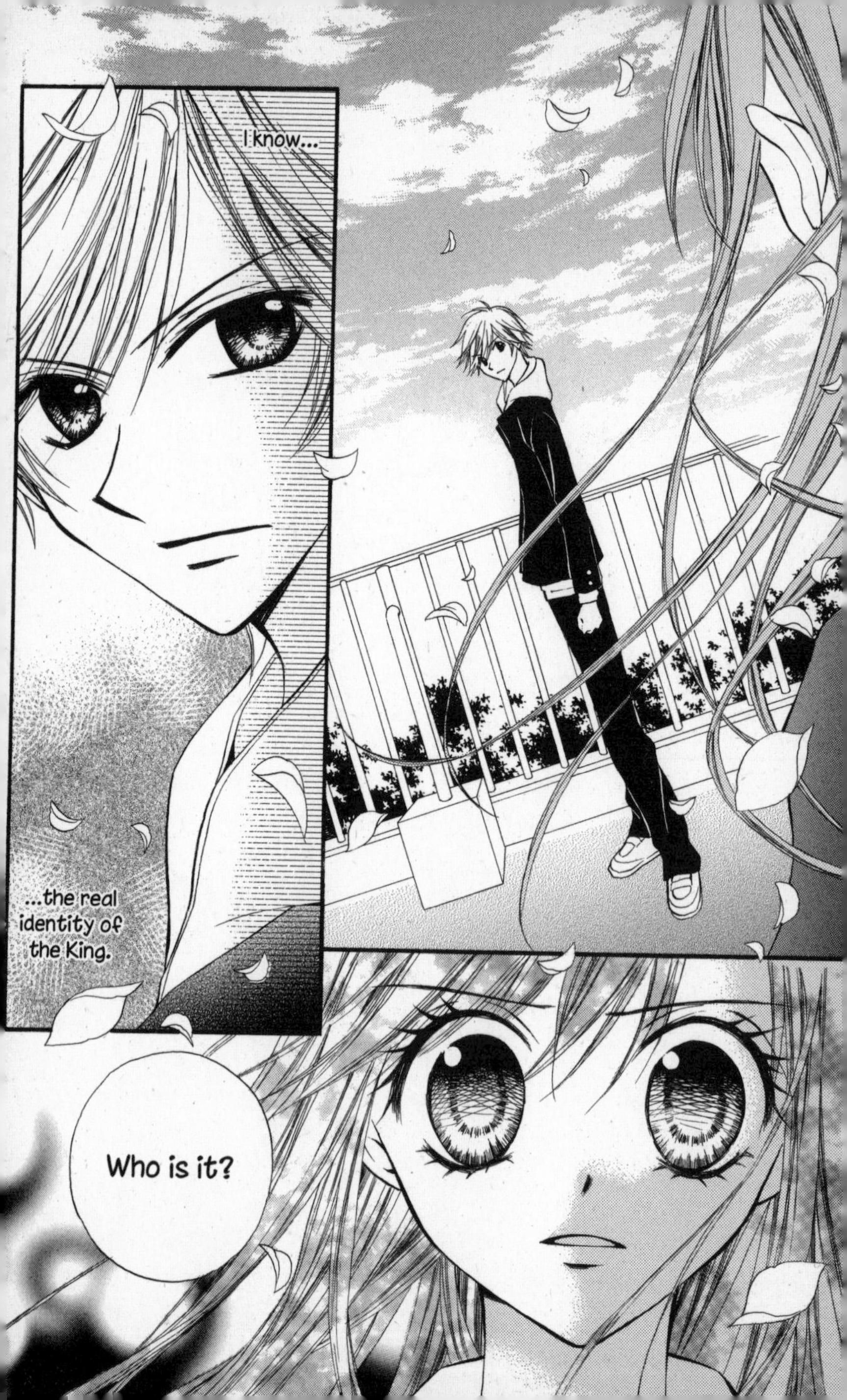
I know...
...the real identity of the King.
Who is it?

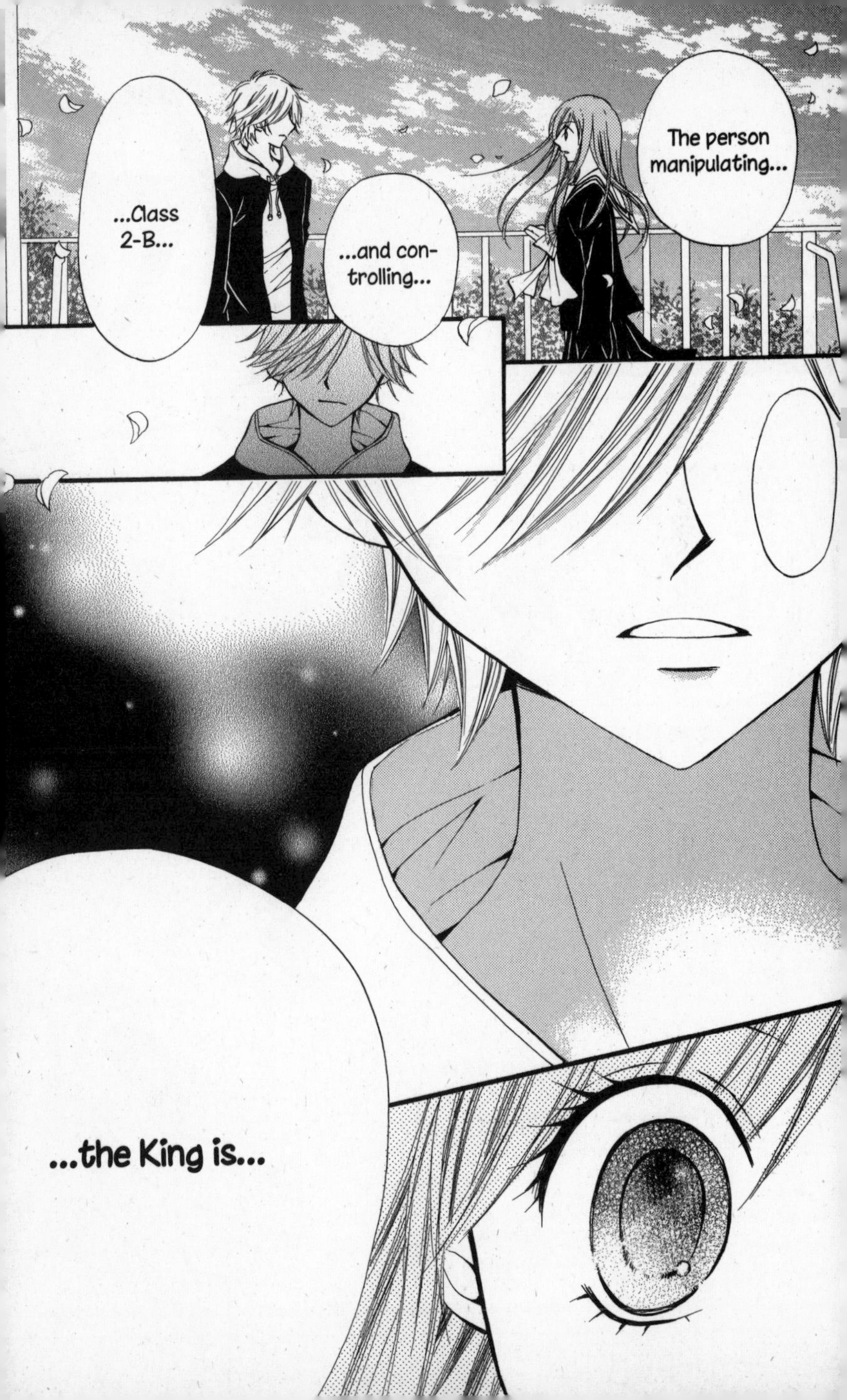
The person manipulating...
...and con-trolling...
...Class 2-B...
...the King is...

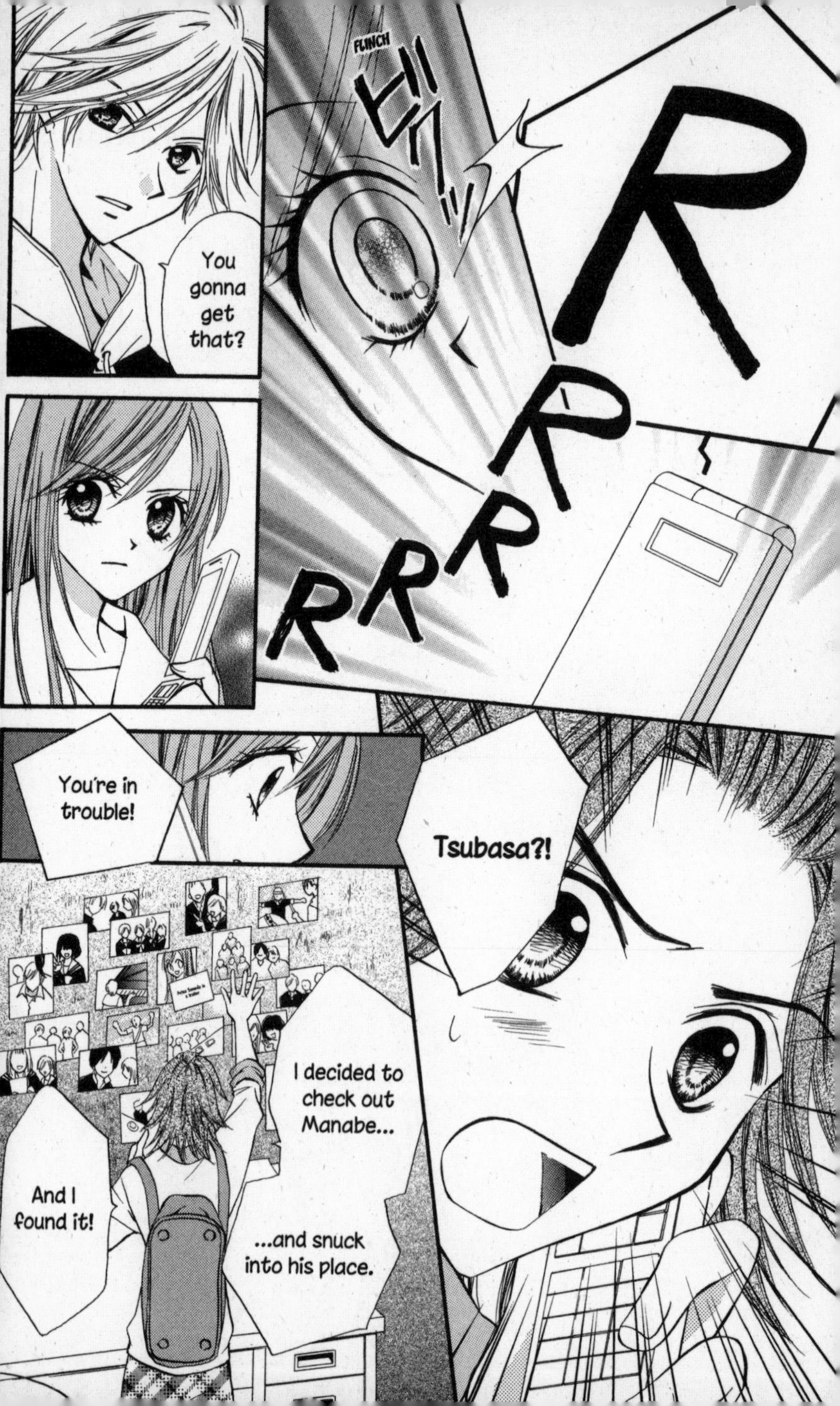
FLINCH
RRRRR
You gonna get that?
Tsubasa?!
You're in trouble!
I decided to check out Manabe...
...and snuck into his place.
And I found it!

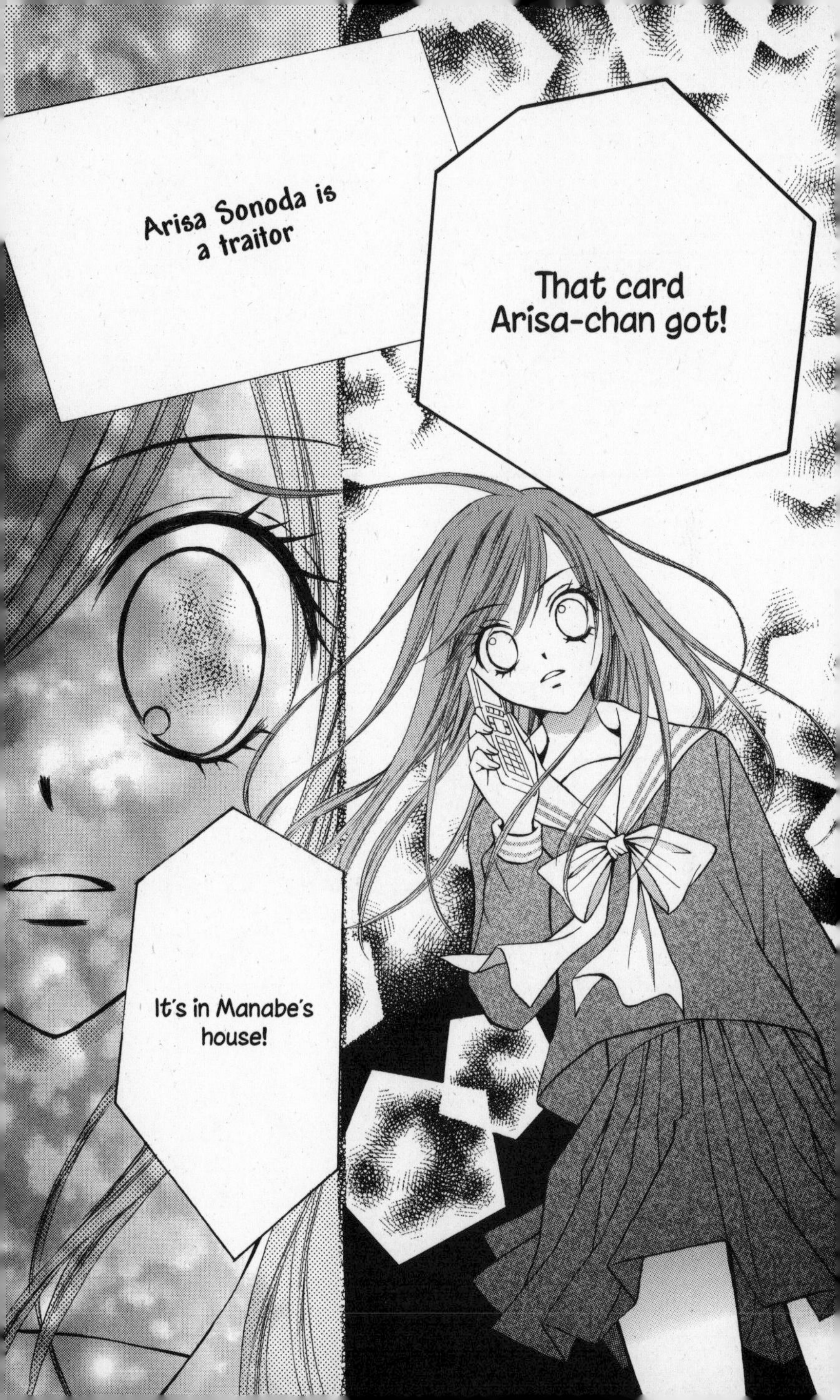
That card Arisa-chan got!
Arisa Sonoda is a traitor
It's in Manabe's house!

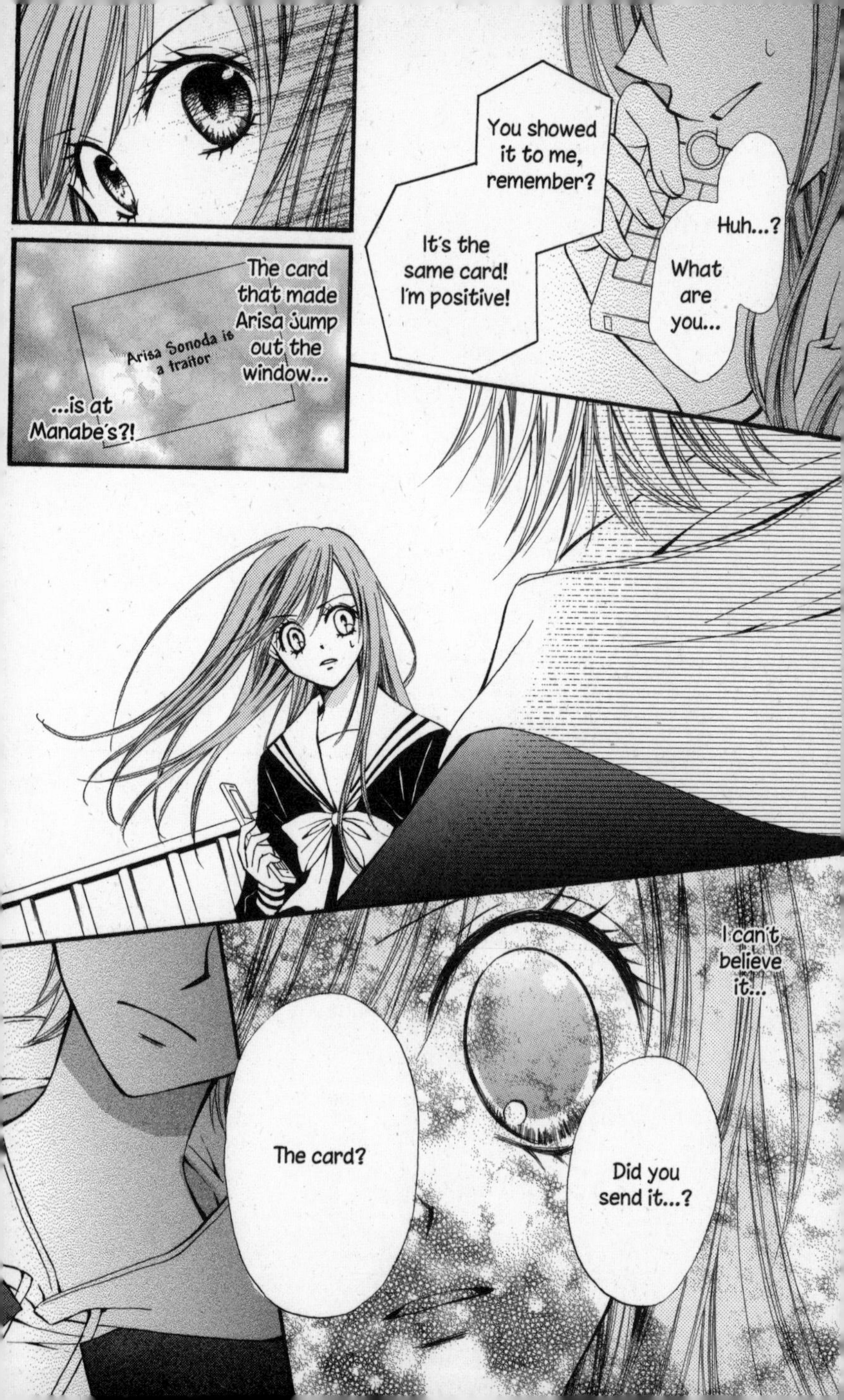

Huh...?
What are you...
You showed it to me, remember?
It's the same card! I'm positive!
The card that made Arisa jump out the window...
Arisa Sonoda is a traitor
...is at Manabe's?!
I can't believe it...
Did you send it...?
The card?

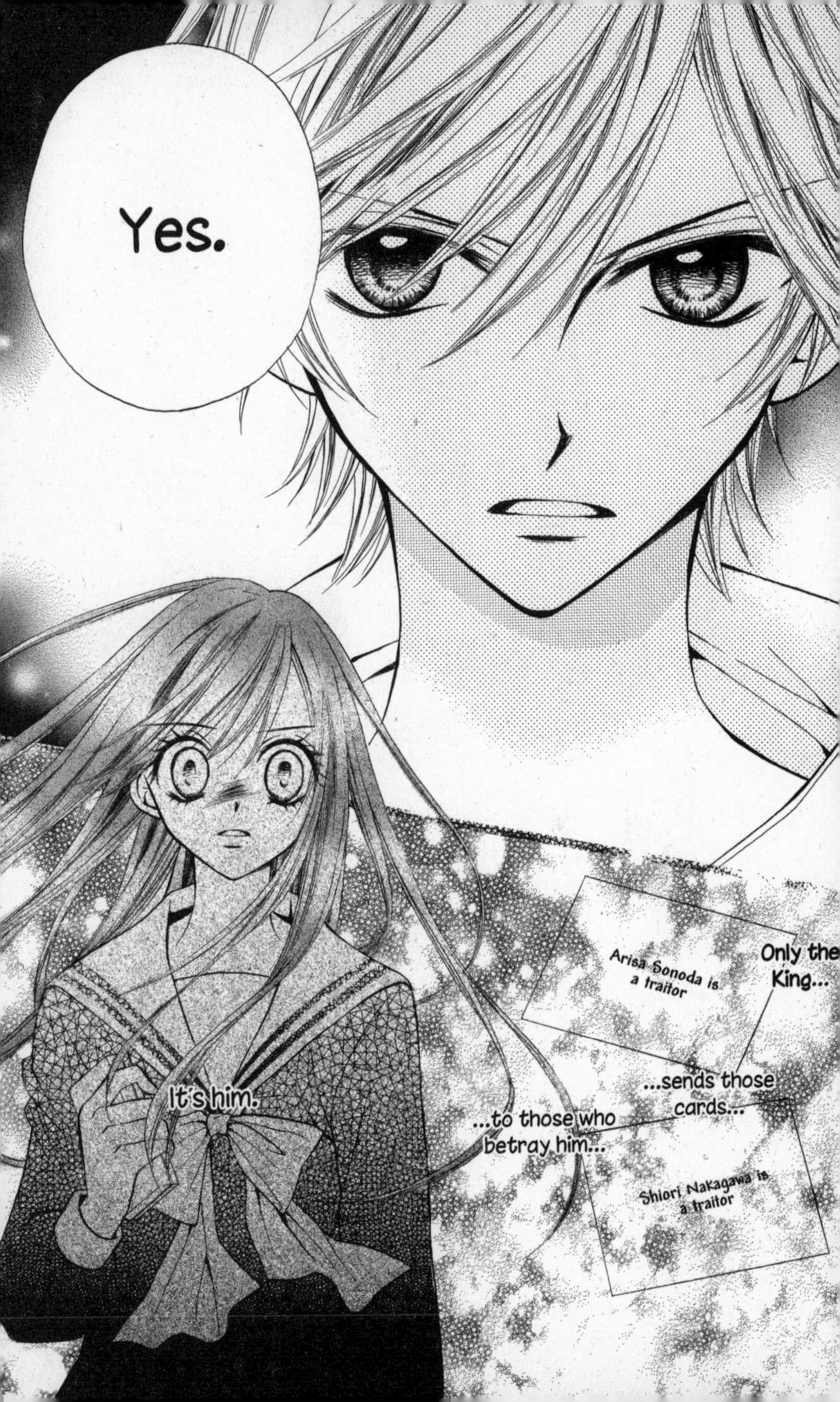
Yes.
Only the King...
Arisa Sonoda is a traitor
...sends those cards...
...to those who betray him...
Shiori Nakagawa is a traitor
It's him.

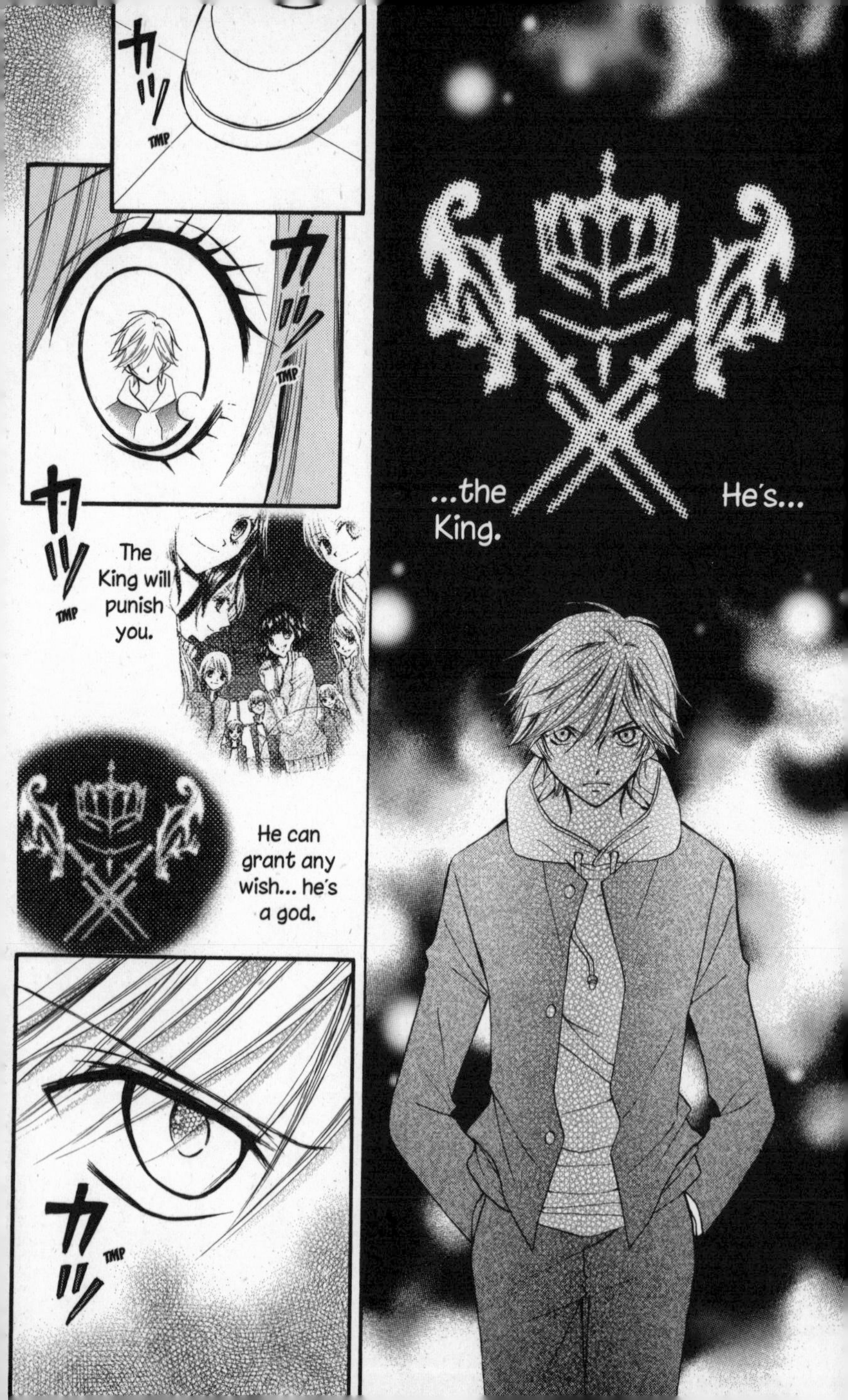
He's...
...the King.
TMP
TMP
TMP
The King will punish you.
He can grant any wish... he's a god.
TMP

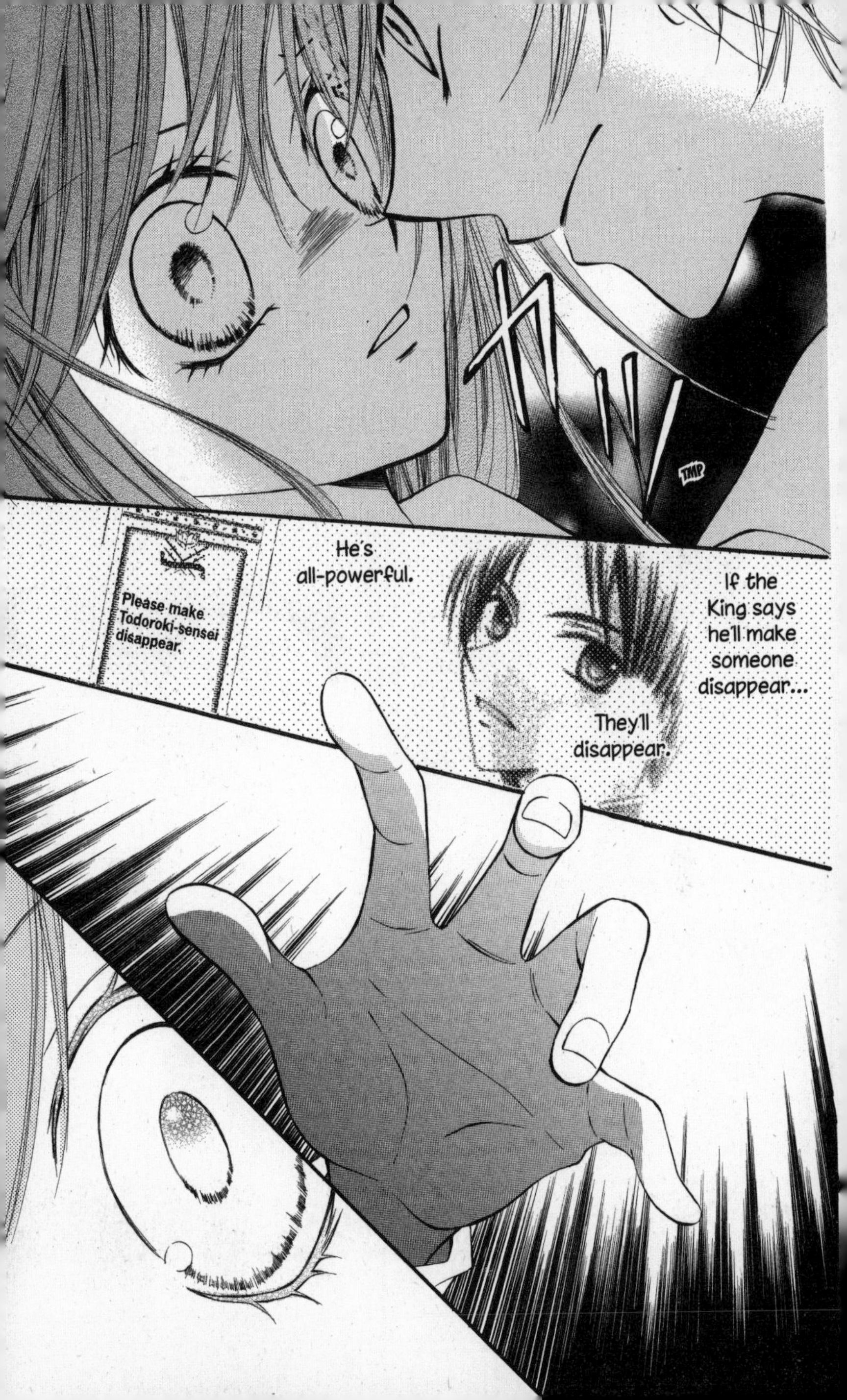
TMP
If the King says he'll make someone disappear...
They'll disappear.
He's all-powerful.
Please make Todoroki-sensei disappear.

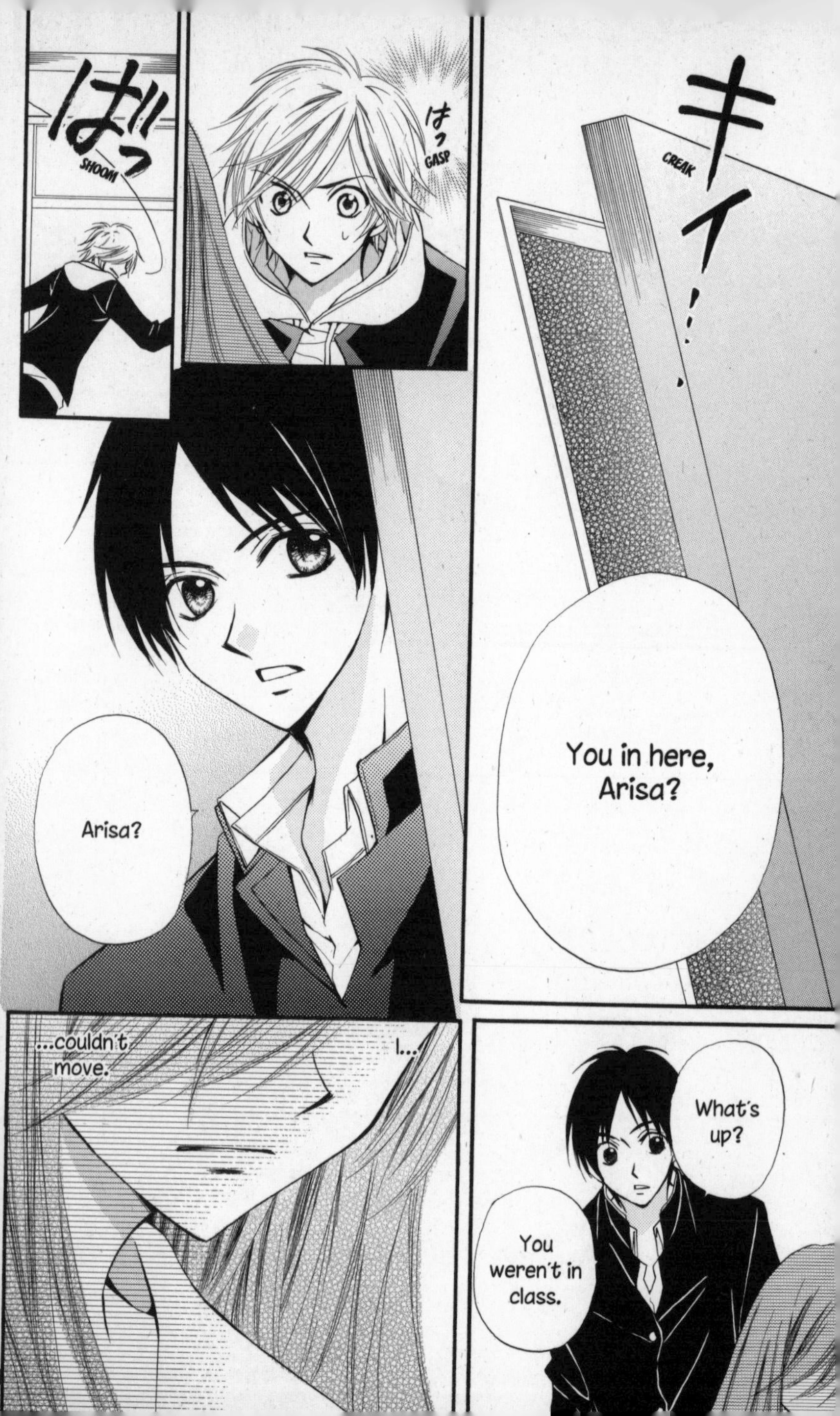
キイ…
CREAK
You in here, Arisa?
はっ
GASP
はっ
SHOOM
Arisa?
What's up?
You weren't in class.
I...
...couldn't move.

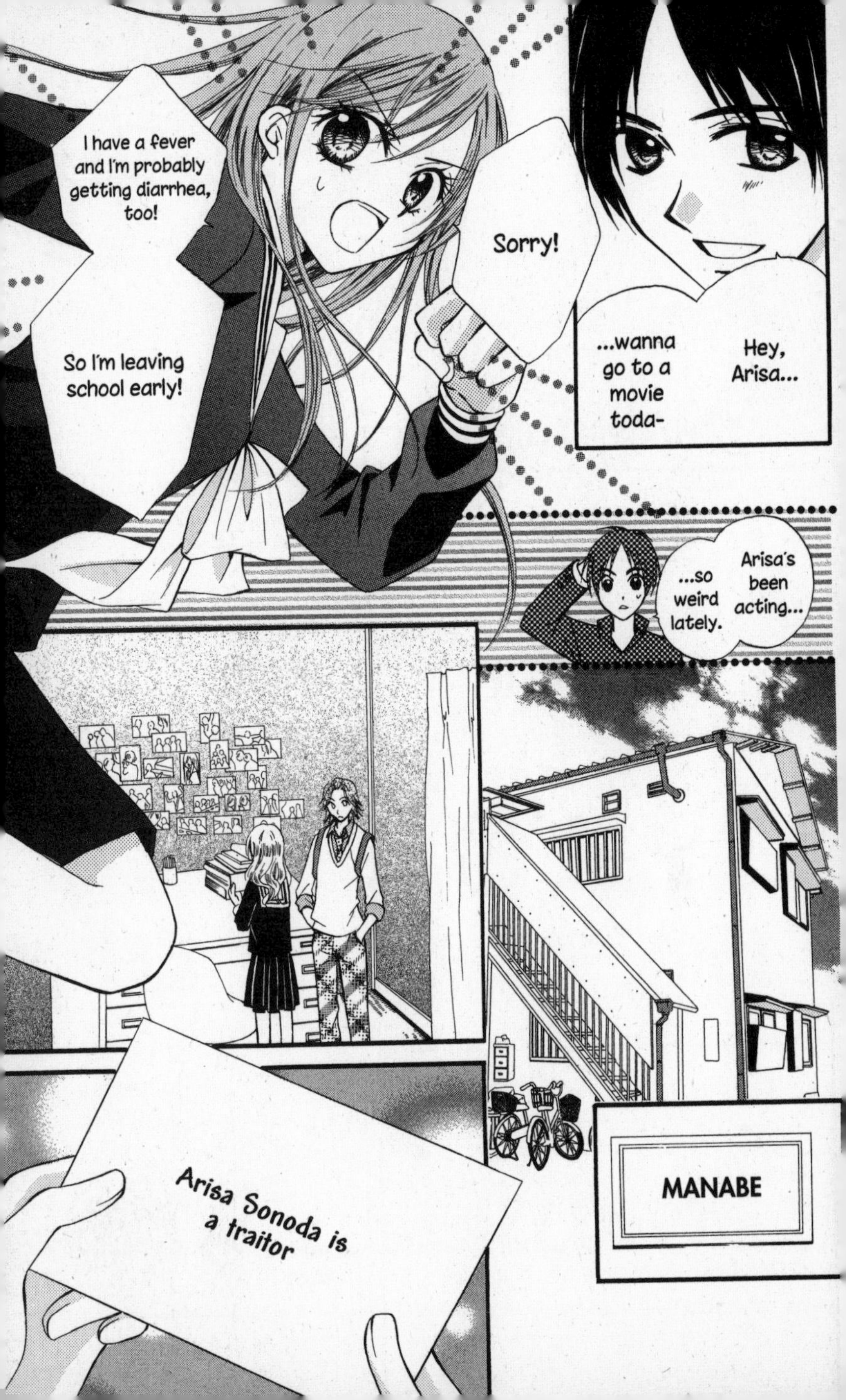
Hey, Arisa...
...wanna go to a movie toda-
Sorry!
I have a fever and I'm probably getting diarrhea, too!
So I'm leaving school early!
Arisa's been acting...
...so weird lately.
MANABE
Arisa Sonoda is a traitor

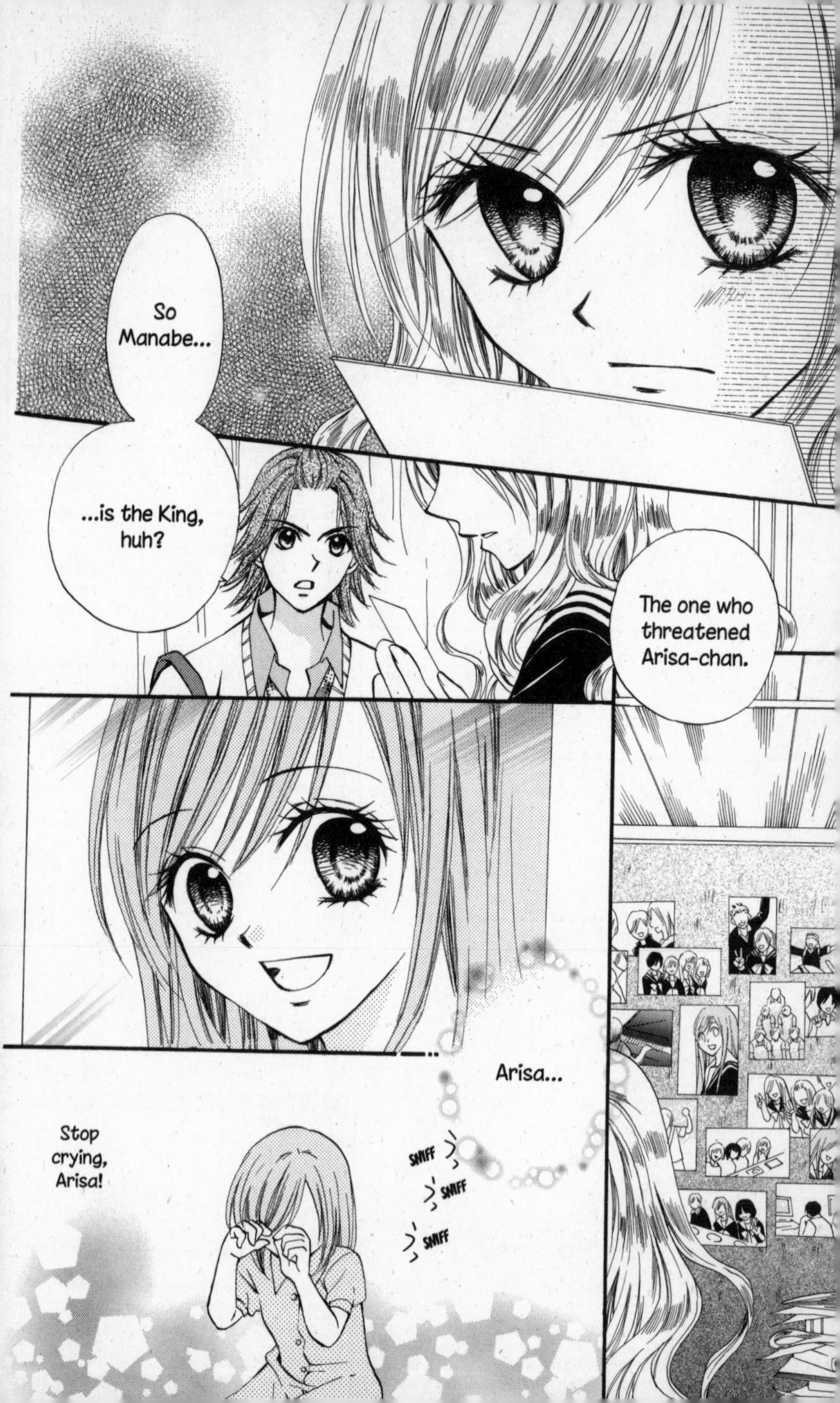
So Manabe...
...is the King, huh?
The one who threatened Arisa-chan.
Arisa...
SNIFF
SNIFF
SNIFF
Stop crying, Arisa!

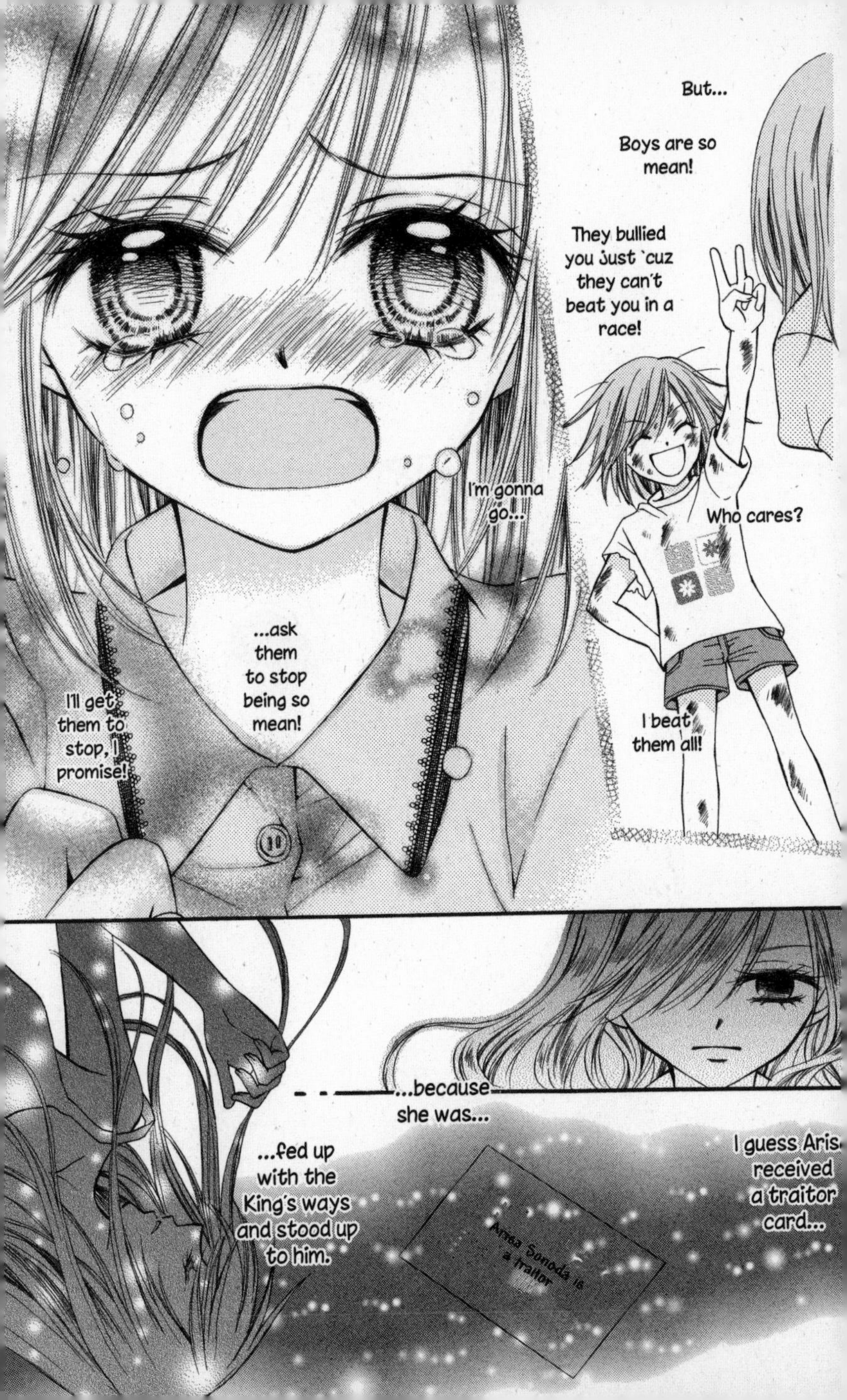
But...
Boys are so mean!
They bullied you just 'cuz they can't beat you in a race!
Who cares?
I beat them all!
I'm gonna go...
...ask them to stop being so mean!
I'll get them to stop, I promise!
I guess Aris received a traitor card...
...because she was...
Arisa Sonoda is a traitor
...fed up with the King's ways and stood up to him.

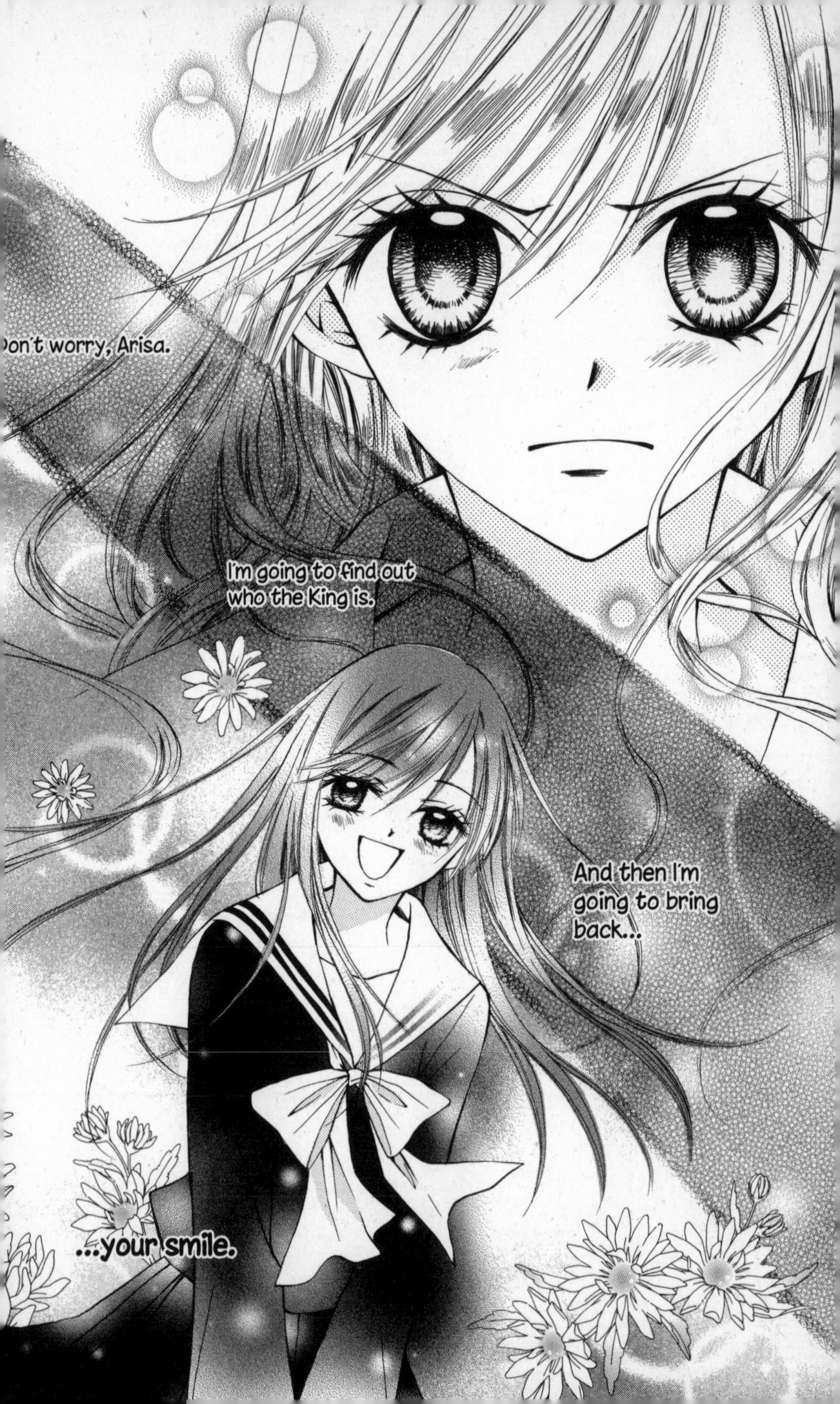

Don't worry, Arisa.
I'm going to find out who the King is.
And then I'm going to bring back...
...your smile.

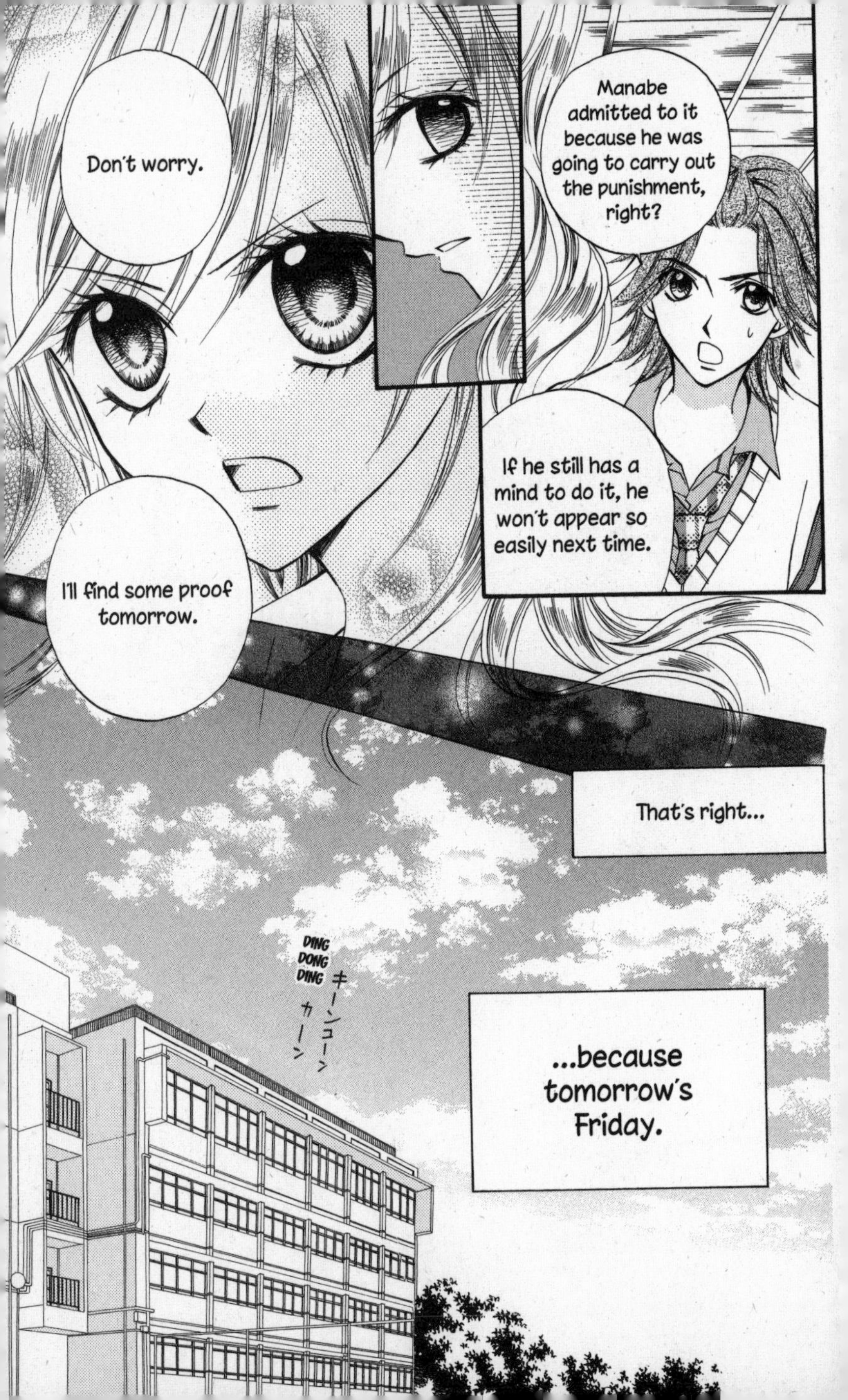

Manabe admitted to it because he was going to carry out the punishment, right?
If he still has a mind to do it, he won't appear so easily next time.
Don't worry.
I'll find some proof tomorrow.
That's right...
DING DONG DING
キーンコーン カーン
...because tomorrow's Friday.

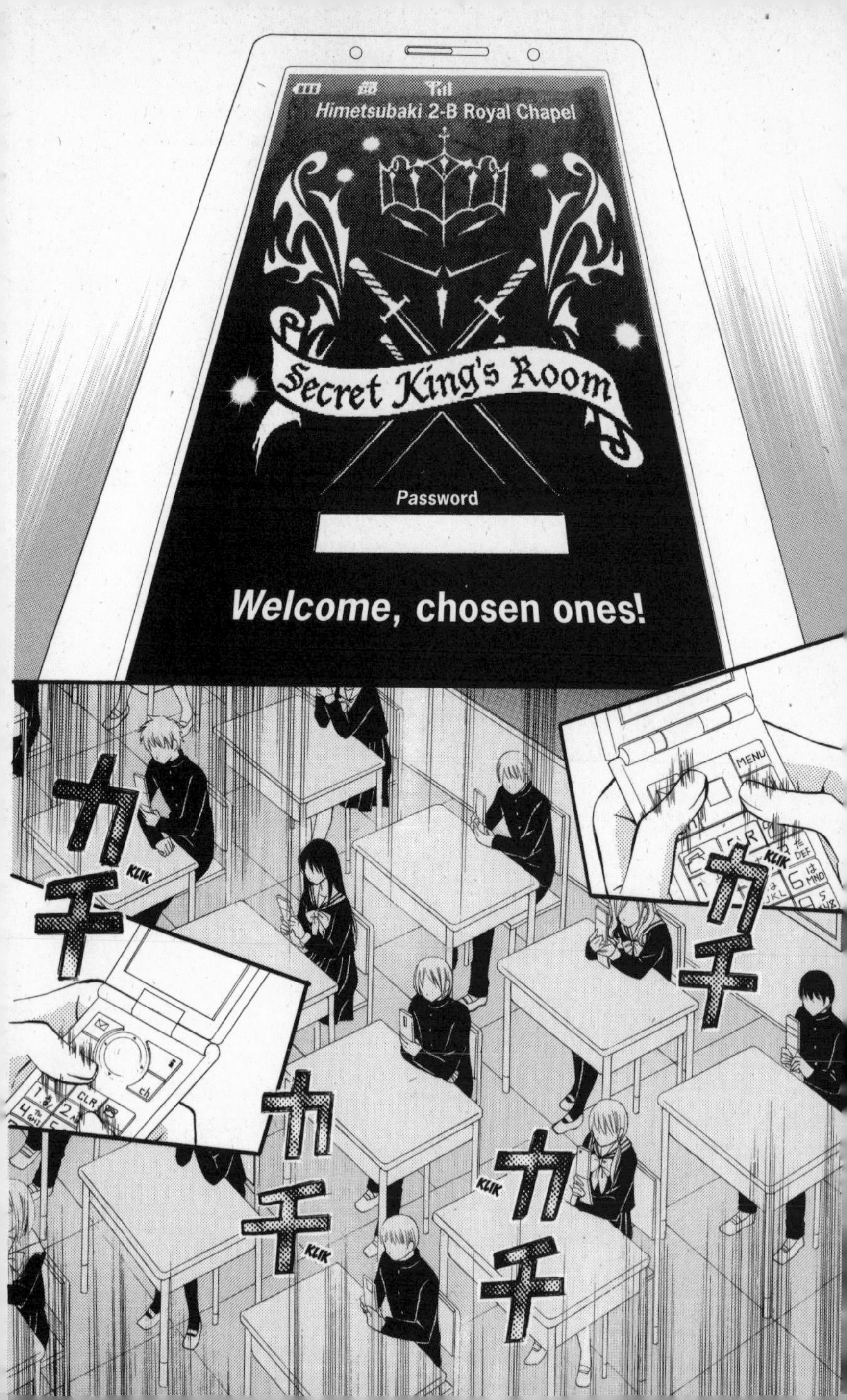
Himetsubaki 2-B Royal Chapel
Secret King's Room
Password
Welcome, chosen ones!
MENU
カチ
KLIK
カチ
KLIK
カチ
KLIK
カチ
KLIK
CLR

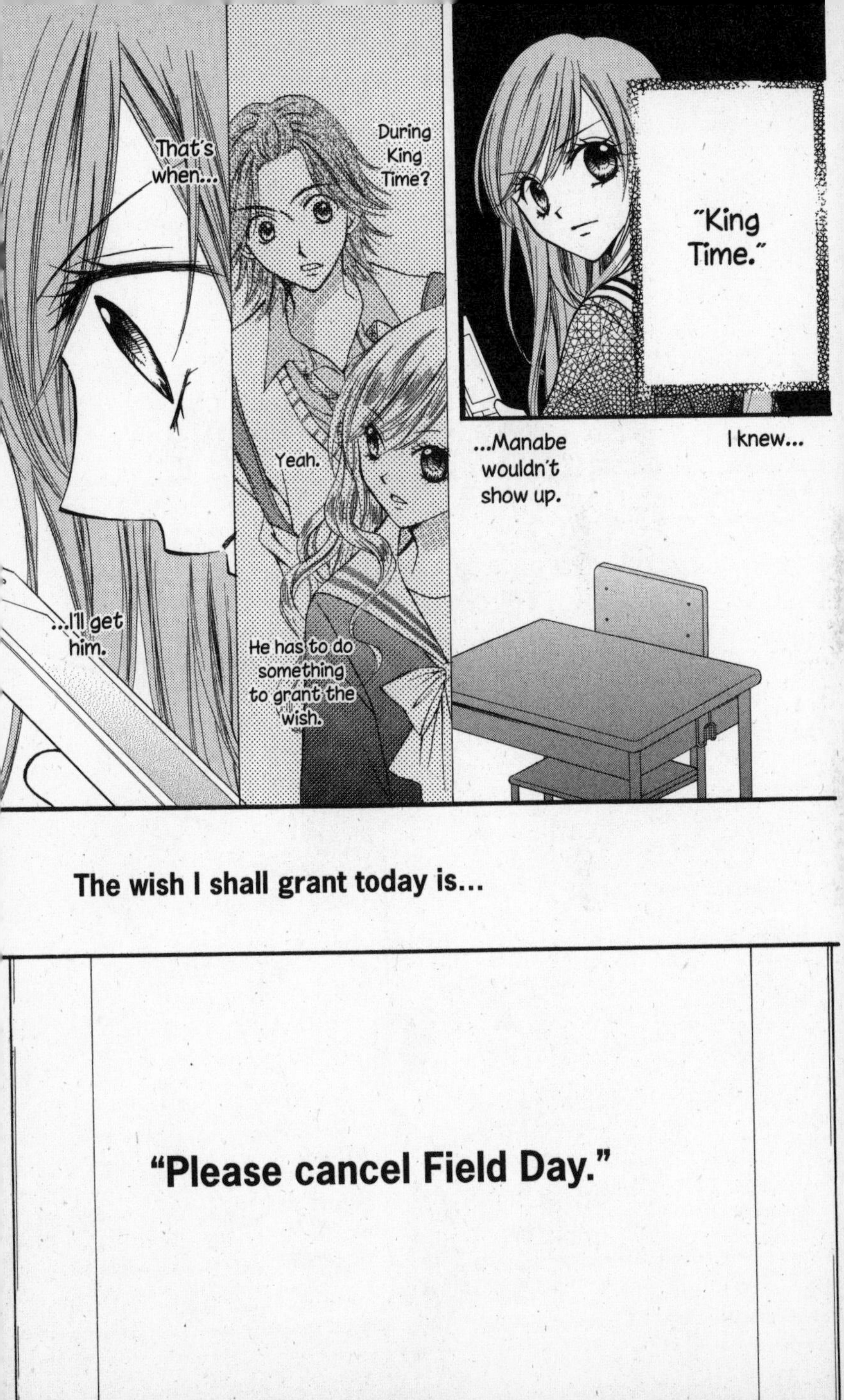
"King Time."
I knew...
...Manabe wouldn't show up.
During King Time?
Yeah.
He has to do something to grant the wish.
That's when...
...I'll get him.
The wish I shall grant today is...
"Please cancel Field Day."

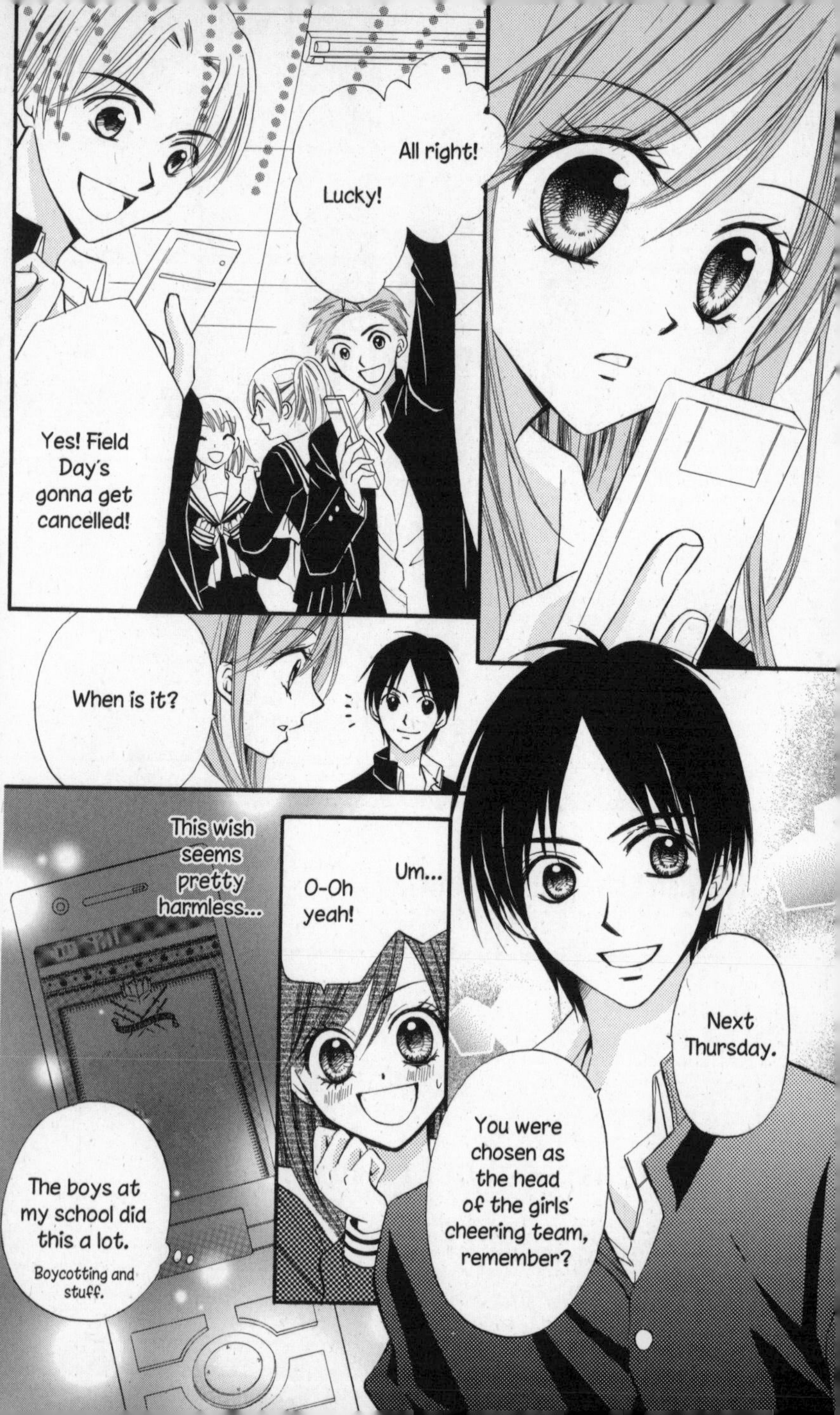
All right!
Lucky!
Yes! Field Day's gonna get cancelled!
When is it?
Next Thursday.
You were chosen as the head of the girls' cheering team, remember?
Um...
O-Oh yeah!
This wish seems pretty harmless...
The boys at my school did this a lot.
Boycotting and stuff.

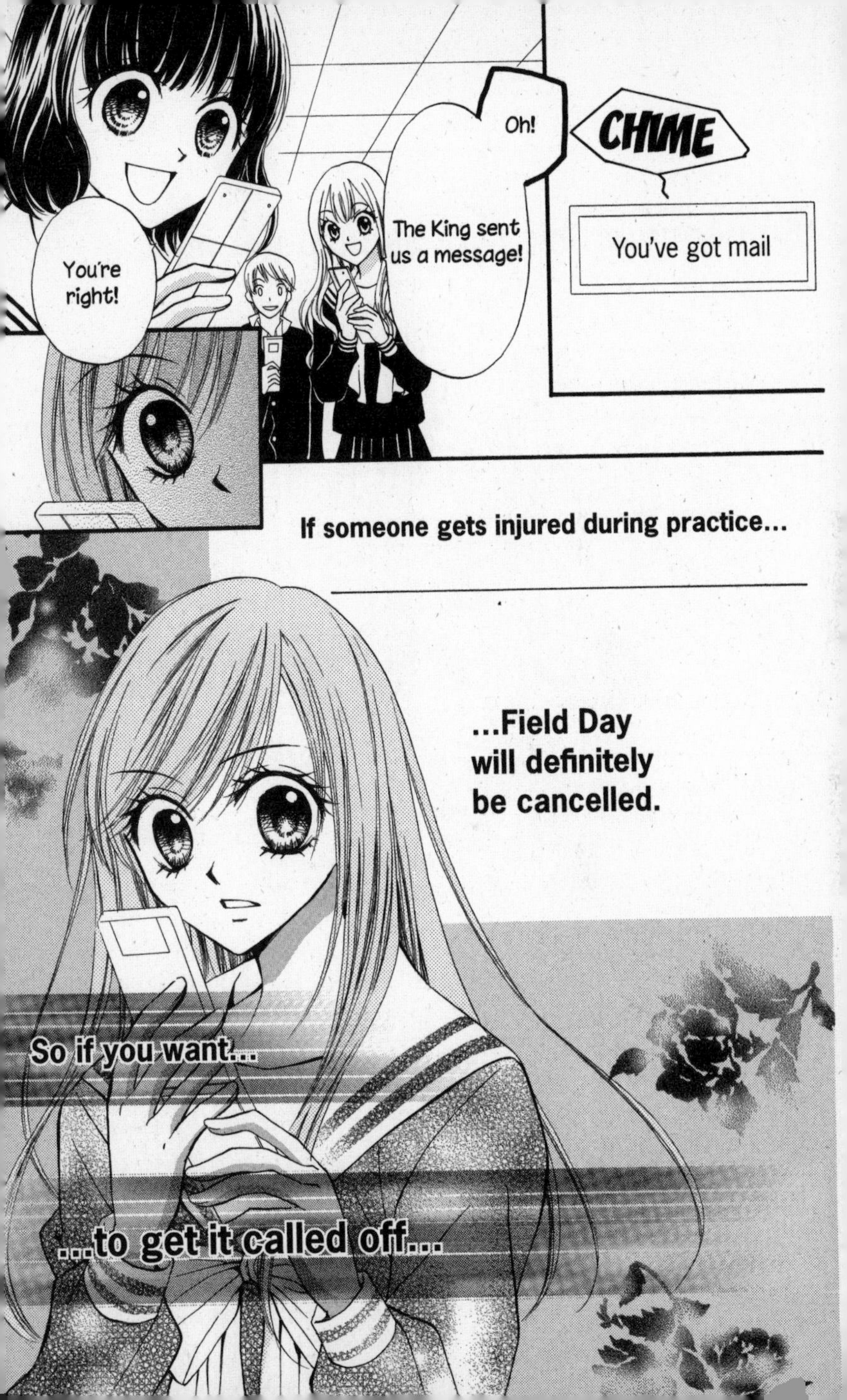
CHIME
You've got mail
Oh!
The King sent us a message!
You're right!
If someone gets injured during practice...
...Field Day will definitely be cancelled.
So if you want...
...to get it called off...

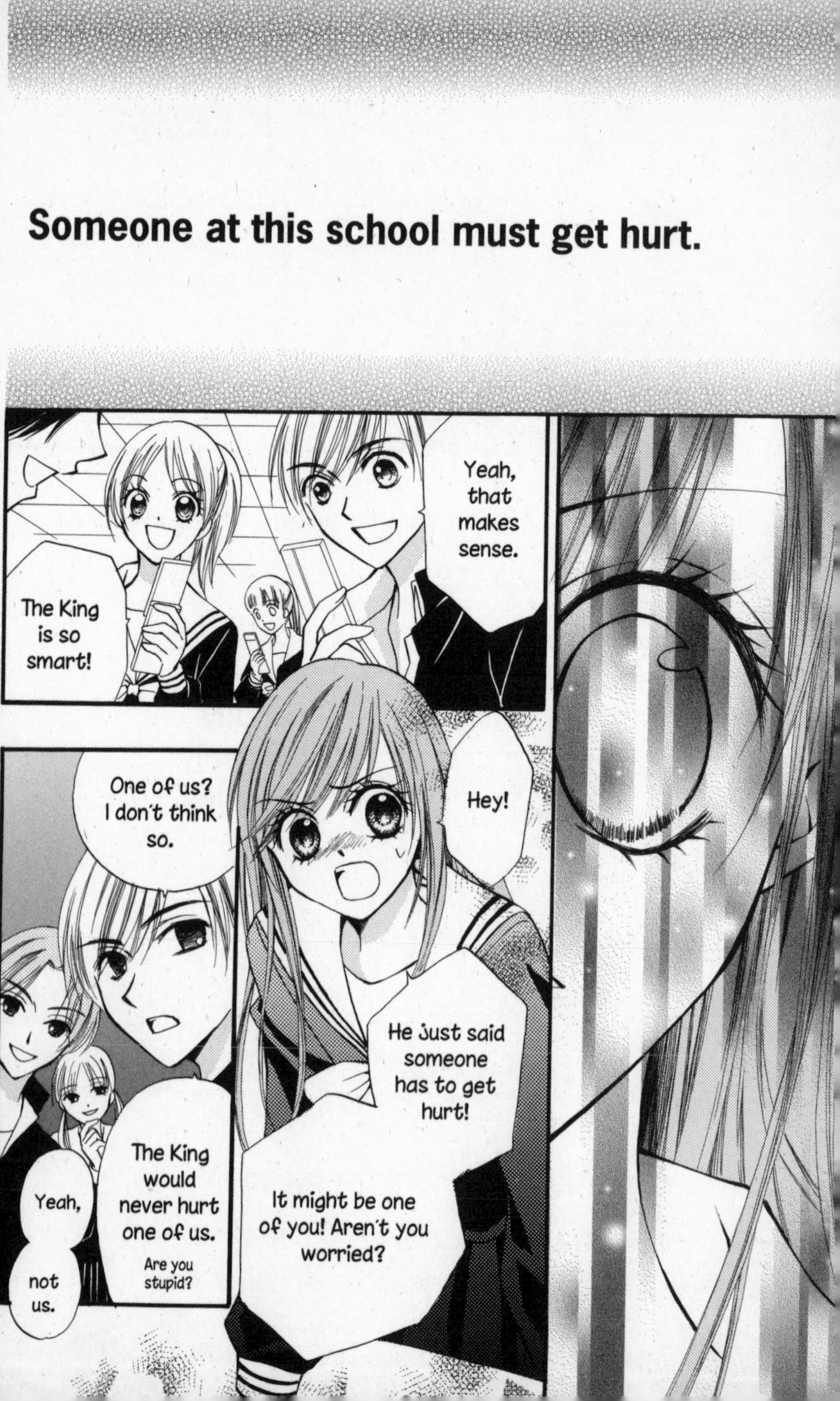
Someone at this school must get hurt.
Yeah, that makes sense.
The King is so smart!
Hey!
One of us? I don't think so.
He just said someone has to get hurt!
It might be one of you! Aren't you worried?
The King would never hurt one of us.
Are you stupid?
Yeah,
not us.

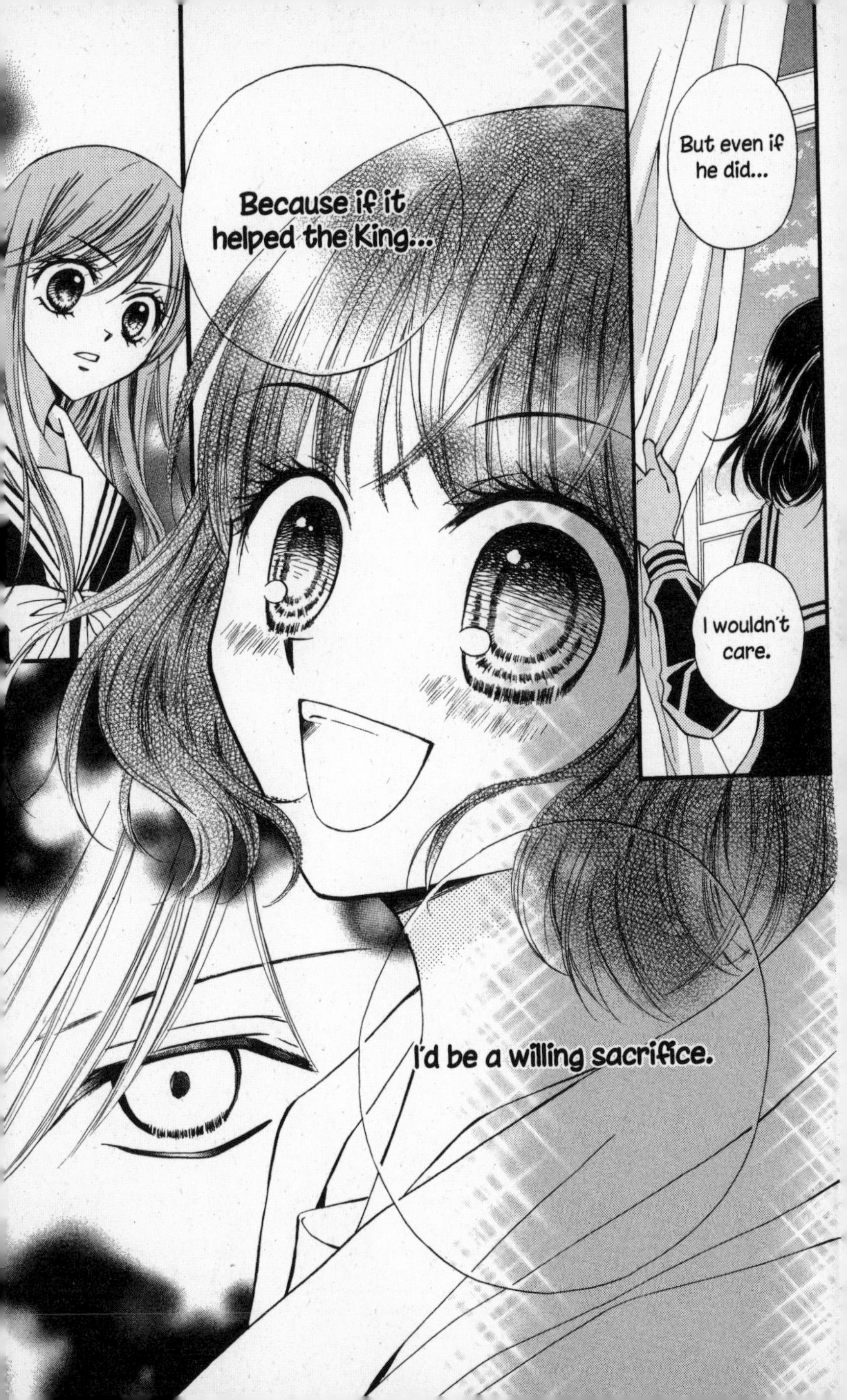
But even if he did...
I wouldn't care.
Because if it helped the King...
I'd be a willing sacrifice.

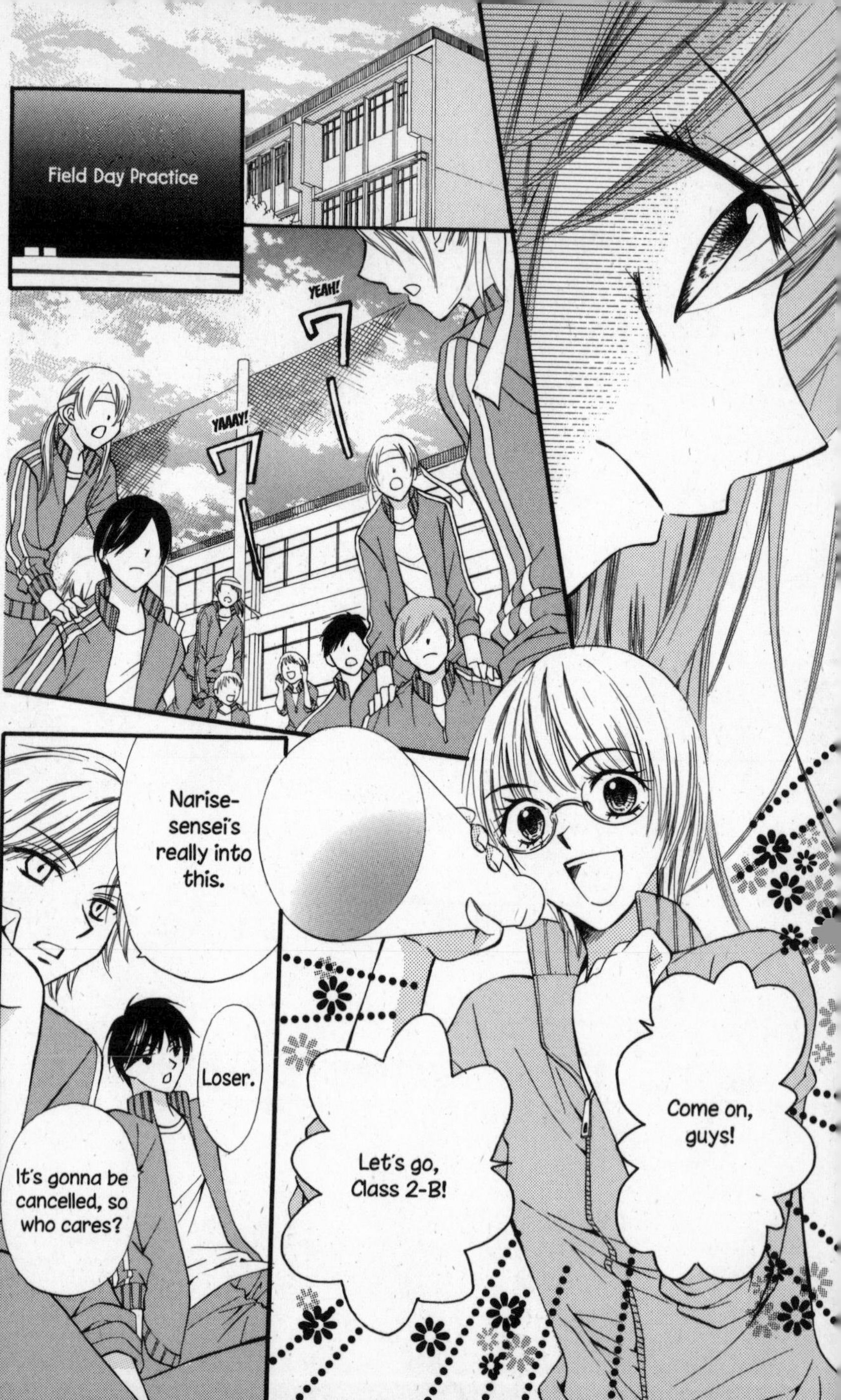
Field Day Practice
YEAH!
YAAAY!
Come on, guys!
Let's go, Class 2-B!
Narise-sensei's really into this.
Loser.
It's gonna be cancelled, so who cares?

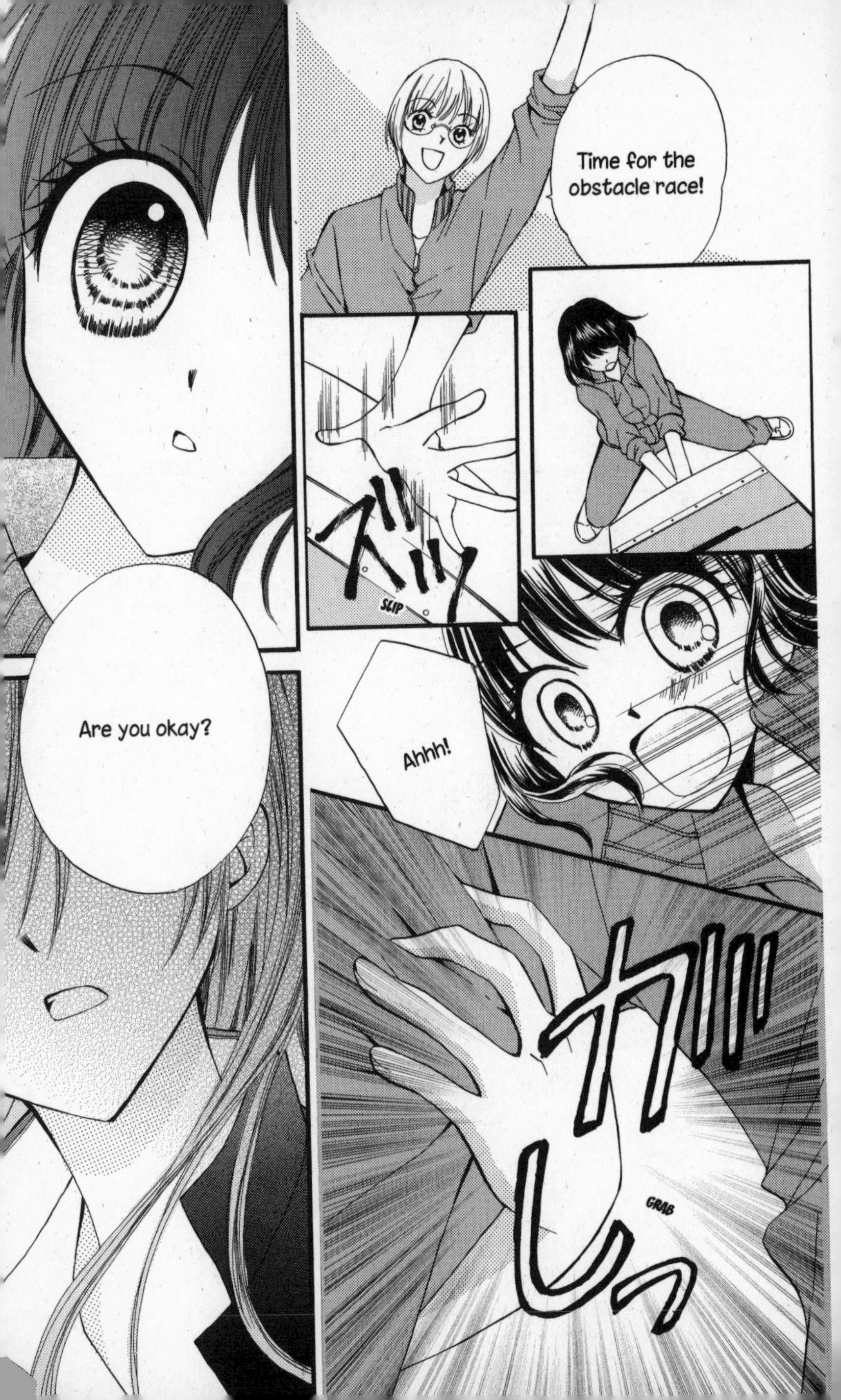
Time for the obstacle race!
SLIP
Ahhh!
GRAB
Are you okay?

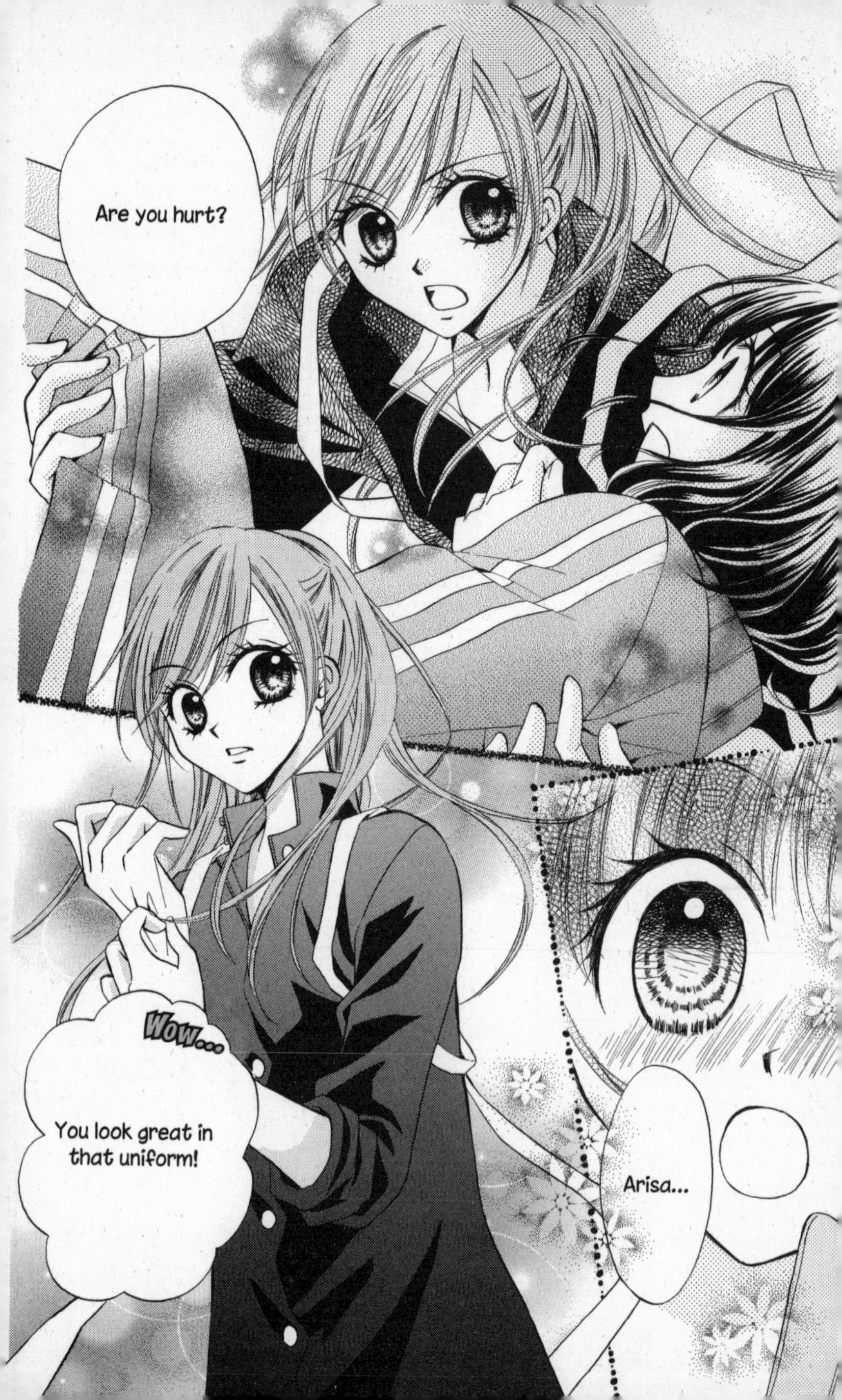
Are you hurt?
Arisa...
Wow...
You look great in that uniform!

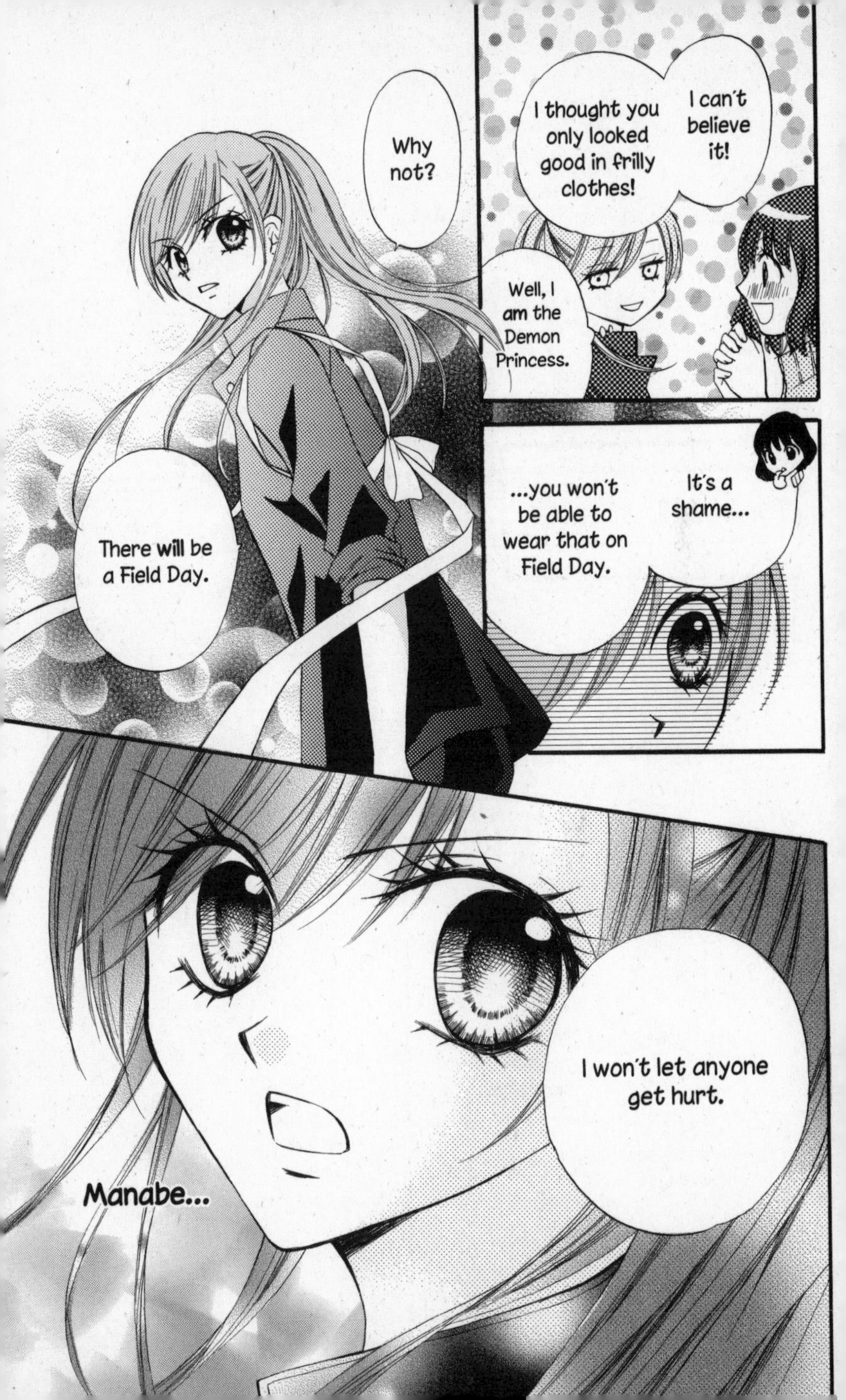
I can't believe it!
I thought you only looked good in frilly clothes!
Well, I am the Demon Princess.
It's a shame...
...you won't be able to wear that on Field Day.
Why not?
There will be a Field Day.
I won't let anyone get hurt.
Manabe...

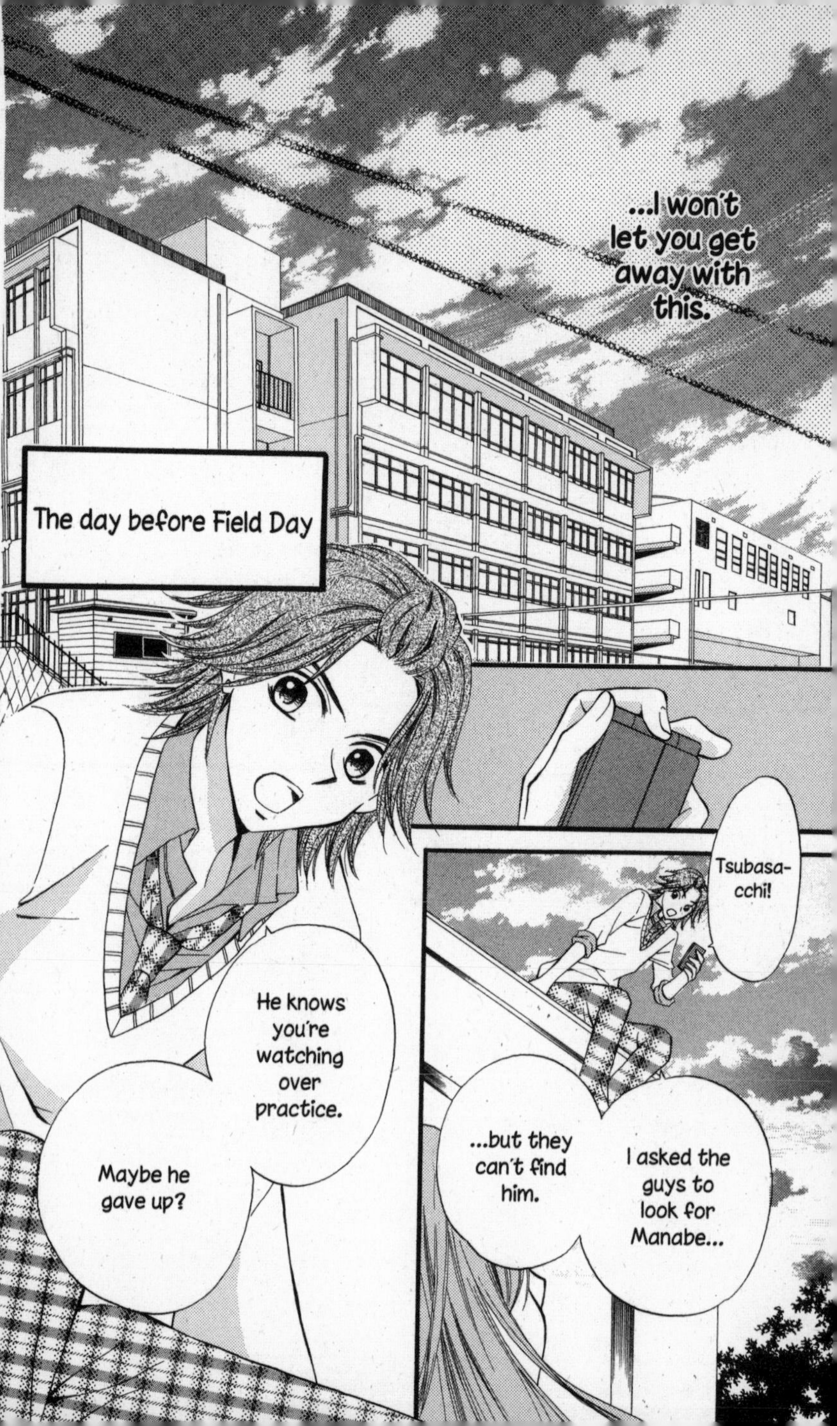
...I won't let you get away with this.
The day before Field Day
Tsubasa-cchi!
I asked the guys to look for Manabe...
...but they can't find him.
He knows you're watching over practice.
Maybe he gave up?

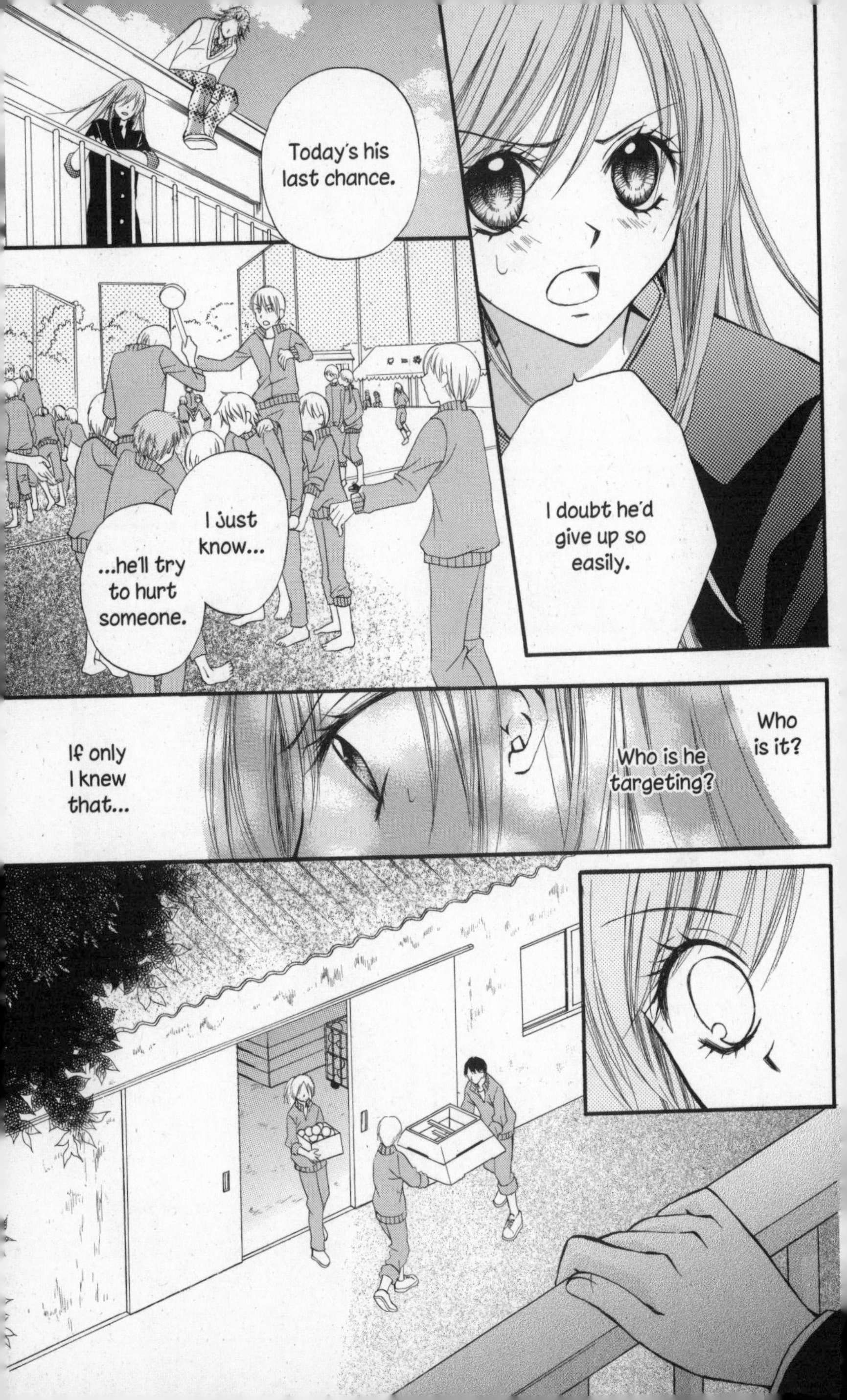
I doubt he'd give up so easily.
Today's his last chance.
I just know...
...he'll try to hurt someone.
Who is it?
Who is he targeting?
If only I knew that...

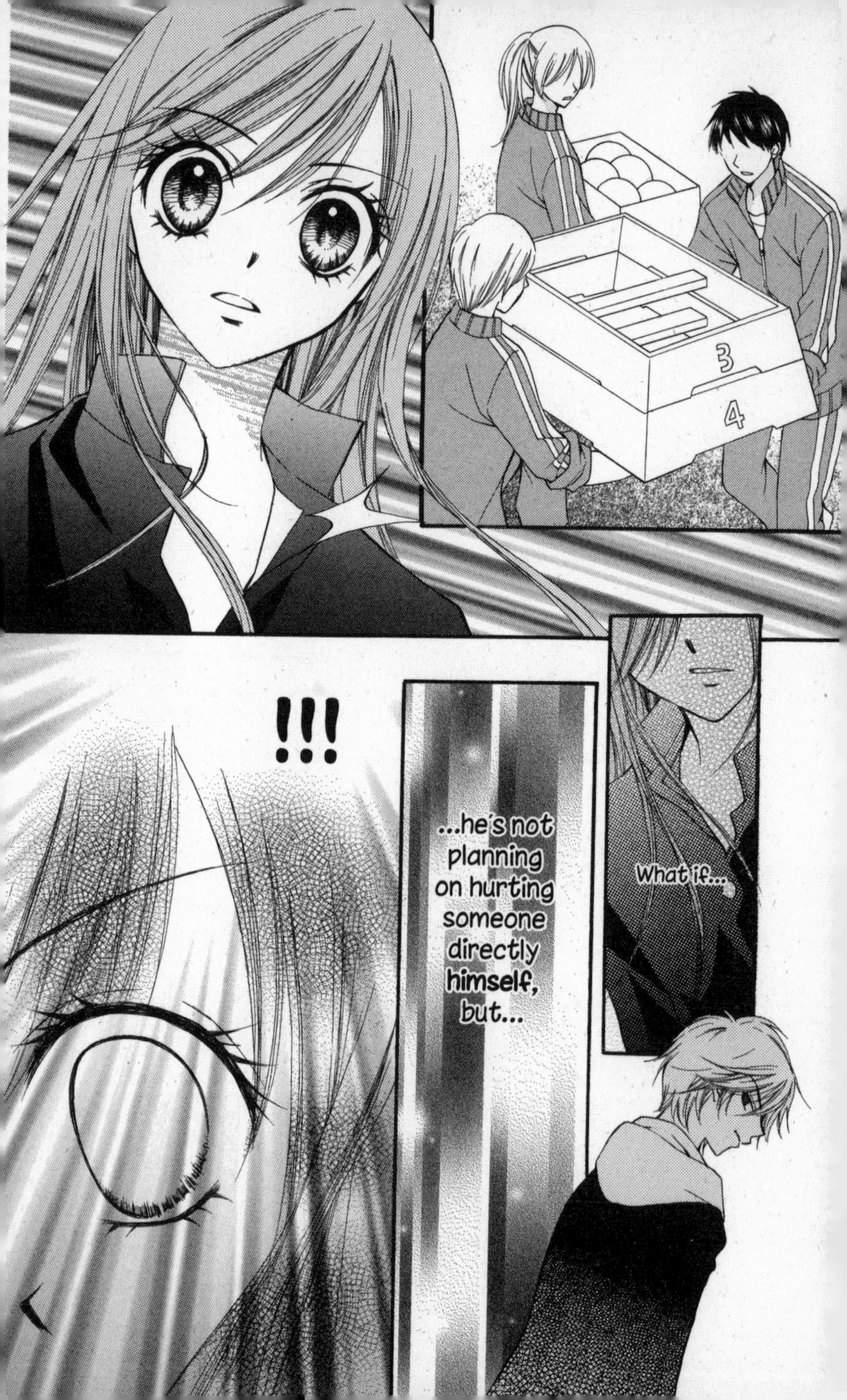
3
4
What if...
...he's not planning on hurting someone directly himself, but...
!!!

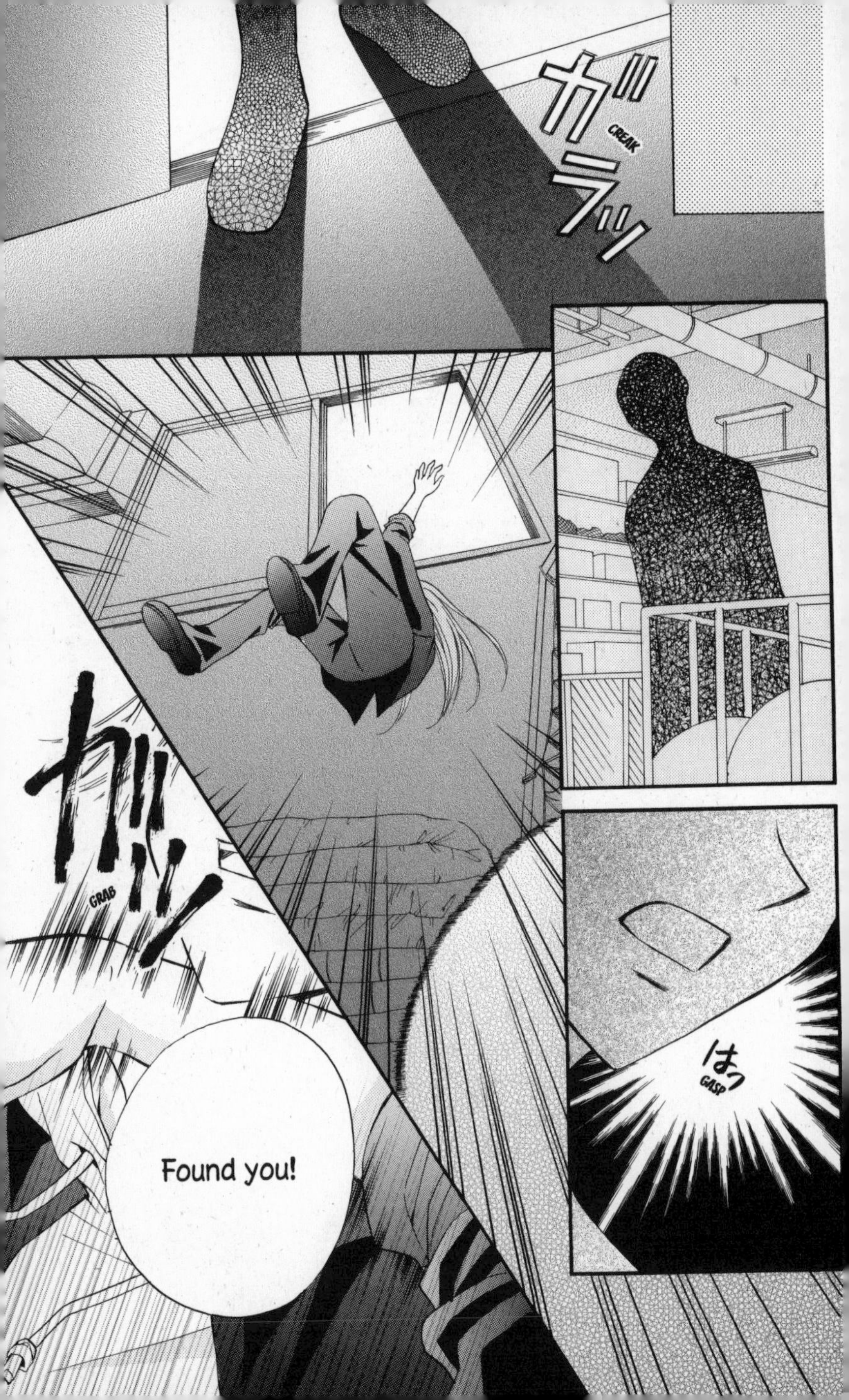
ガラッ
CREAK
はっ
GASP
ガシッ
GRAB
Found you!

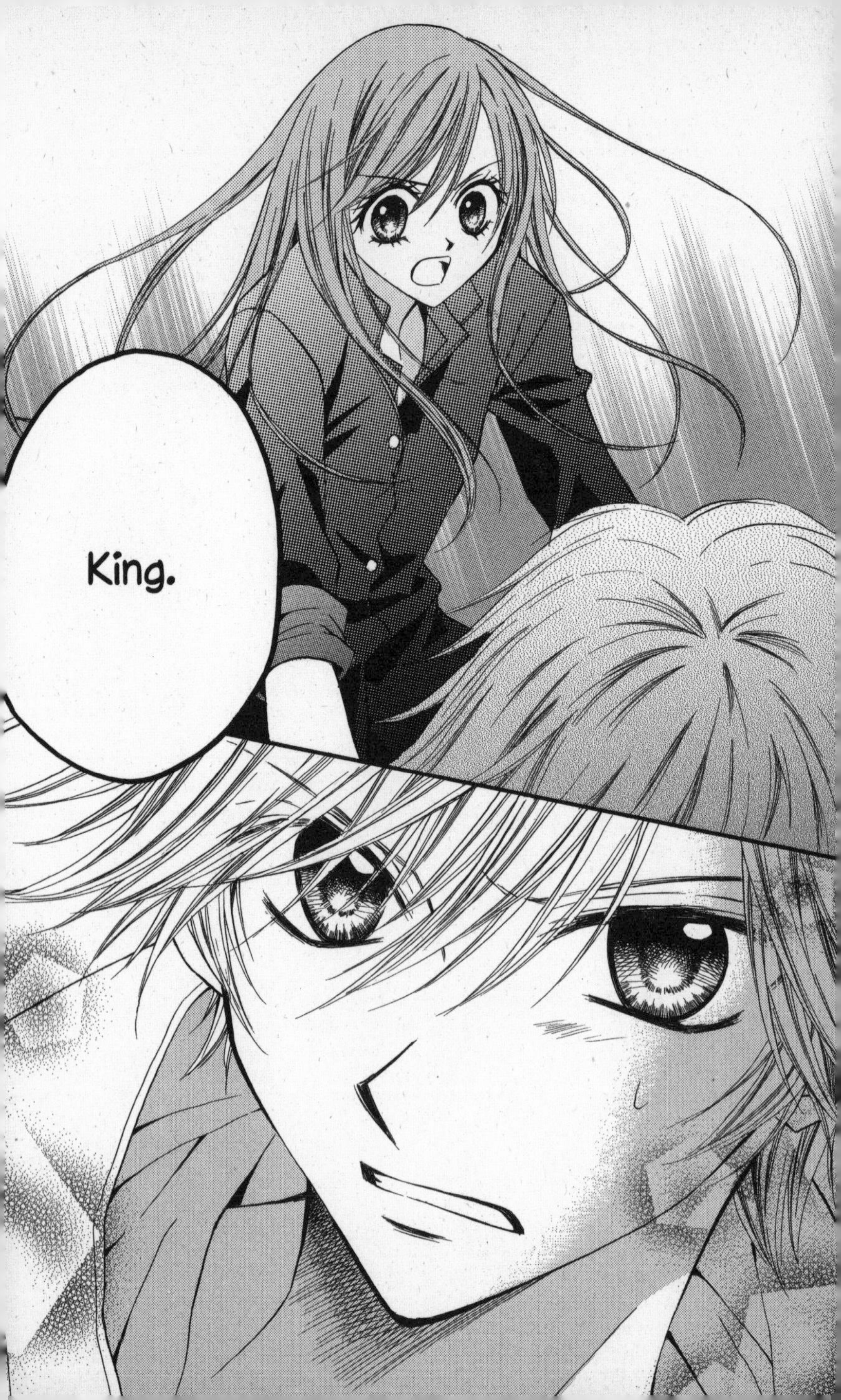
King.

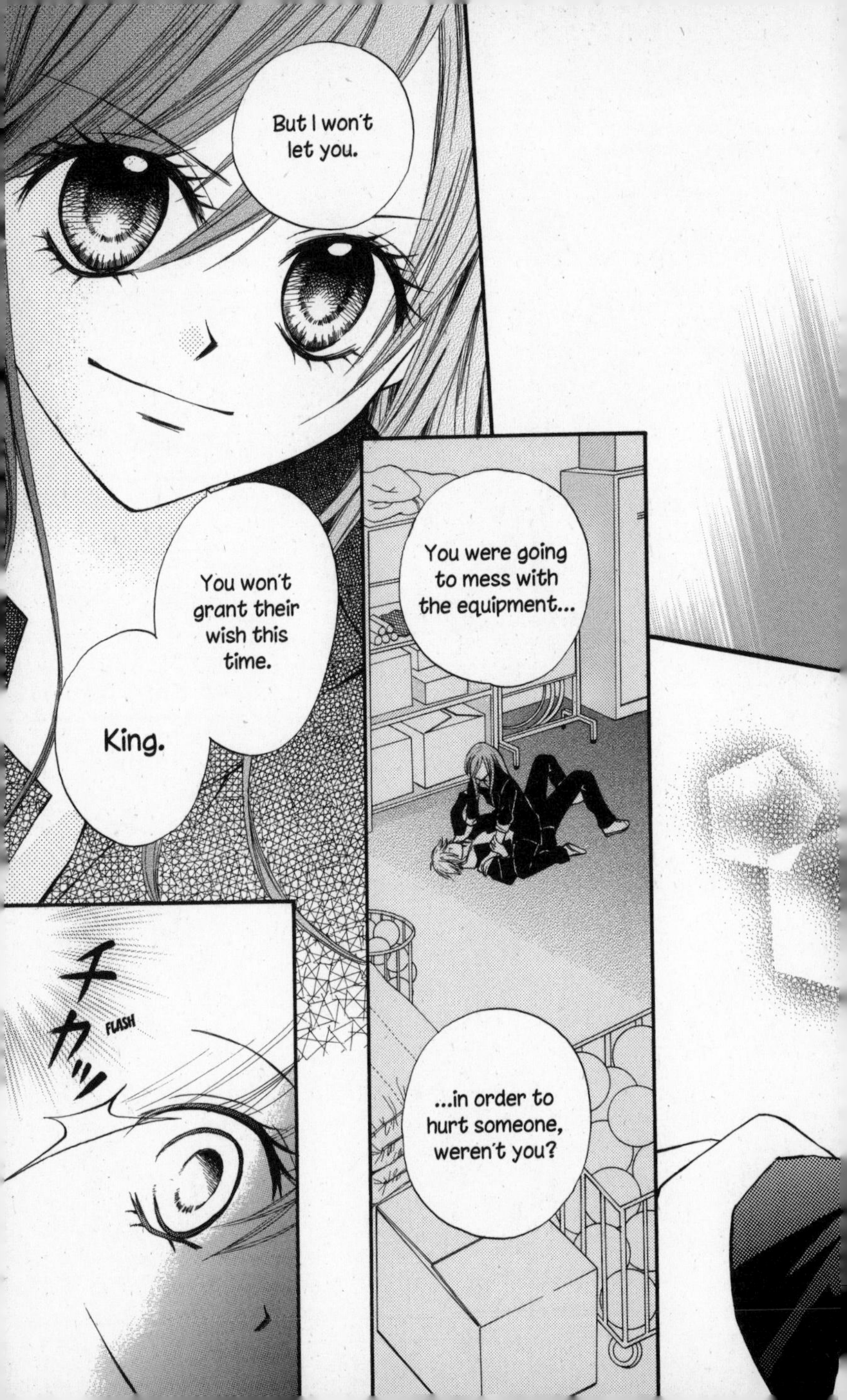
But I won't let you.
You won't grant their wish this time.
King.
You were going to mess with the equipment...
...in order to hurt someone, weren't you?
チカッ
FLASH

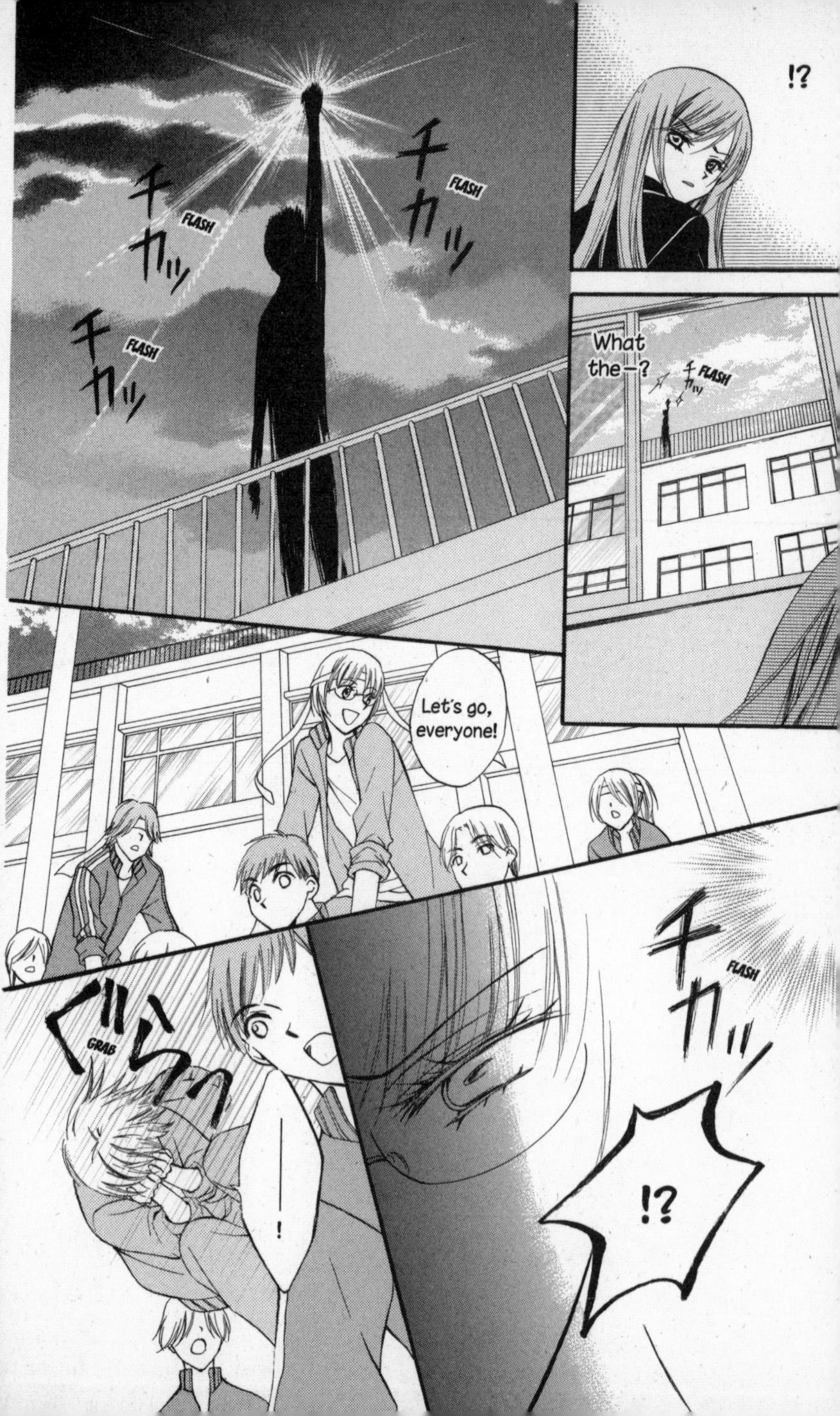
!?
What the—?
チカッ
FLASH
チカッ
FLASH
チカッ
FLASH
チカッ
FLASH
Let's go, everyone!
チカッ
FLASH
!?
ぐらっ
GRAB
—!

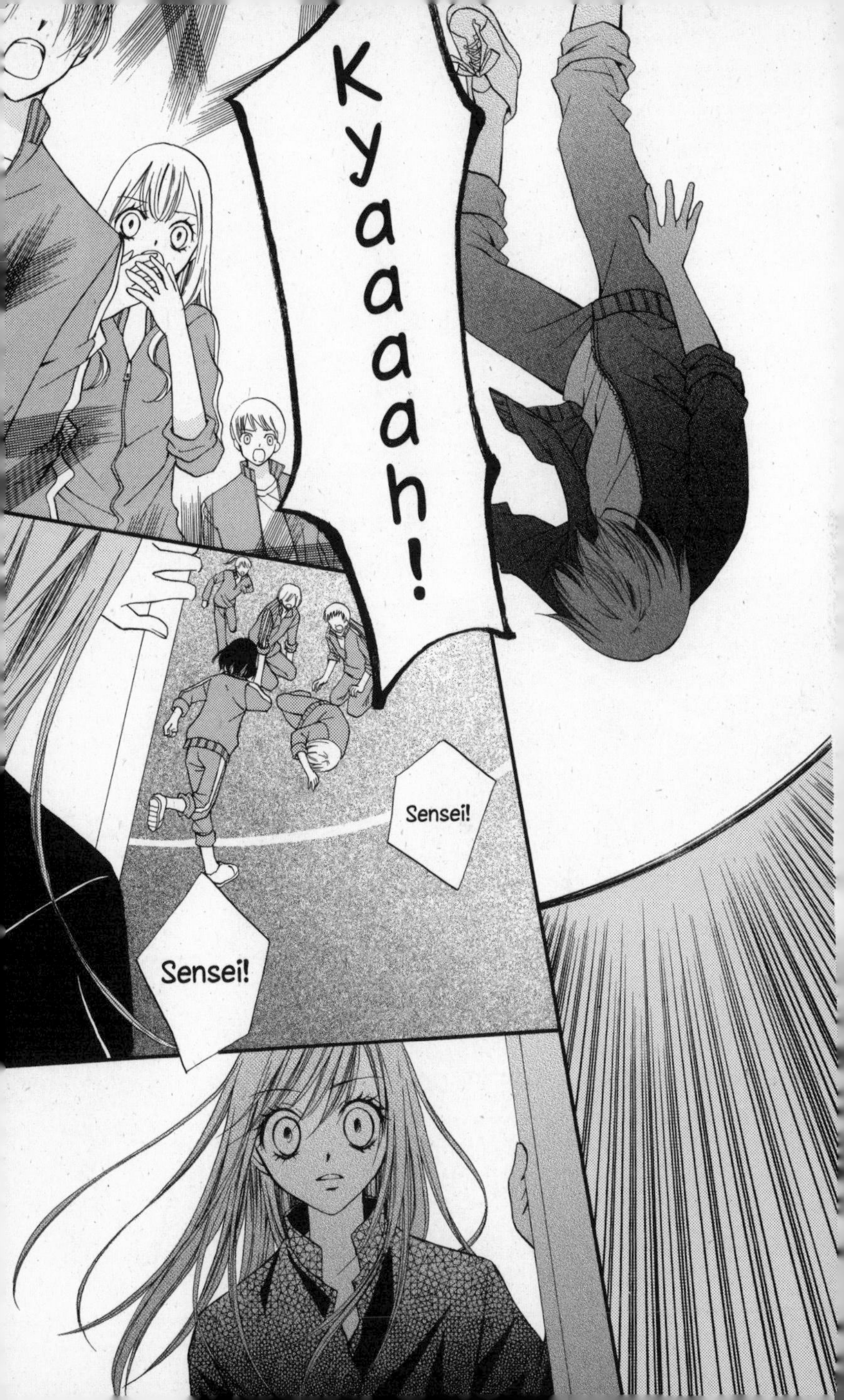
Kyaaah!
Sensei!
Sensei!

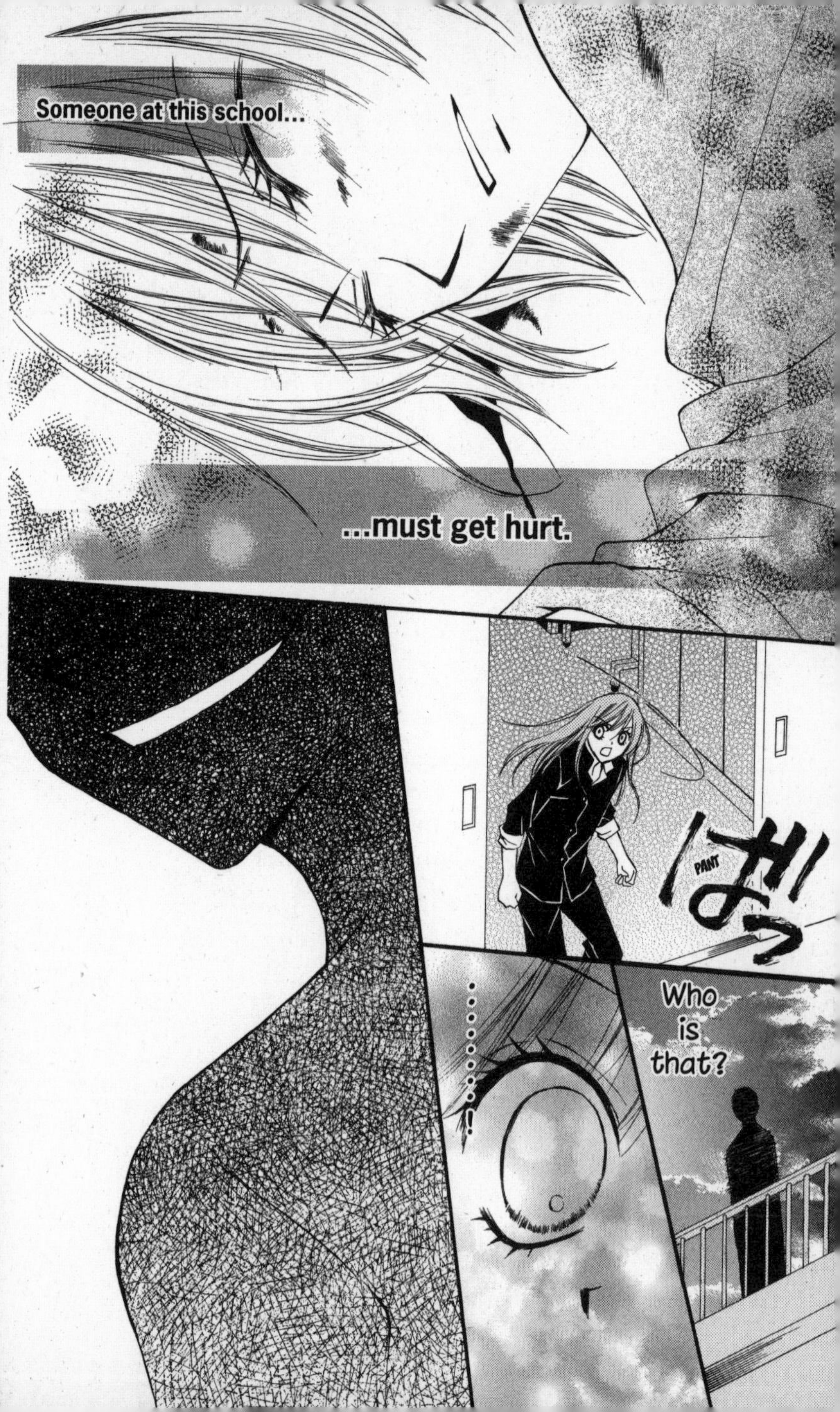
Someone at this school...
...must get hurt.
はっ
PANT
Who is that?
..........!

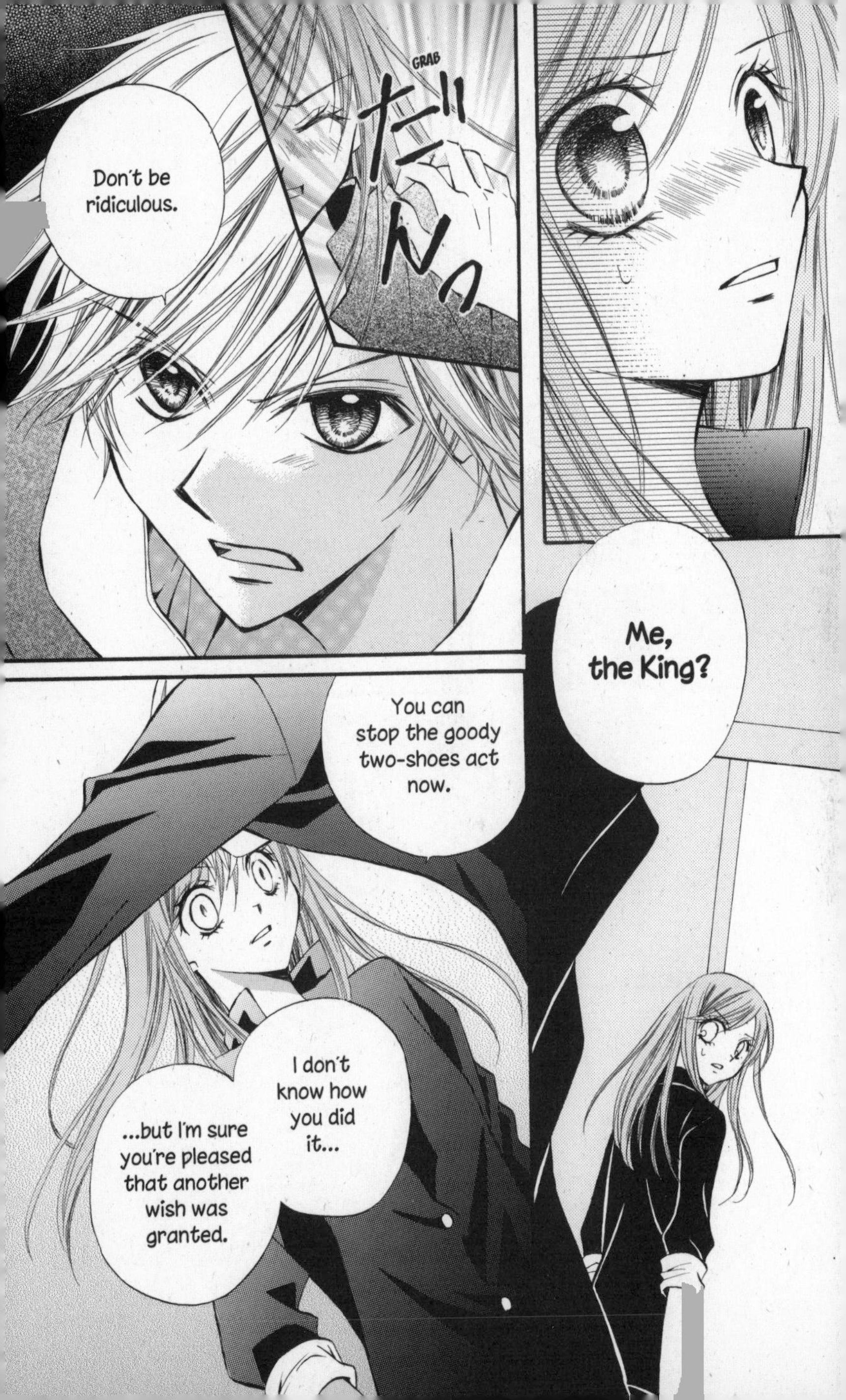
Me, the King?
GRAB
Don't be ridiculous.
You can stop the goody two-shoes act now.
I don't know how you did it...
...but I'm sure you're pleased that another wish was granted.

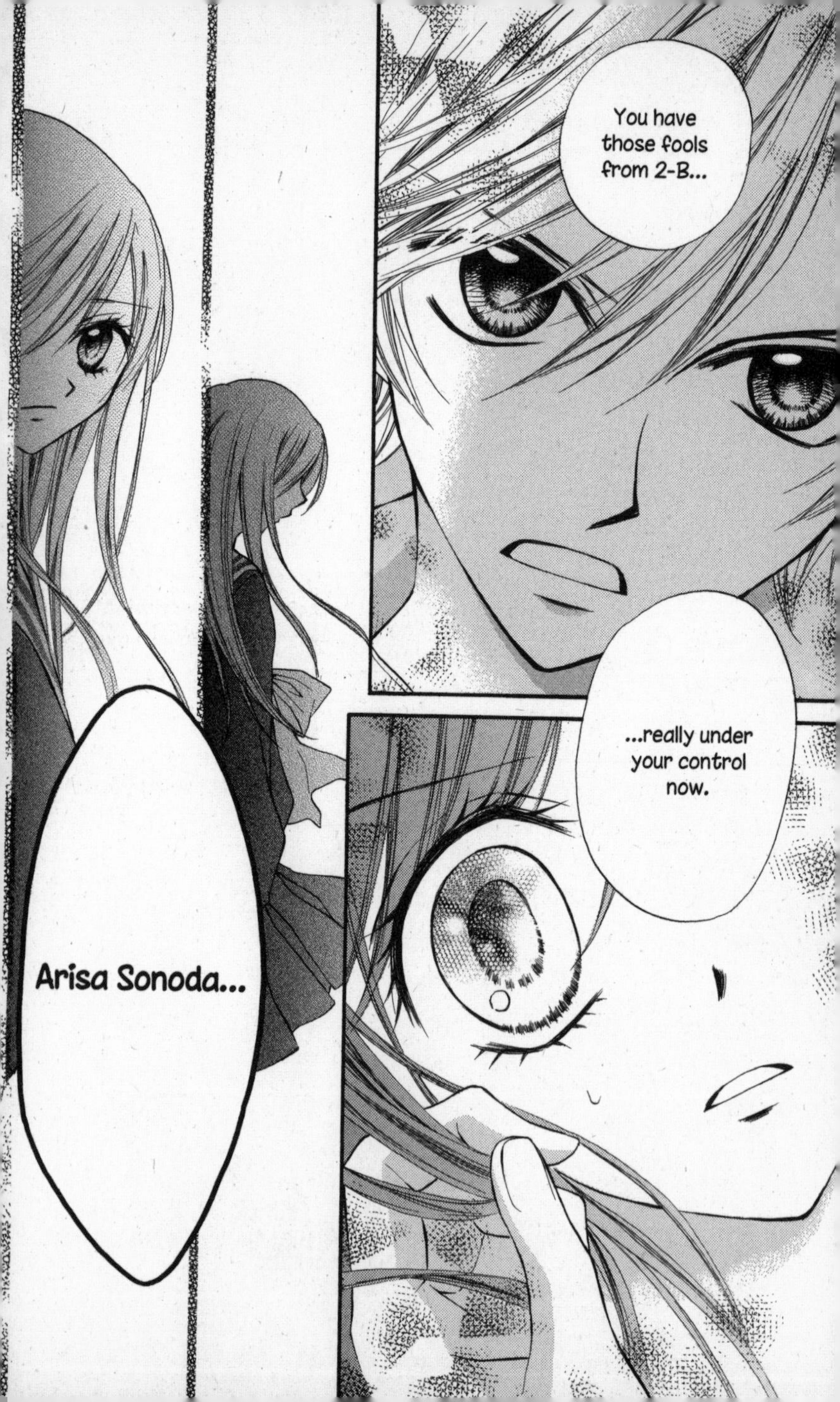
You have those fools from 2-B...
...really under your control now.
Arisa Sonoda...

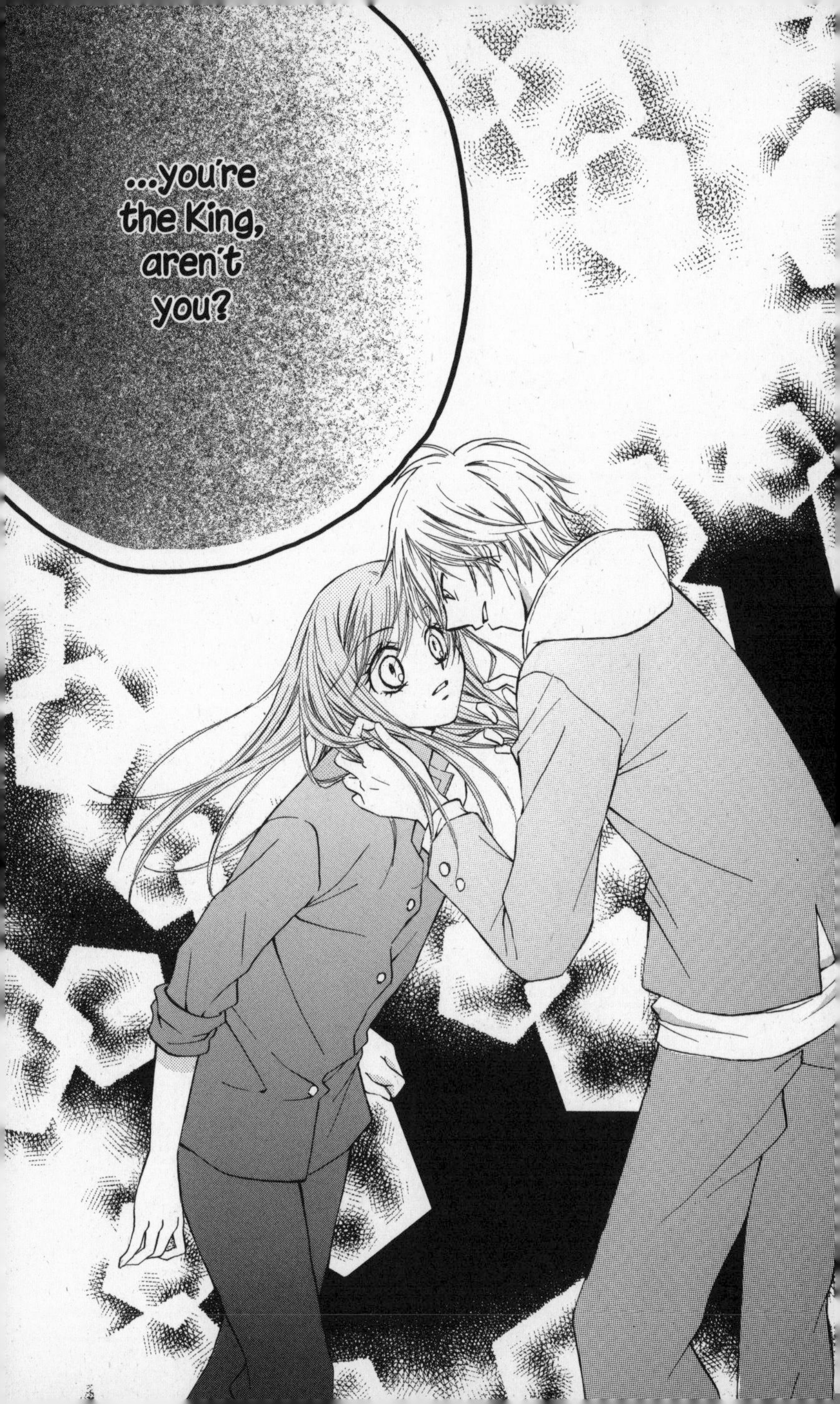
...you're the King, aren't you?

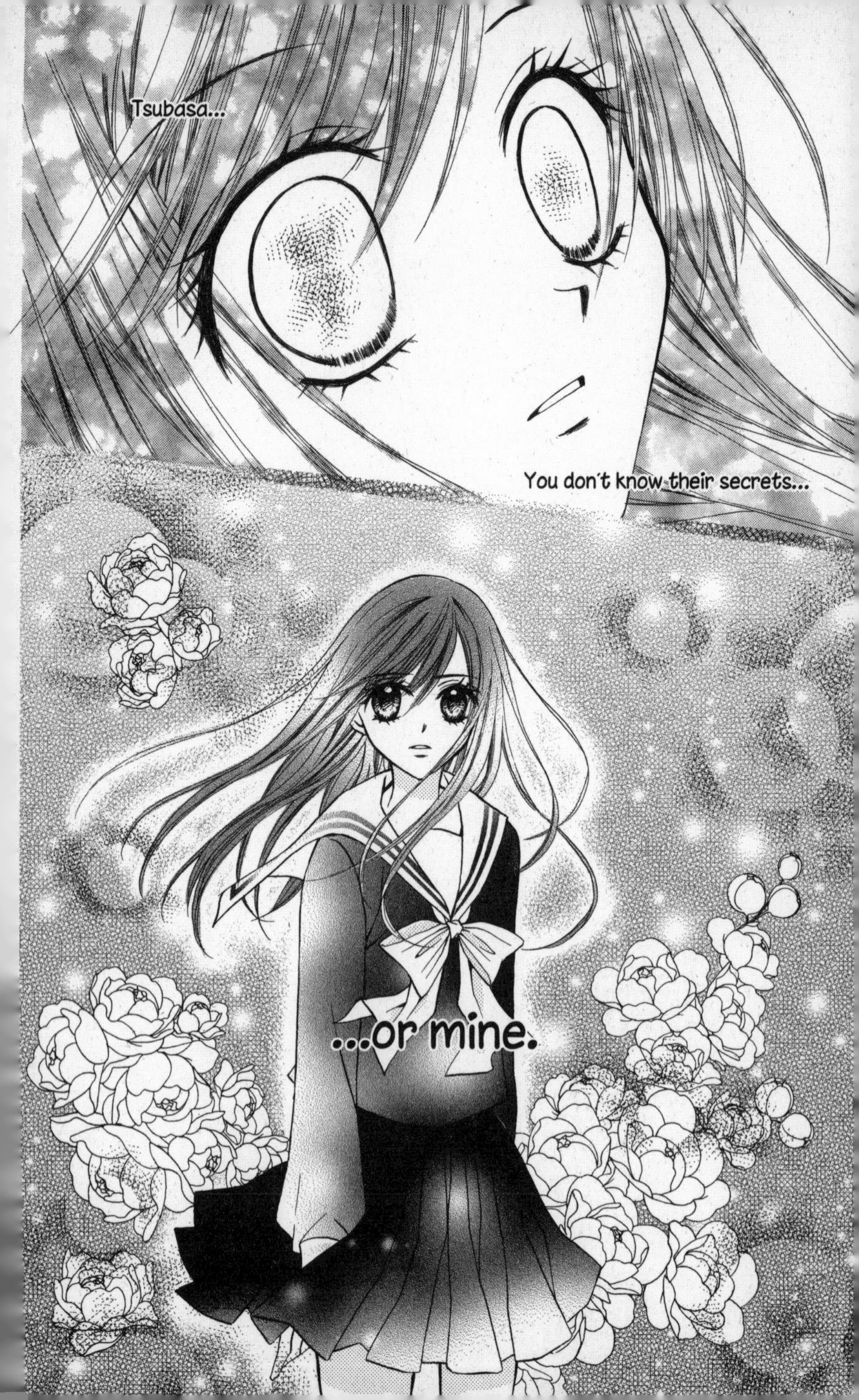
Tsubasa...
You don't know their secrets...
...or mine.

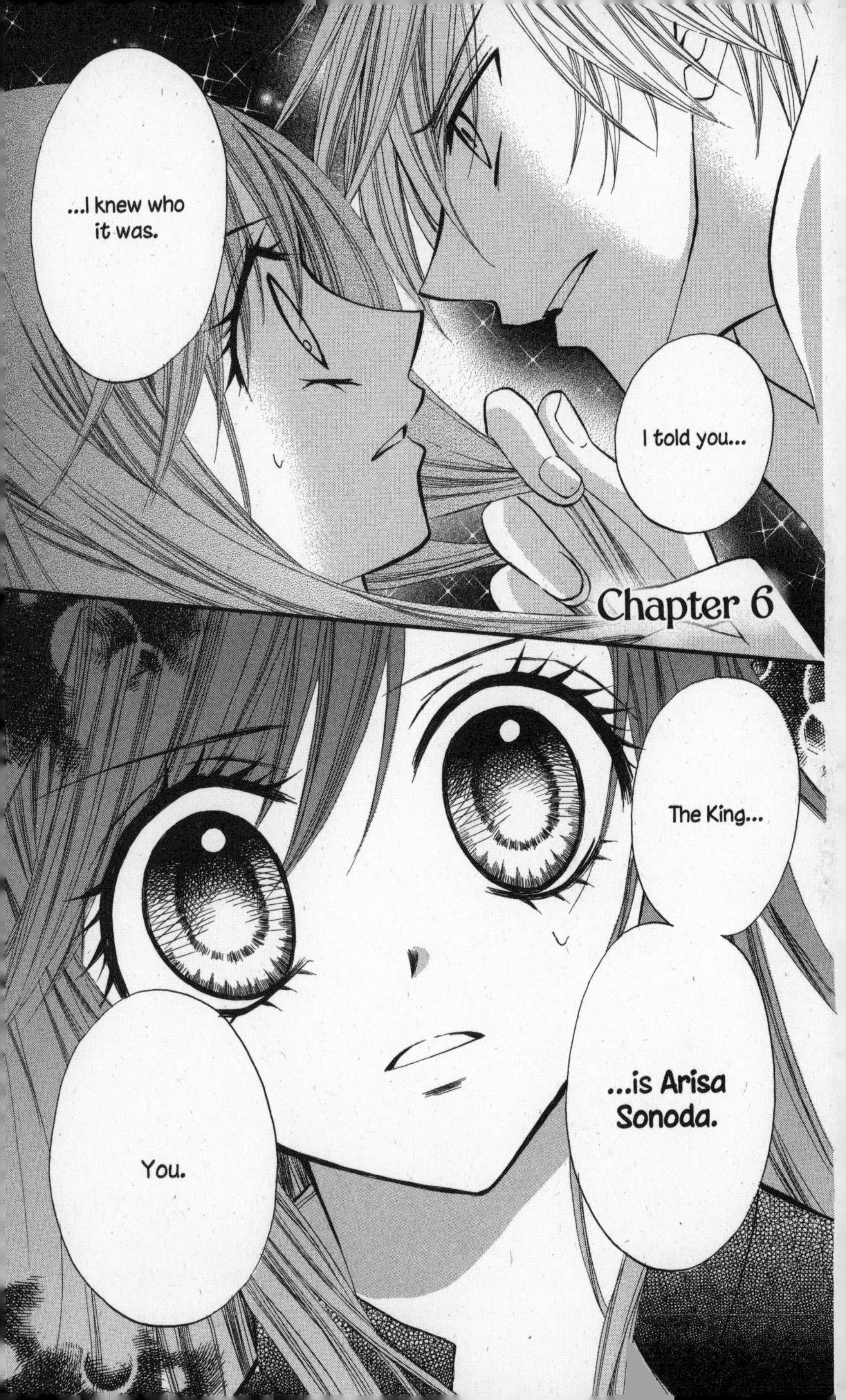
I told you...
...I knew who it was.
Chapter 6
The King...
...is Arisa Sonoda.
You.

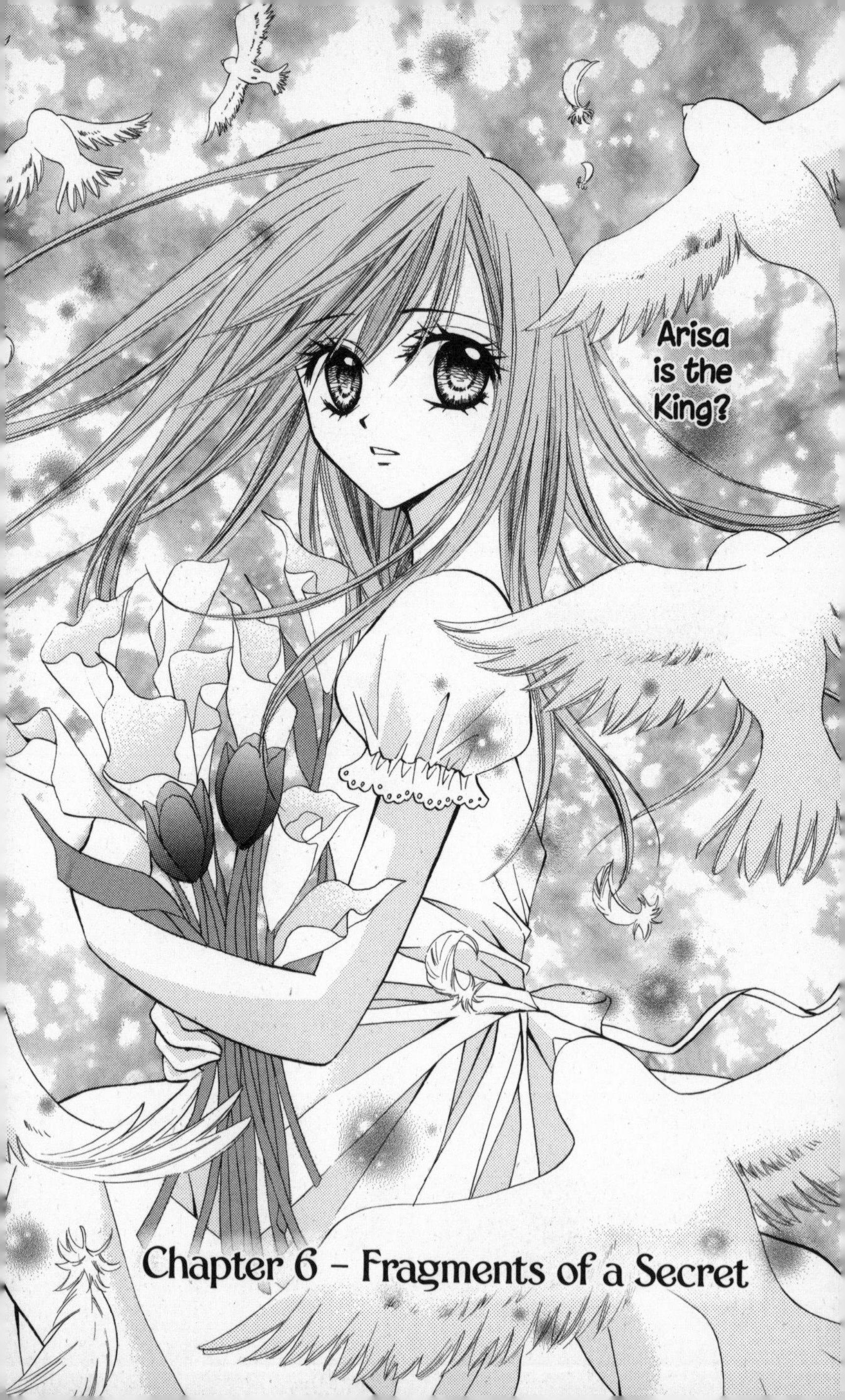
Arisa is the King?
Chapter 6 - Fragments of a Secret

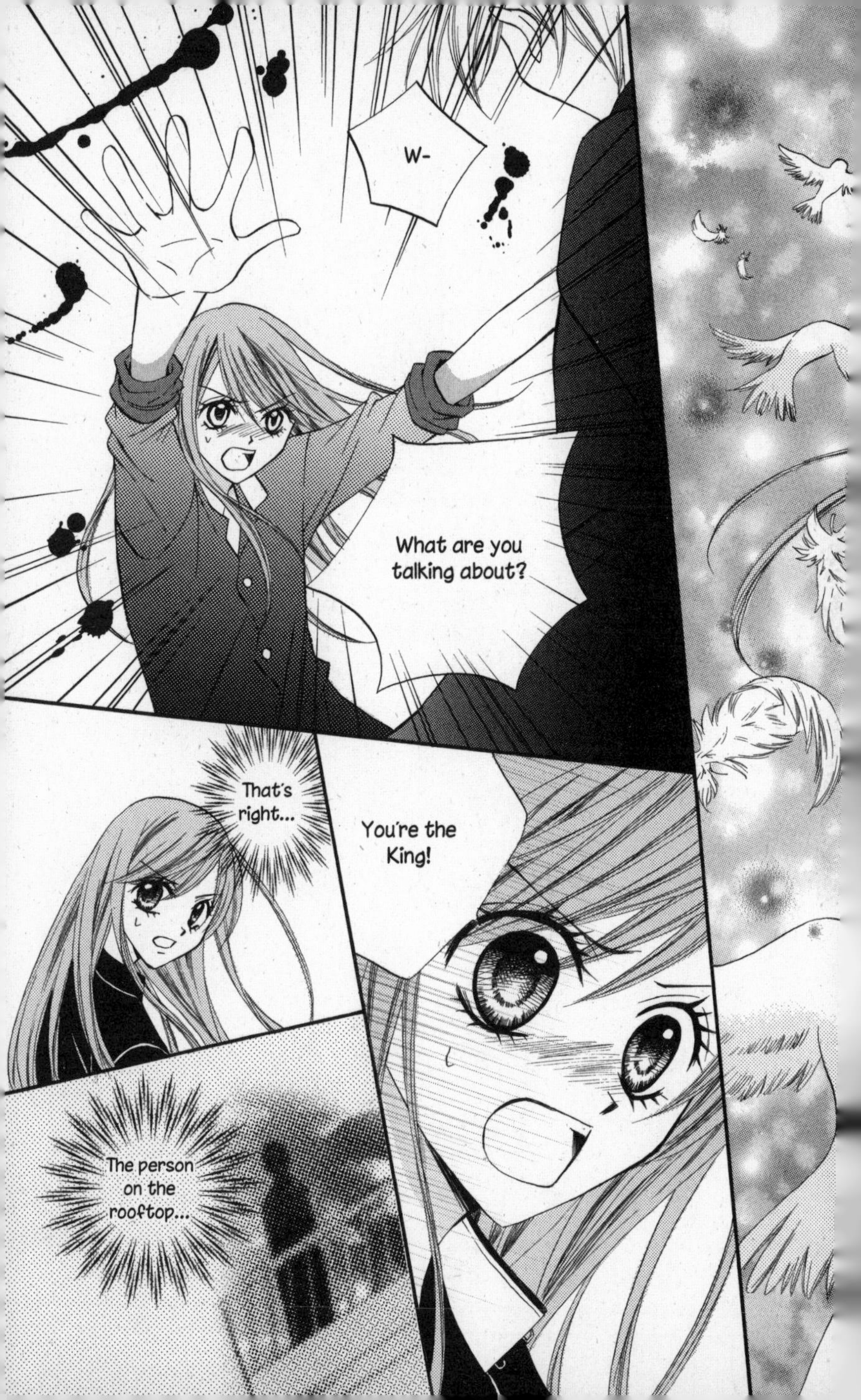
W-
What are you talking about?
You're the King!
That's right...
The person on the rooftop...

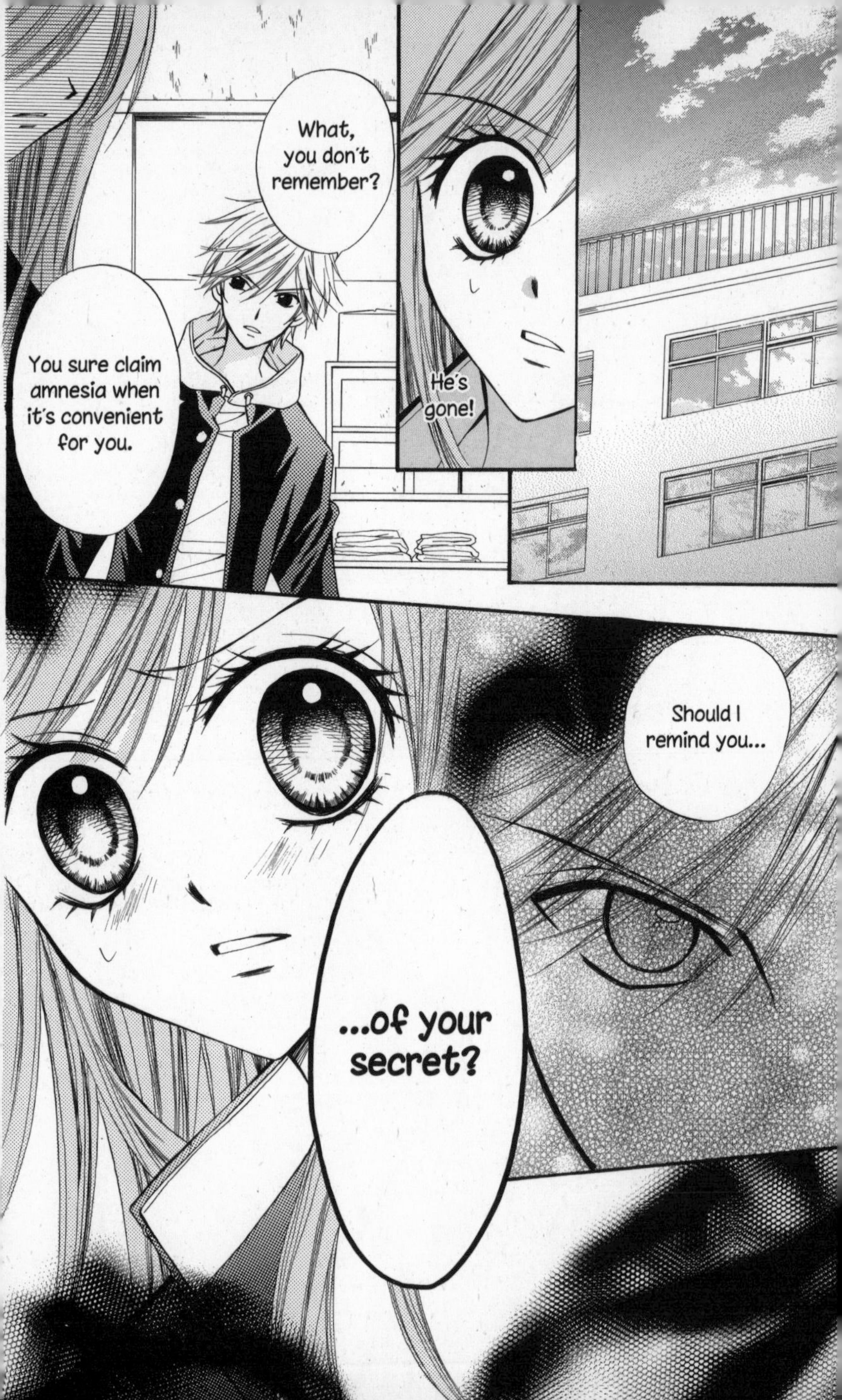
He's gone!
What, you don't remember?
You sure claim amnesia when it's convenient for you.
Should I remind you...
...of your secret?

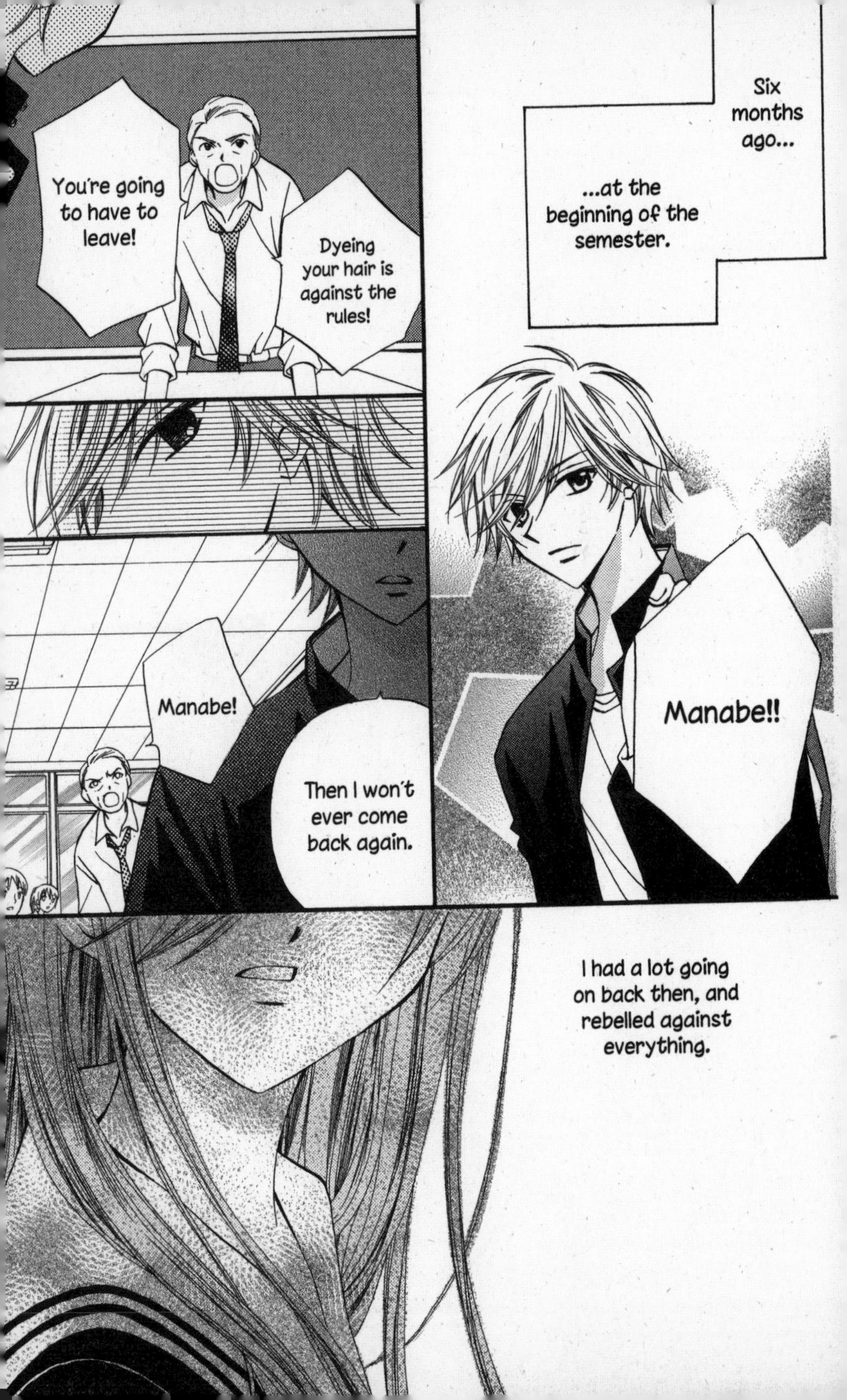
Six months ago...
...at the beginning of the semester.
Dyeing your hair is against the rules!
You're going to have to leave!
Then I won't ever come back again.
Manabe!
Manabe!!
I had a lot going on back then, and rebelled against everything.

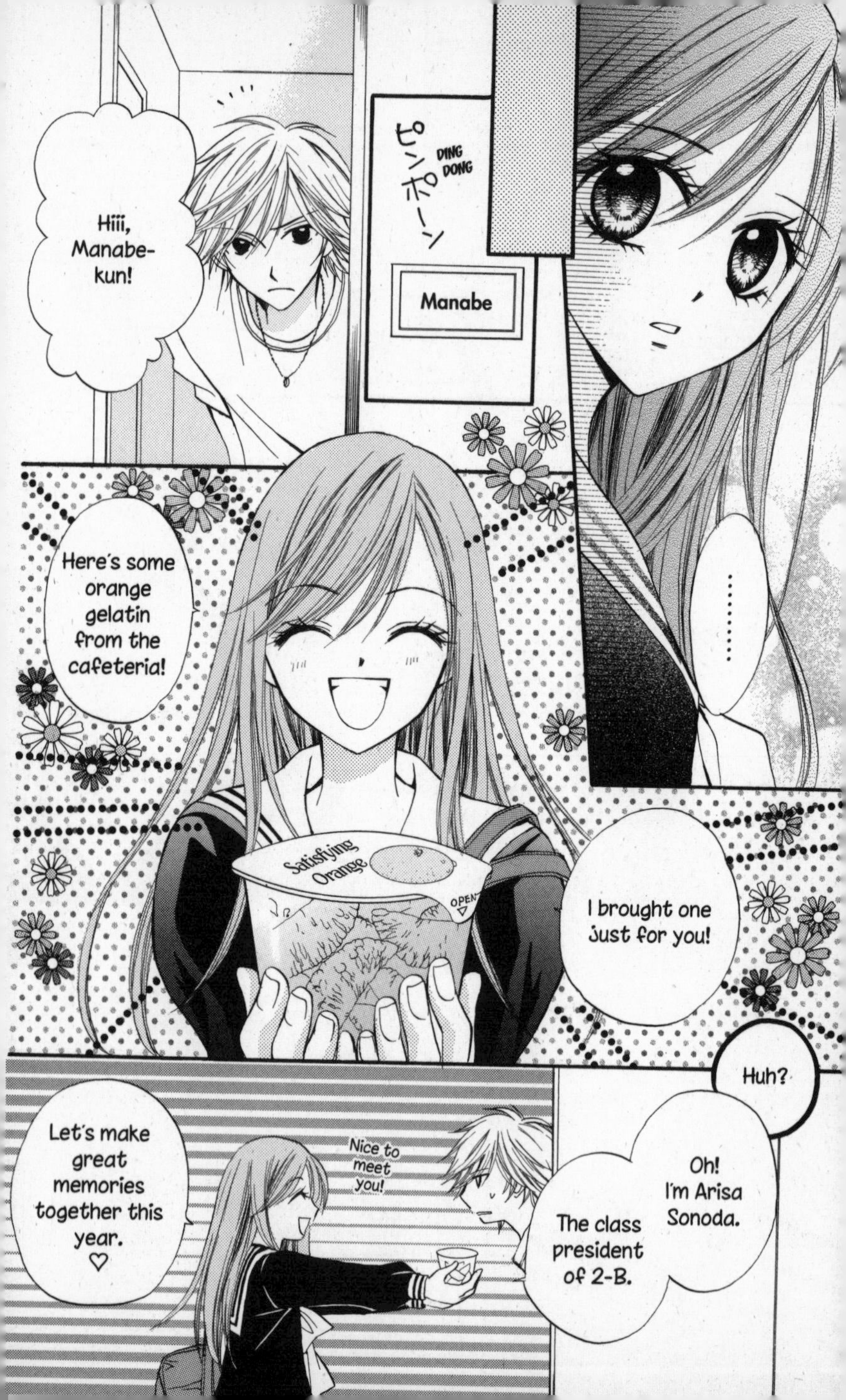
......
ピンポーン
DING DONG
Manabe
Hiii, Manabe-kun!
Here's some orange gelatin from the cafeteria!
Satisfying Orange
OPEN
I brought one just for you!
Huh?
Oh! I'm Arisa Sonoda.
The class president of 2-B.
Nice to meet you!
Let's make great memories together this year. ♡

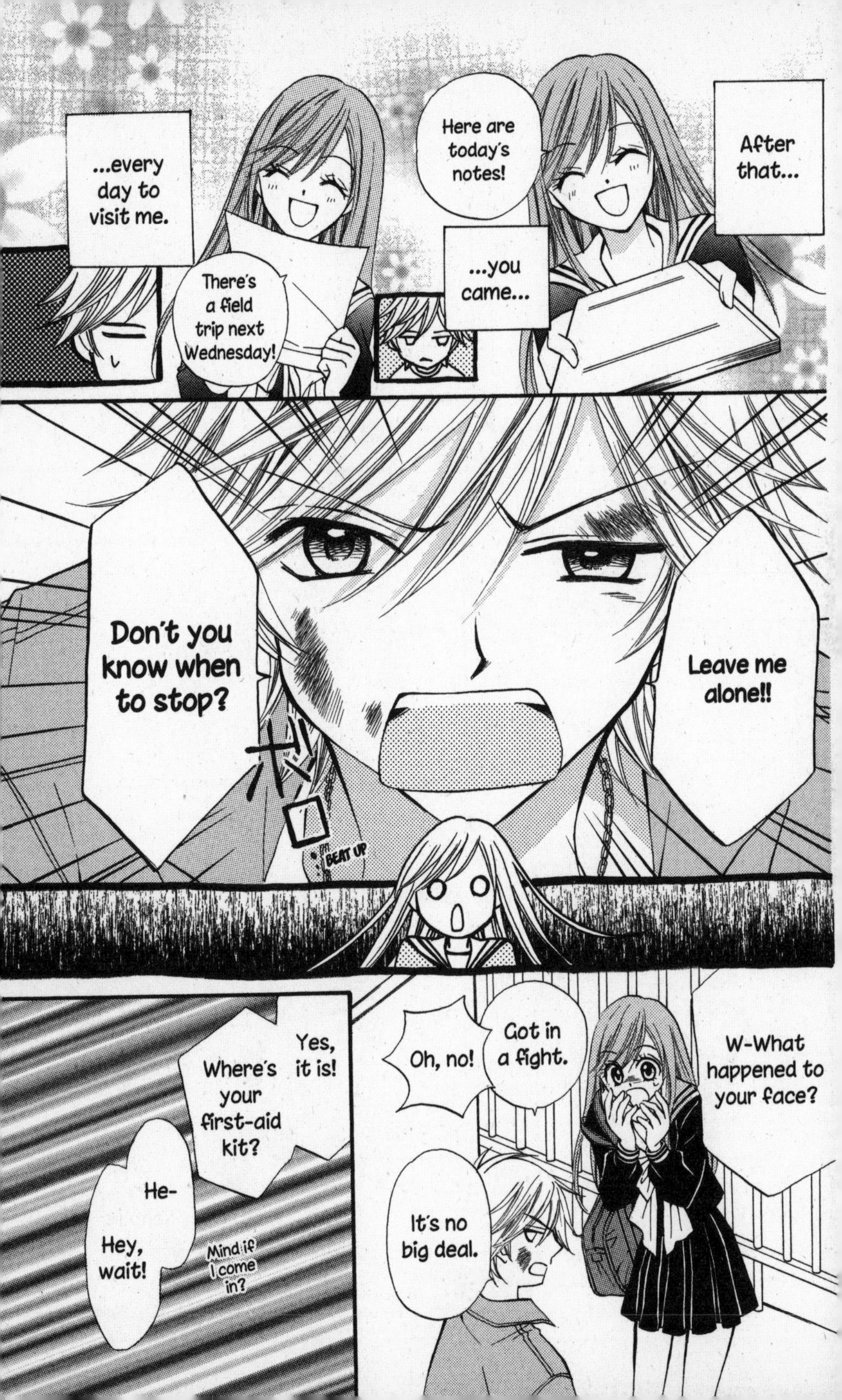
After that...
Here are today's notes!
...you came...
...every day to visit me.
There's a field trip next Wednesday!
Leave me alone!!
Don't you know when to stop?
BEAT UP
W-What happened to your face?
Got in a fight.
Oh, no!
It's no big deal.
Yes, it is!
Where's your first-aid kit?
He-
Hey, wait!
Mind if I come in?

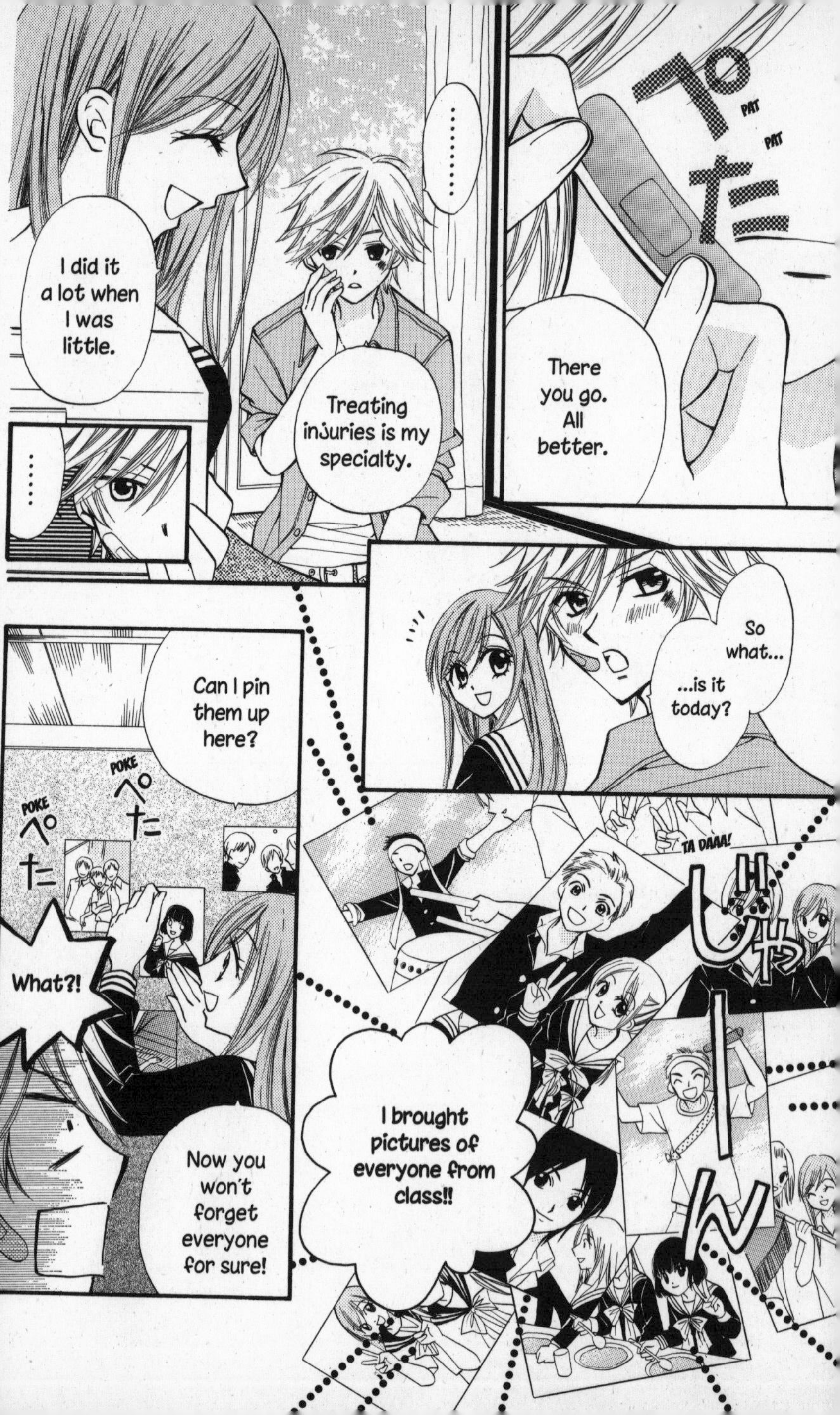
PAT
PAT
ぺたー
There you go. All better.
......
Treating injuries is my specialty.
I did it a lot when I was little.
......
So what...
...is it today?
TA DAAA!
しゃーん
I brought pictures of everyone from class!!
Can I pin them up here?
POKE
ぺた
POKE
ぺた
What?!
Now you won't forget everyone for sure!

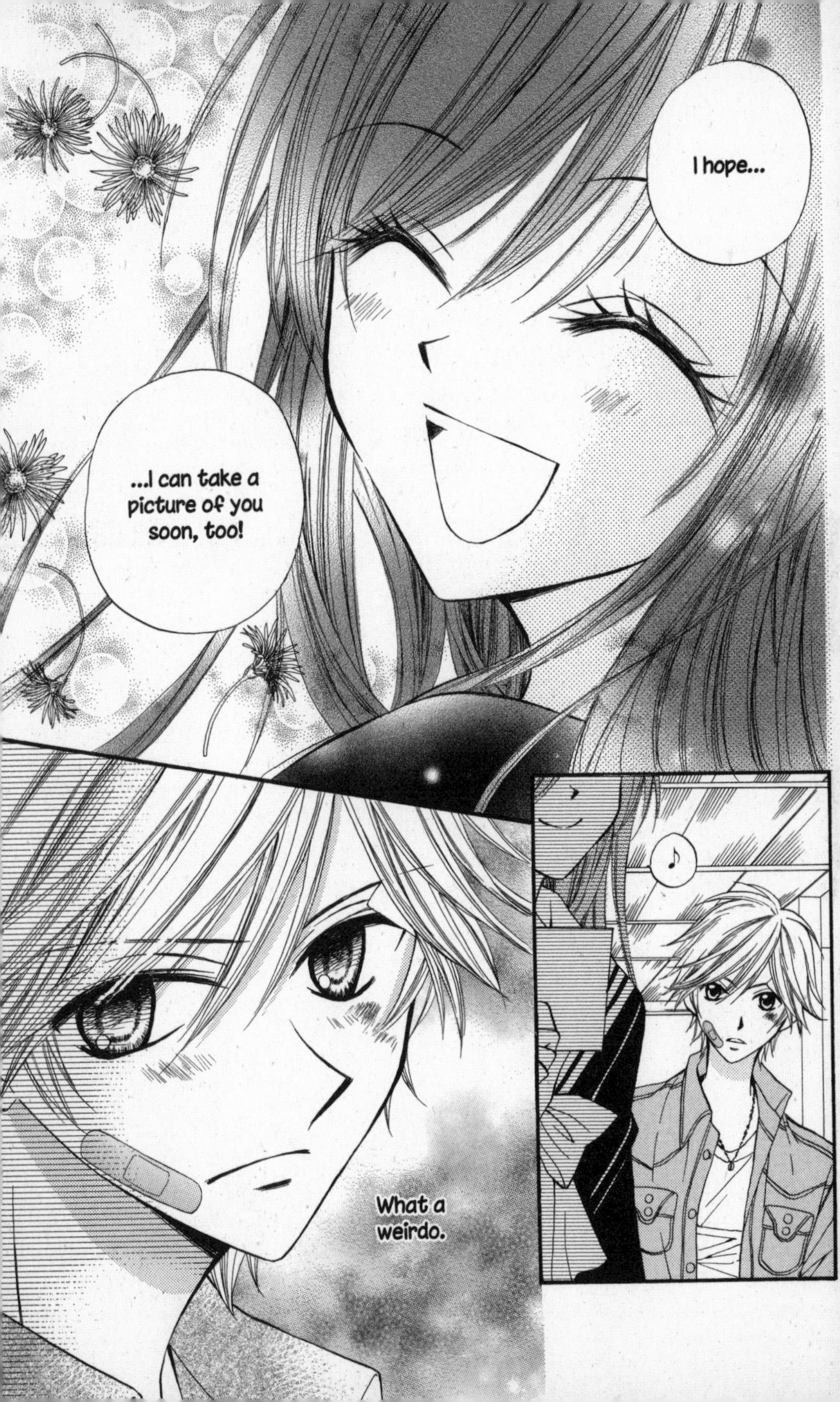
I hope...
...I can take a picture of you soon, too!
♪
What a weirdo.

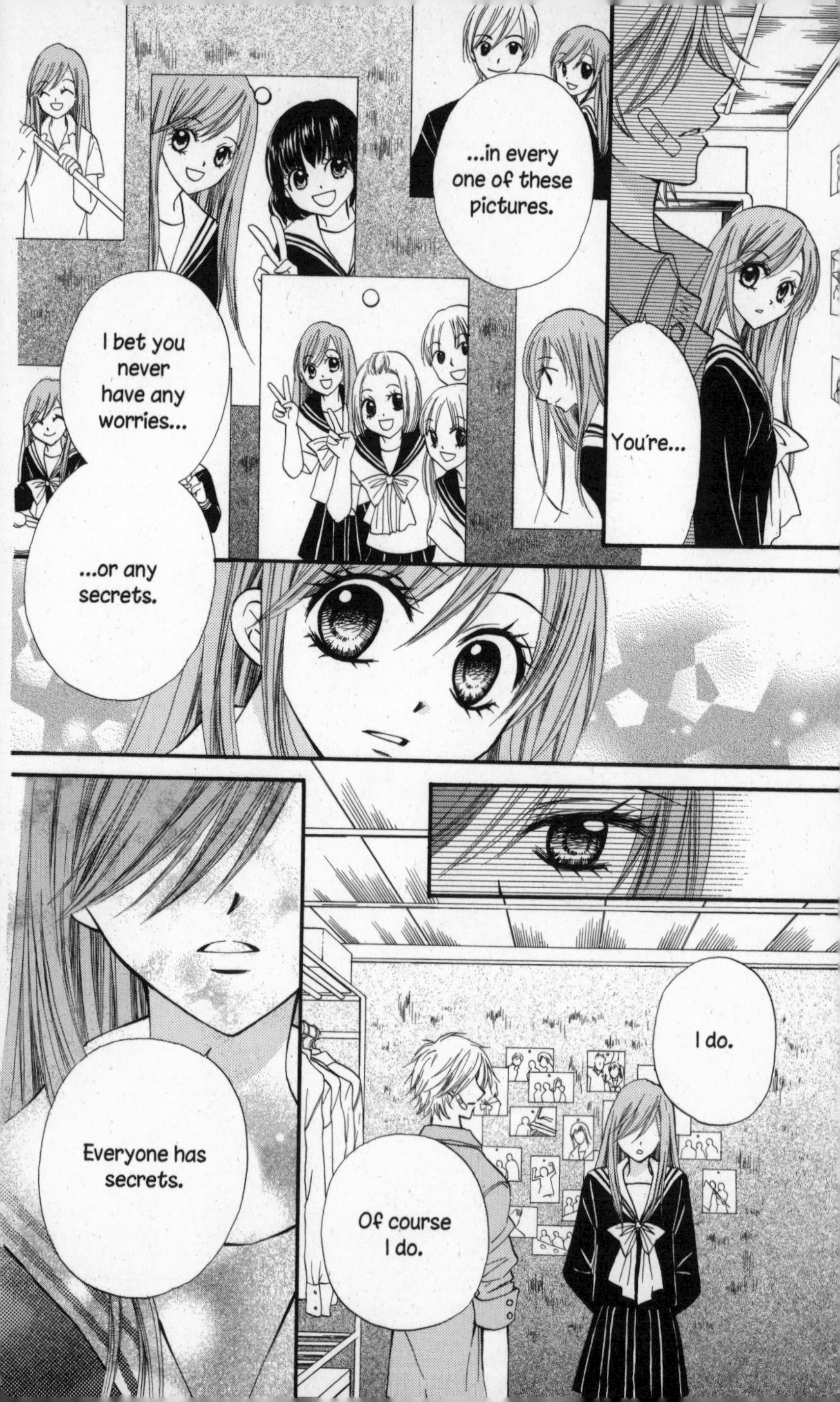
You're...
...in every one of these pictures.
I bet you never have any worries...
...or any secrets.
I do.
Of course I do.
Everyone has secrets.

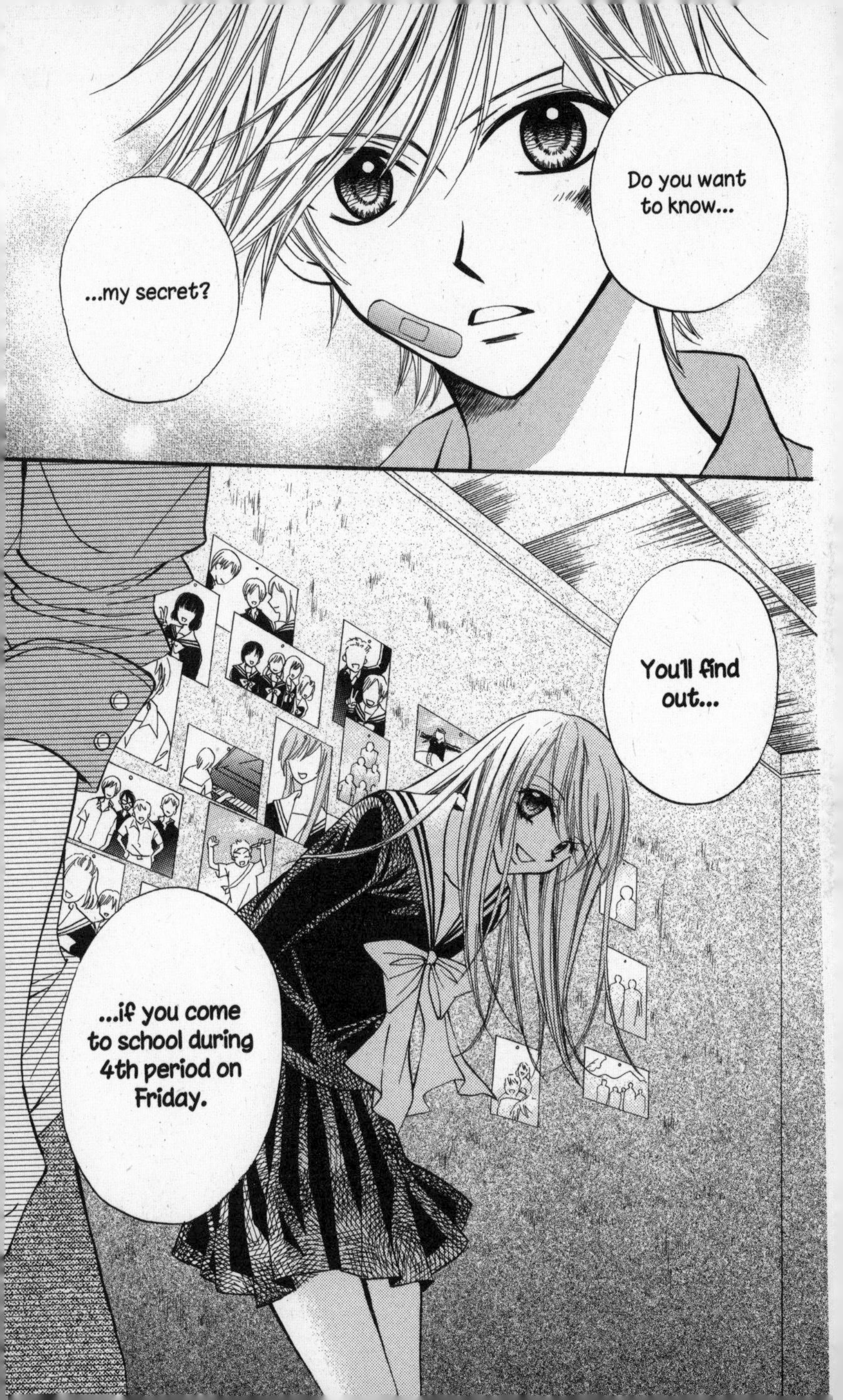
Do you want to know...
...my secret?
You'll find out...
...if you come to school during 4th period on Friday.

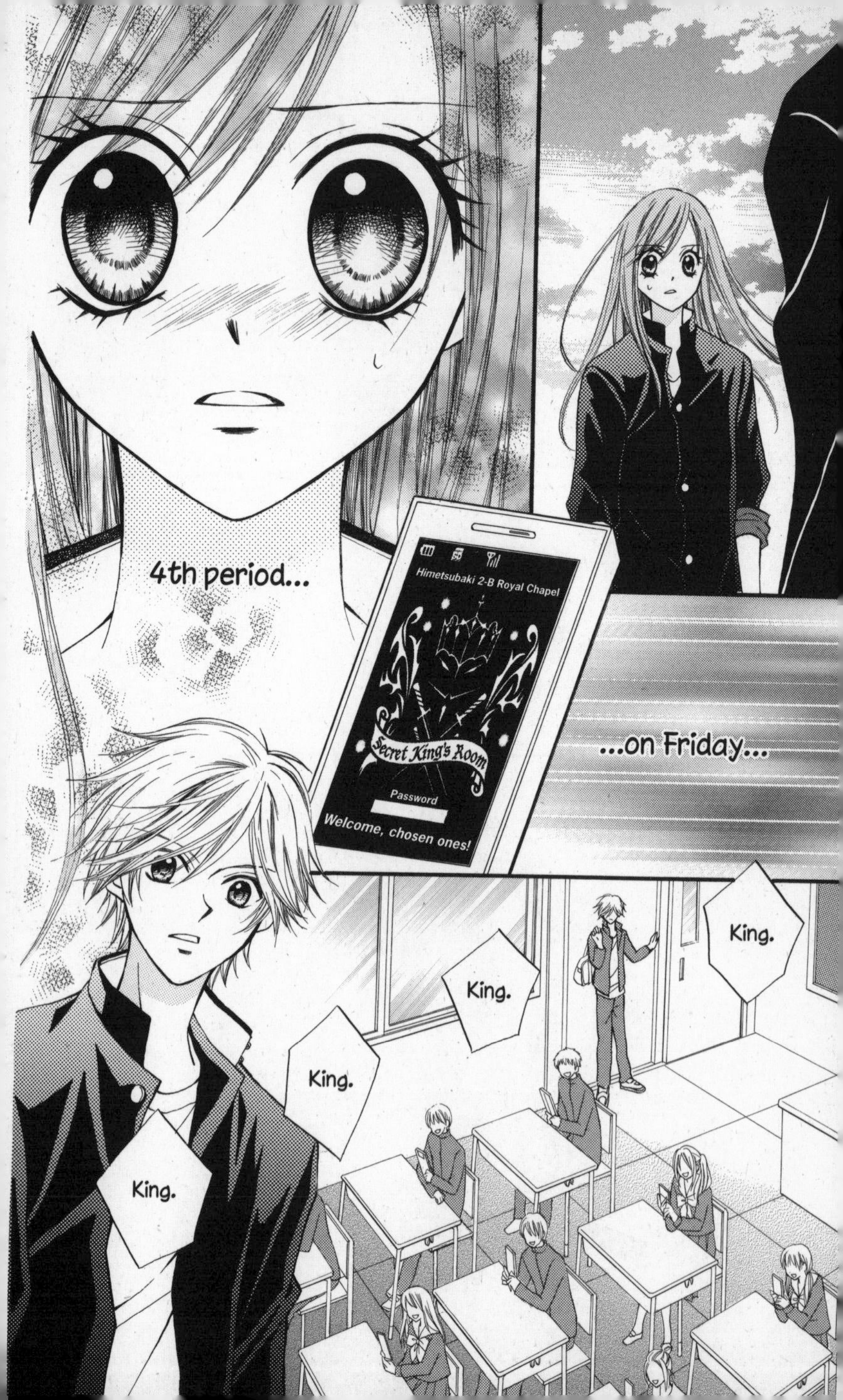
4th period...
Himetsubaki 2-B Royal Chapel
Secret King's Room
Password
Welcome, chosen ones!
...on Friday...
King.
King.
King.
King.

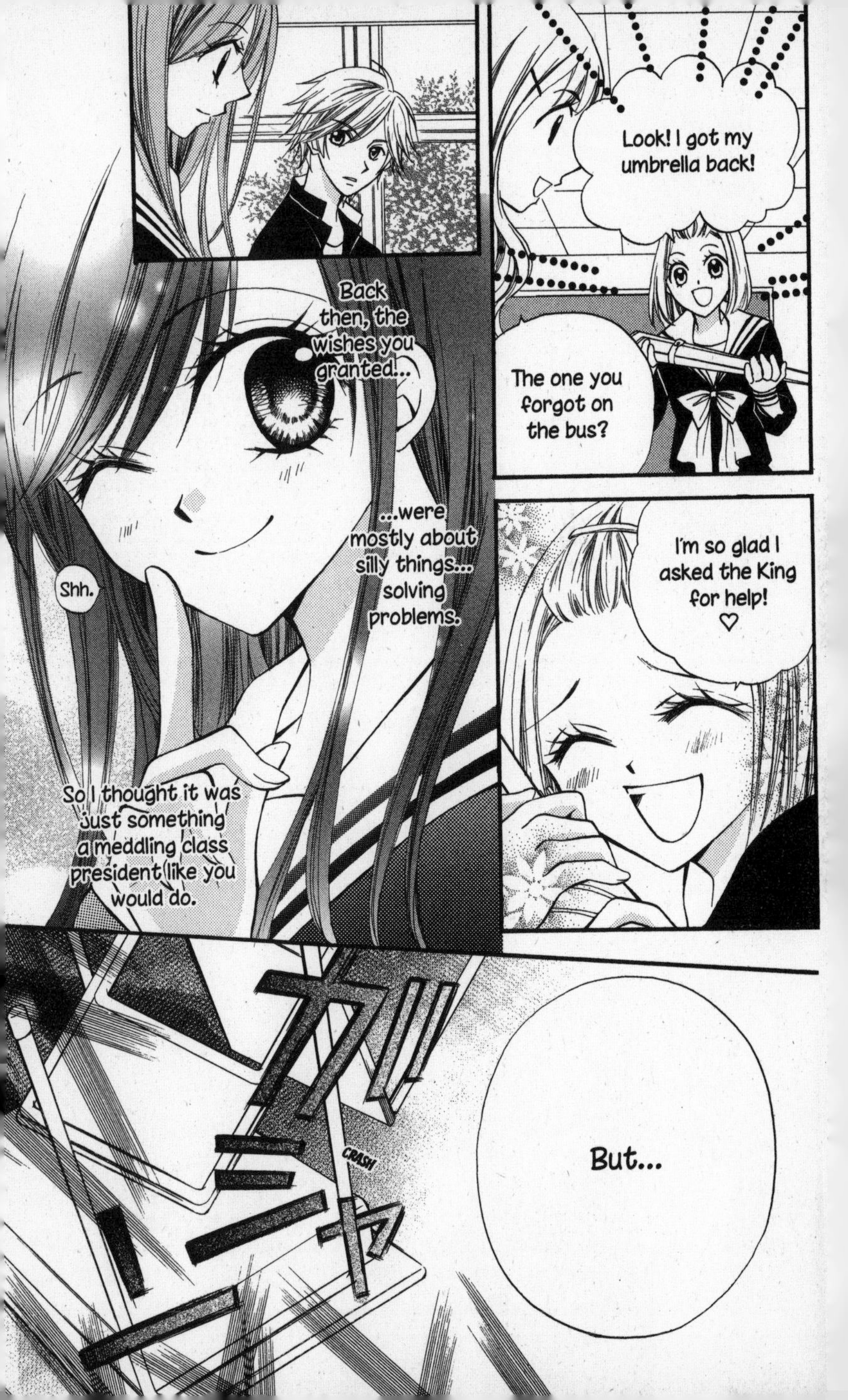

Look! I got my umbrella back!
The one you forgot on the bus?
I'm so glad I asked the King for help! ♡
Back then, the wishes you granted...
...were mostly about silly things... solving problems.
Shh.
So I thought it was just something a meddling class president like you would do.
But...
CRASH

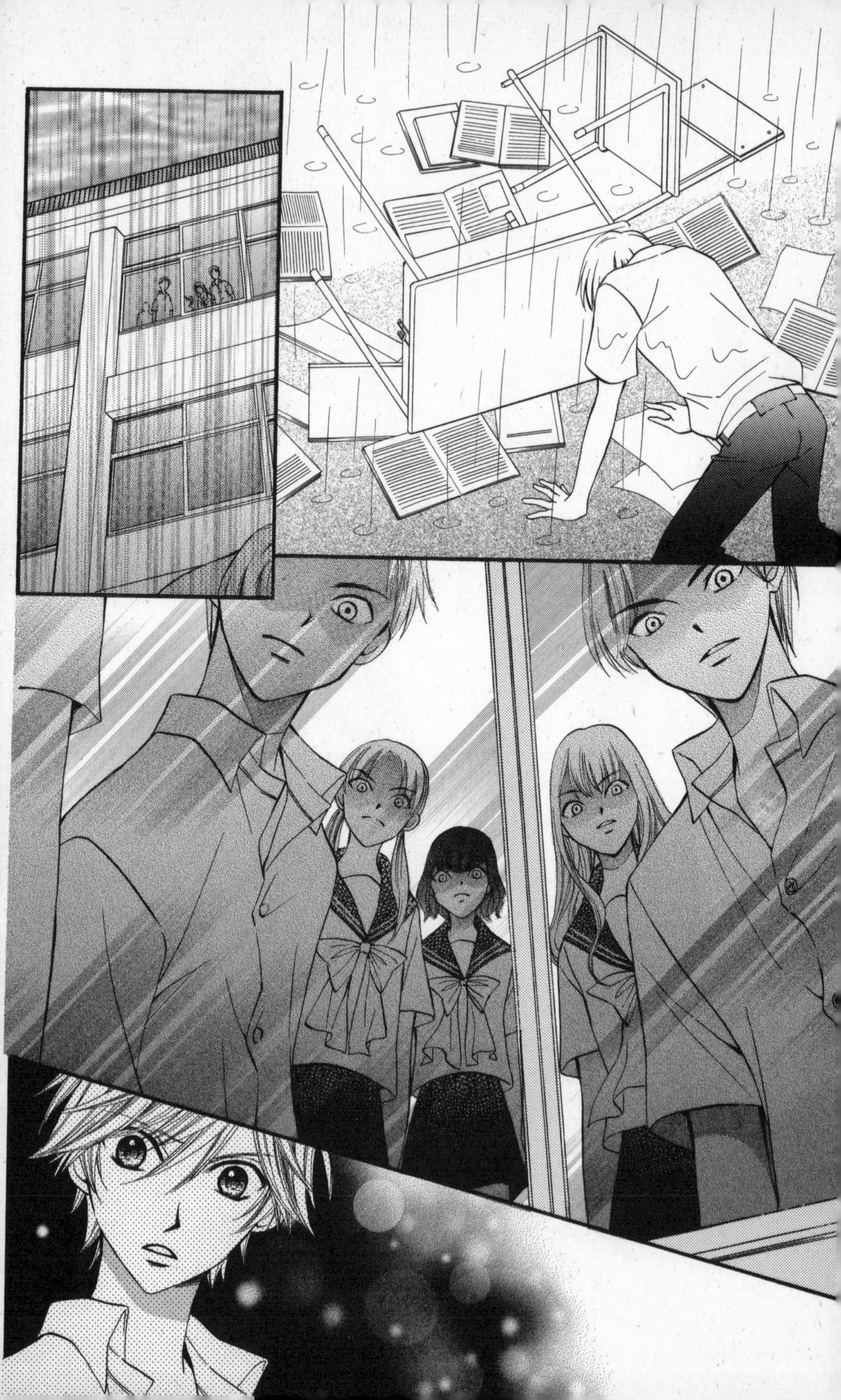

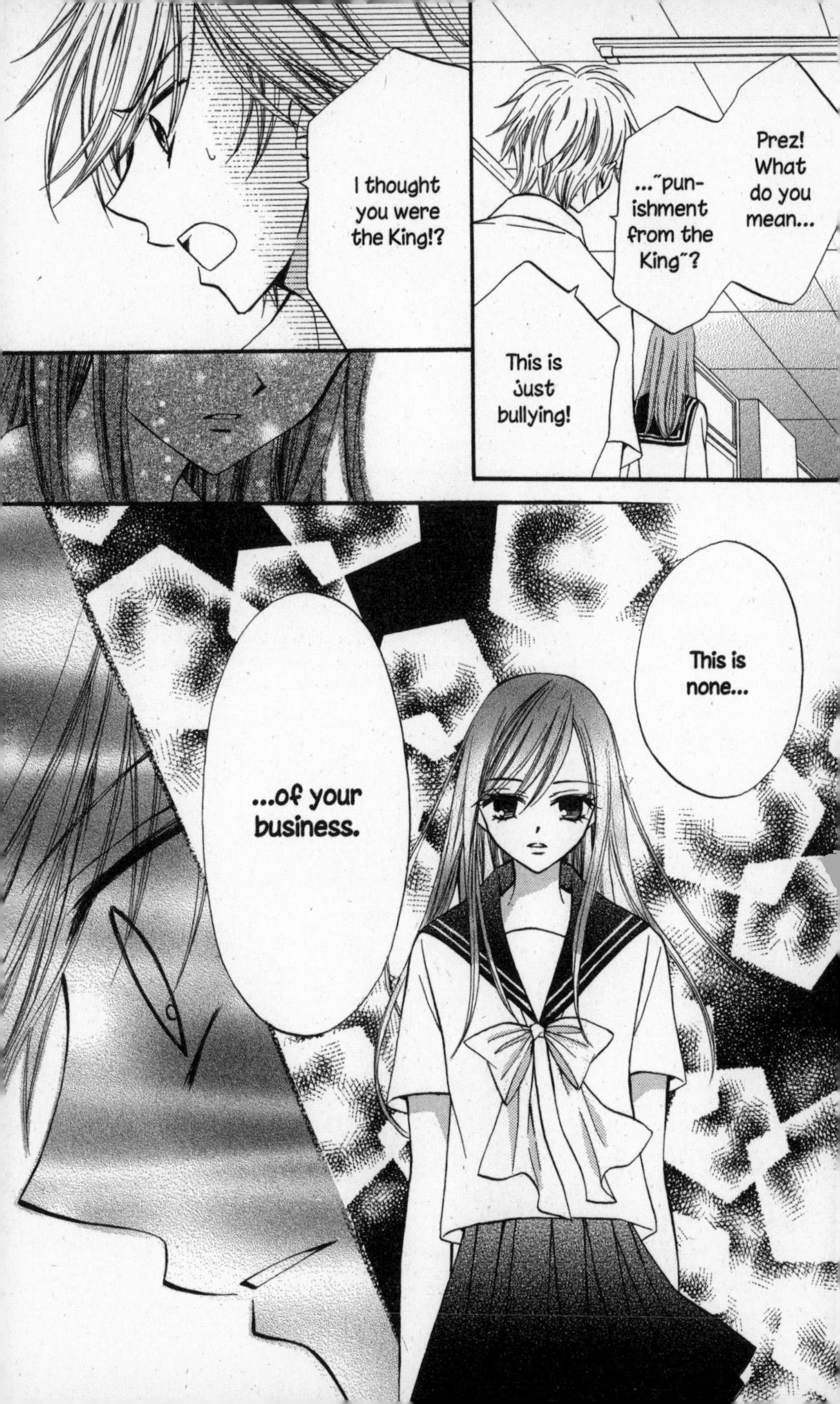
Prez! What do you mean...
..."punishment from the King"?
This is just bullying!
I thought you were the King!?
This is none...
...of your business.

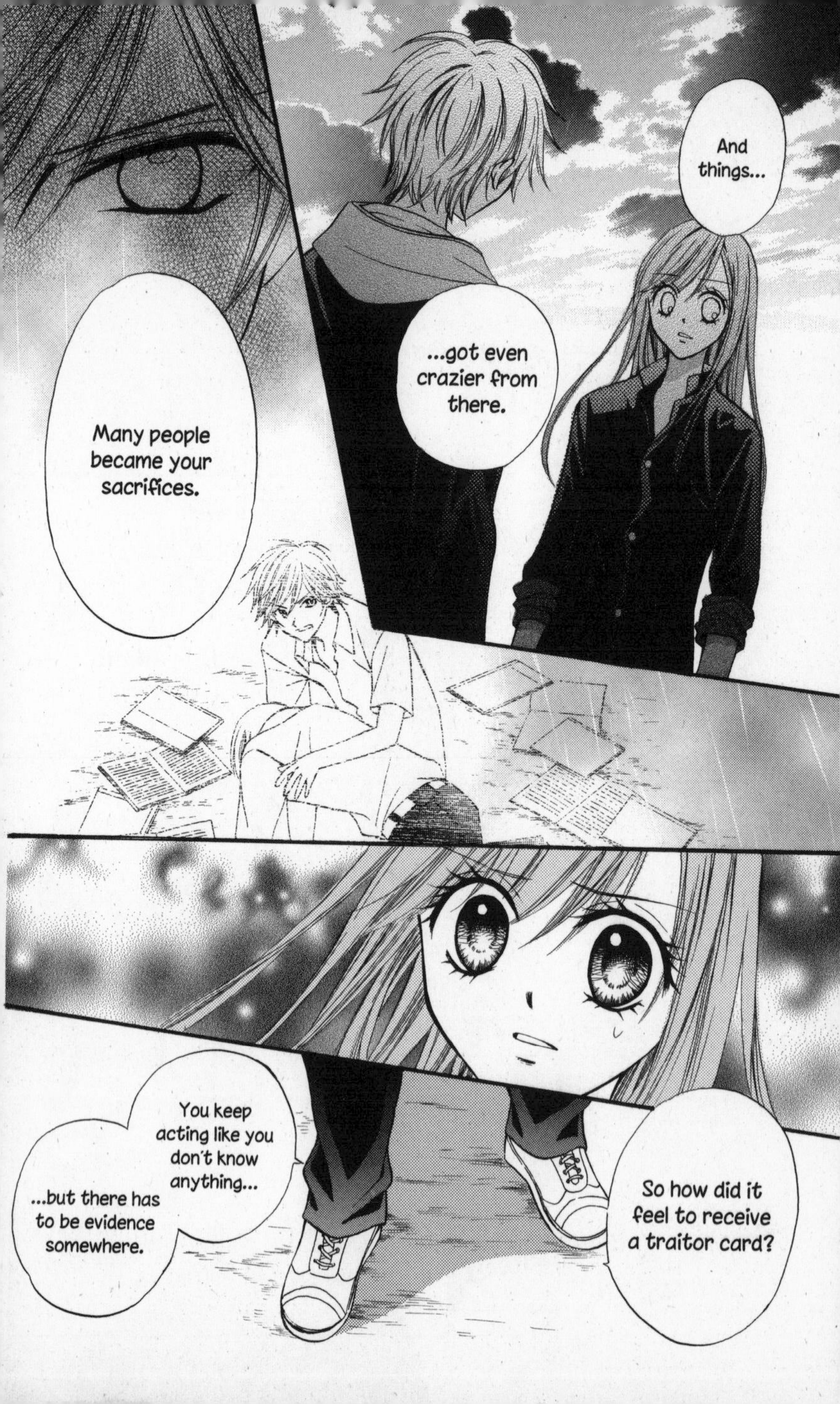
And things...
...got even crazier from there.
Many people became your sacrifices.
So how did it feel to receive a traitor card?
You keep acting like you don't know anything...
...but there has to be evidence somewhere.

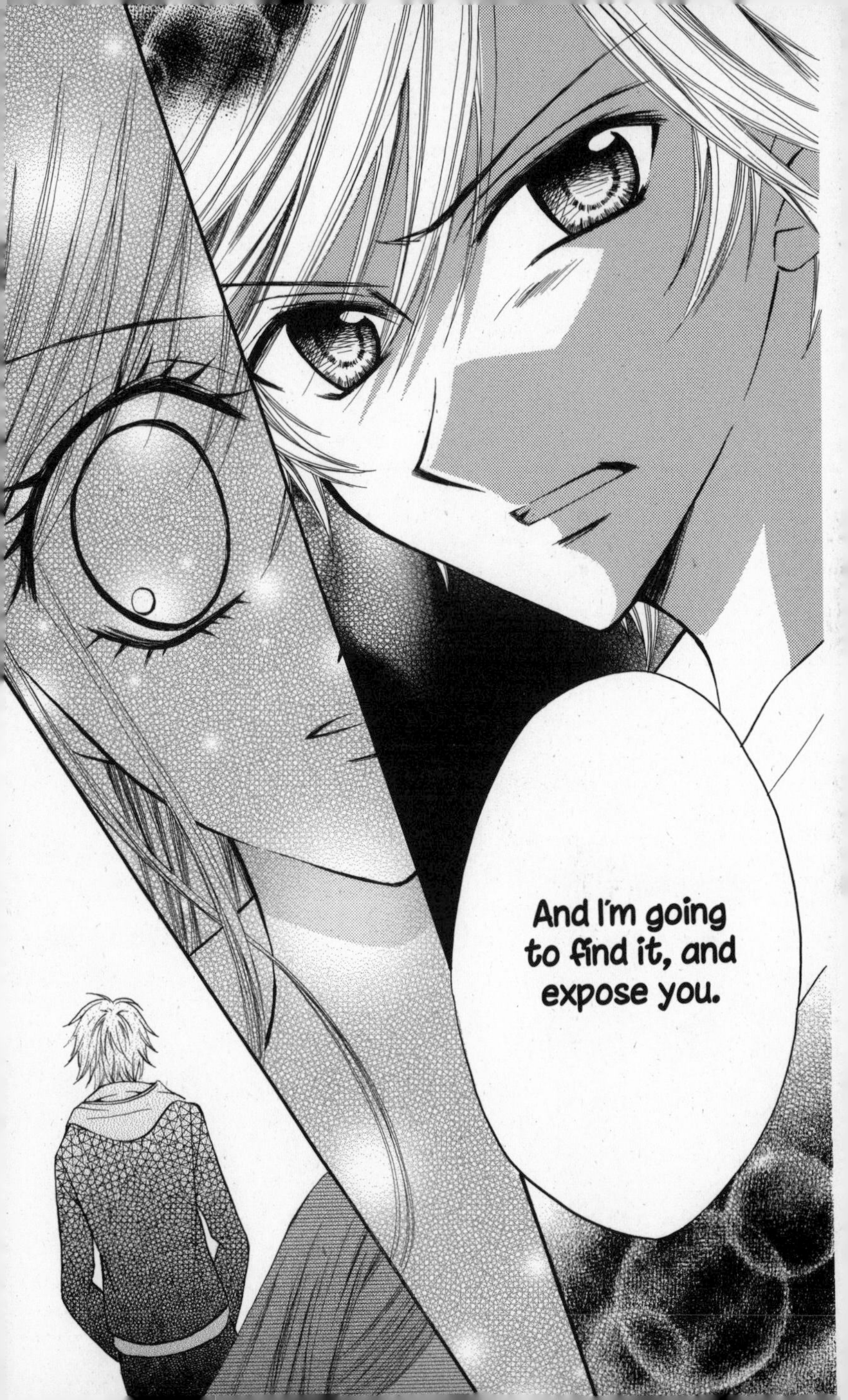
And I'm going to find it, and expose you.

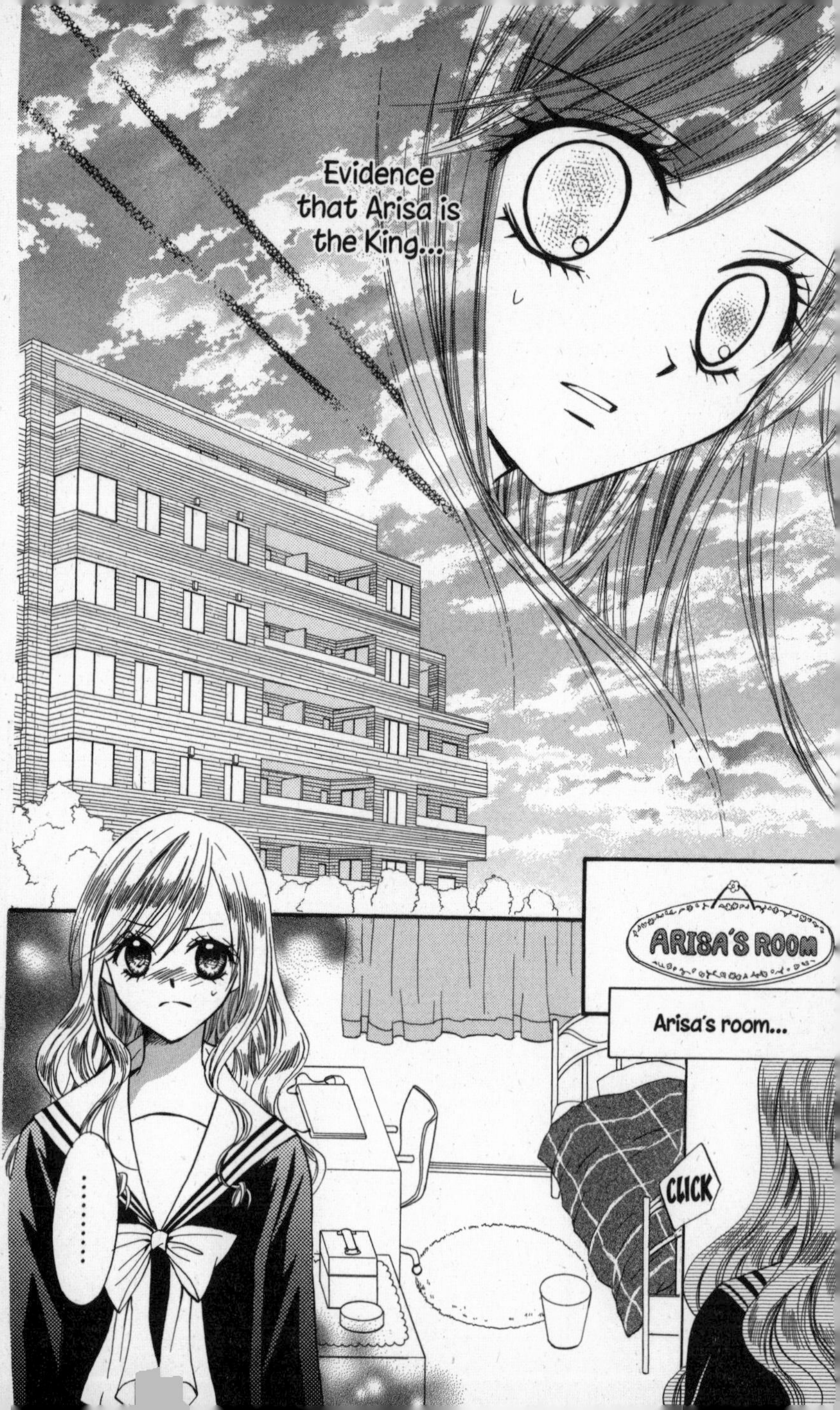

Evidence that Arisa is the King...
ARISA'S ROOM
Arisa's room...
CLICK
......

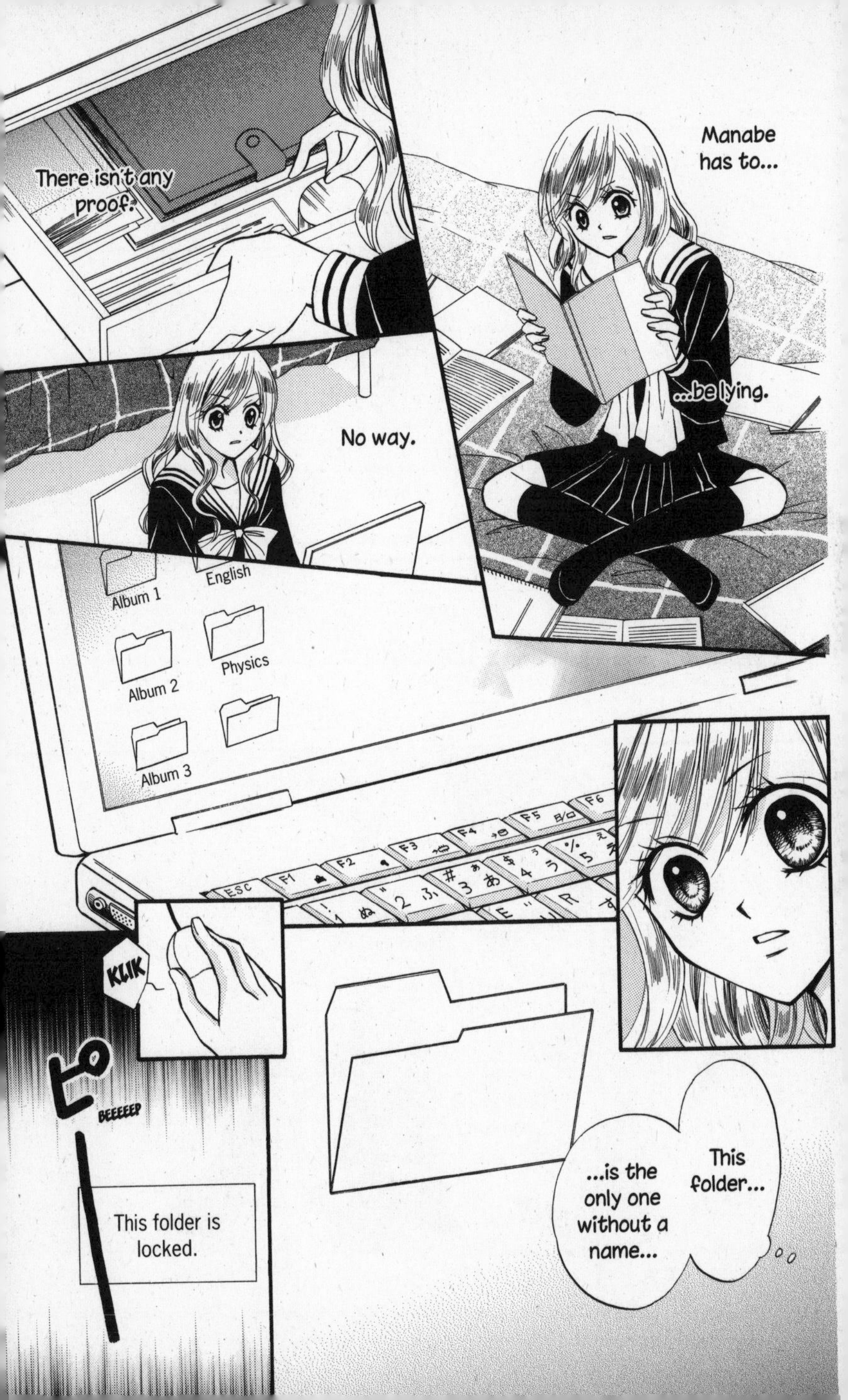
Manabe has to...
...be lying.
There isn't any proof.
No way.
English
Album 1
Physics
Album 2
Album 3
This folder...
...is the only one without a name...
KLIK
BEEEEEP
This folder is locked.

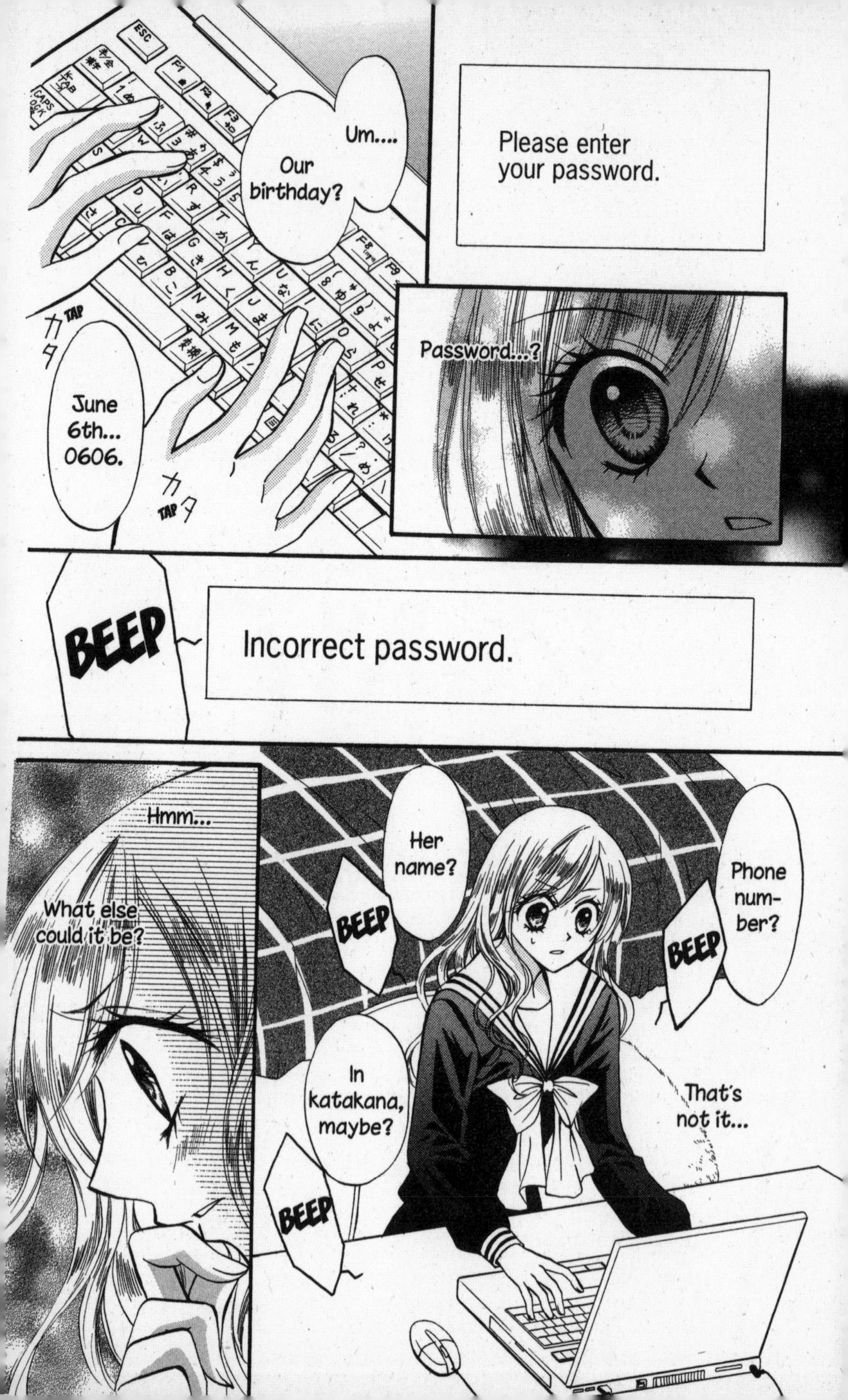

Please enter your password.
Password...?
Um.... Our birthday?
カタ TAP
June 6th... 0606.
カタ TAP
Incorrect password.
BEEP~
Phone num- ber?
BEEP
Her name?
BEEP
That's not it...
In katakana, maybe?
BEEP
Hmm...
What else could it be?

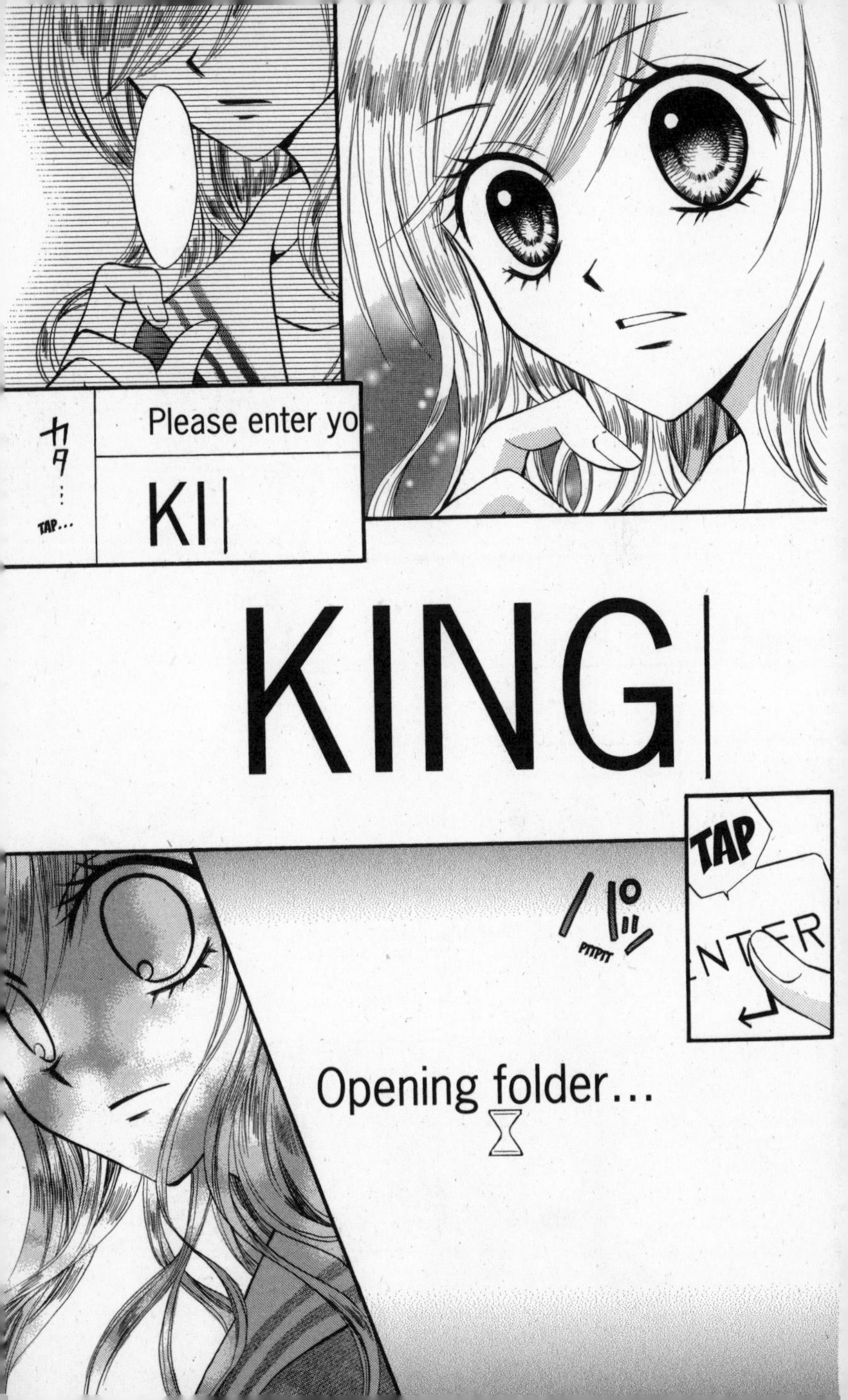
Please enter yo
KI|
カタ…
TAP...
KING|
TAP
ENTER
PITPIT
Opening folder...

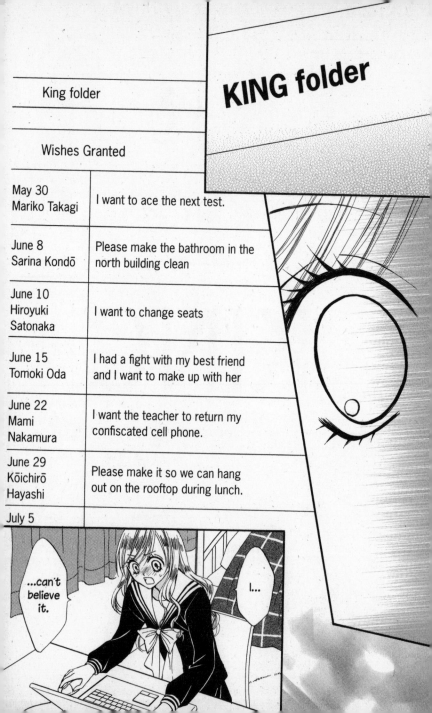

KING folder

King folder

Wishes Granted

May 30 Mariko Takagi	I want to ace the next test.
June 8 Sarina Kondō	Please make the bathroom in the north building clean
June 10 Hiroyuki Satonaka	I want to change seats
June 15 Tomoki Oda	I had a fight with my best friend and I want to make up with her
June 22 Mami Nakamura	I want the teacher to return my confiscated cell phone.
June 29 Kōichirō Hayashi	Please make it so we can hang out on the rooftop during lunch.
July 5	

...can't believe it.

I...

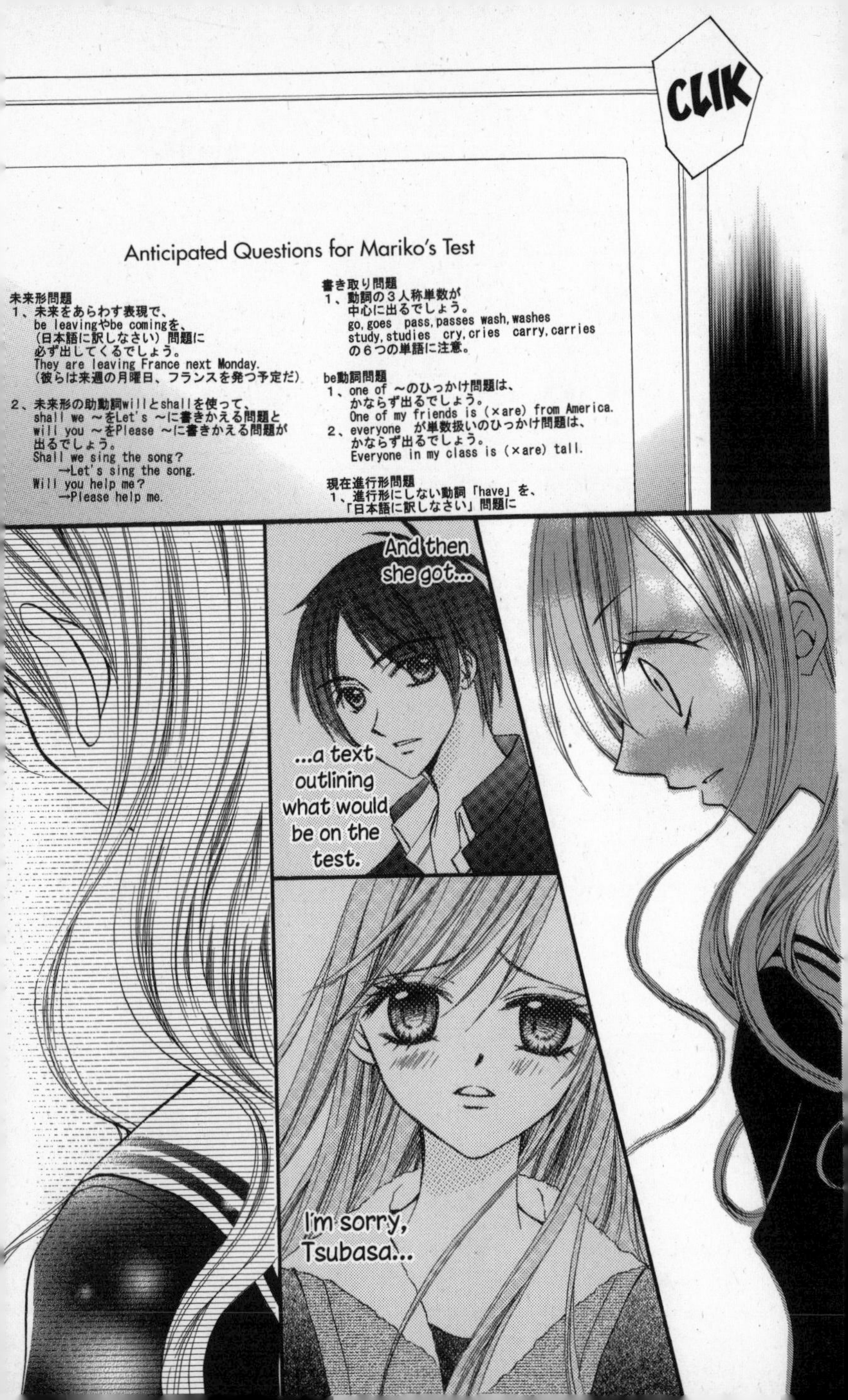
CLIK
Anticipated Questions for Mariko's Test
未来形問題
1、未来をあらわす表現で、
be leavingやbe comingを、
(日本語に訳しなさい) 問題に
必ず出してくるでしょう。
They are leaving France next Monday.
(彼らは来週の月曜日、フランスを発つ予定だ)
2、未来形の助動詞willとshallを使って、
shall we ～をLet's ～に書きかえる問題と
will you ～をPlease ～に書きかえる問題が
出るでしょう。
Shall we sing the song?
→Let's sing the song.
Will you help me?
→Please help me.
書き取り問題
1、動詞の3人称単数が
中心に出るでしょう。
go,goes pass,passes wash,washes
study,studies cry,cries carry,carries
の6つの単語に注意。
be動詞問題
1、one of ～のひっかけ問題は、
かならず出るでしょう。
One of my friends is (×are) from America.
2、everyone が単数扱いのひっかけ問題は、
かならず出るでしょう。
Everyone in my class is (×are) tall.
現在進行形問題
1、進行形にしない動詞「have」を、
「日本語に訳しなさい」問題に
And then she got...
...a text outlining what would be on the test.
I'm sorry, Tsubasa...

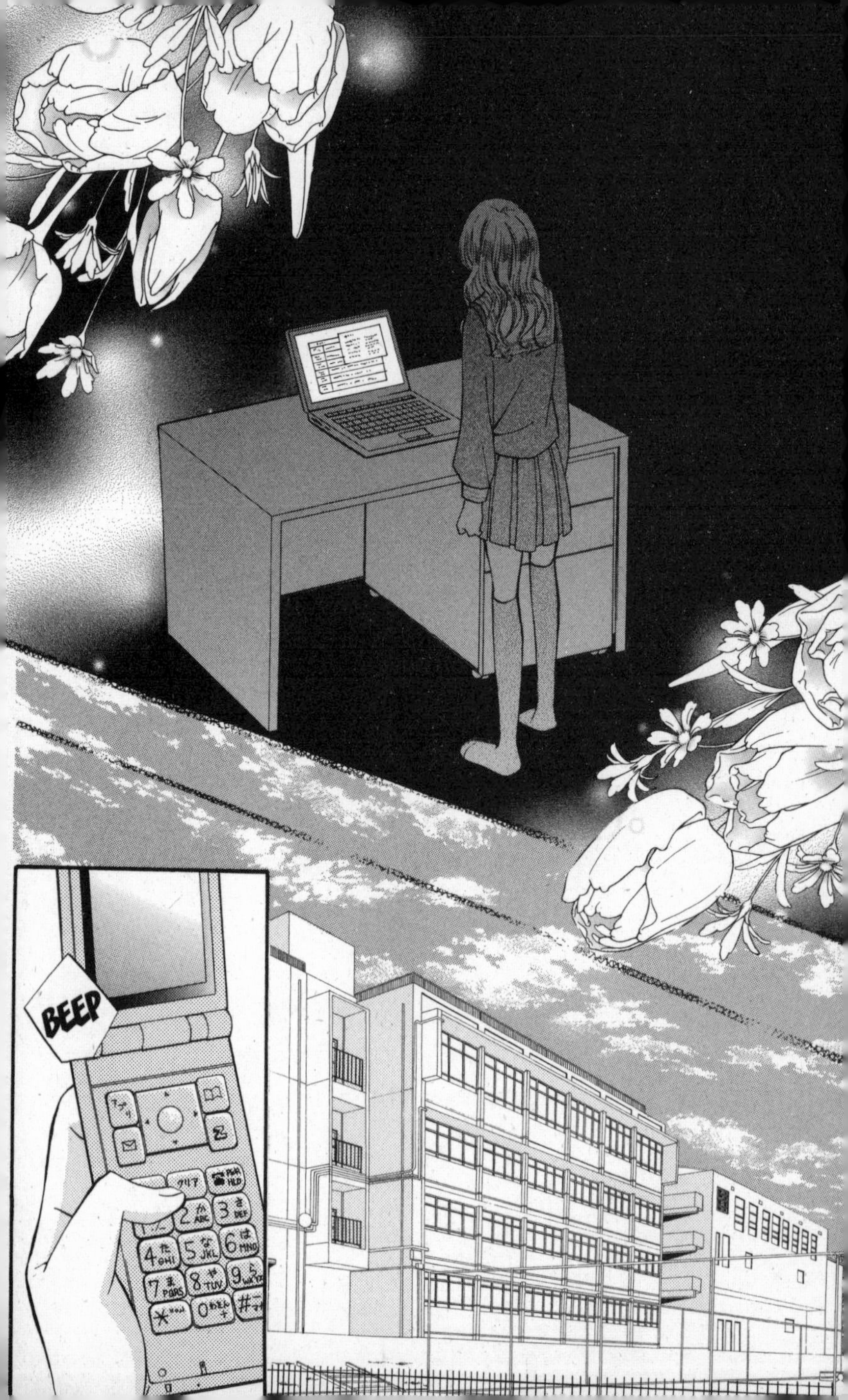
BEEP

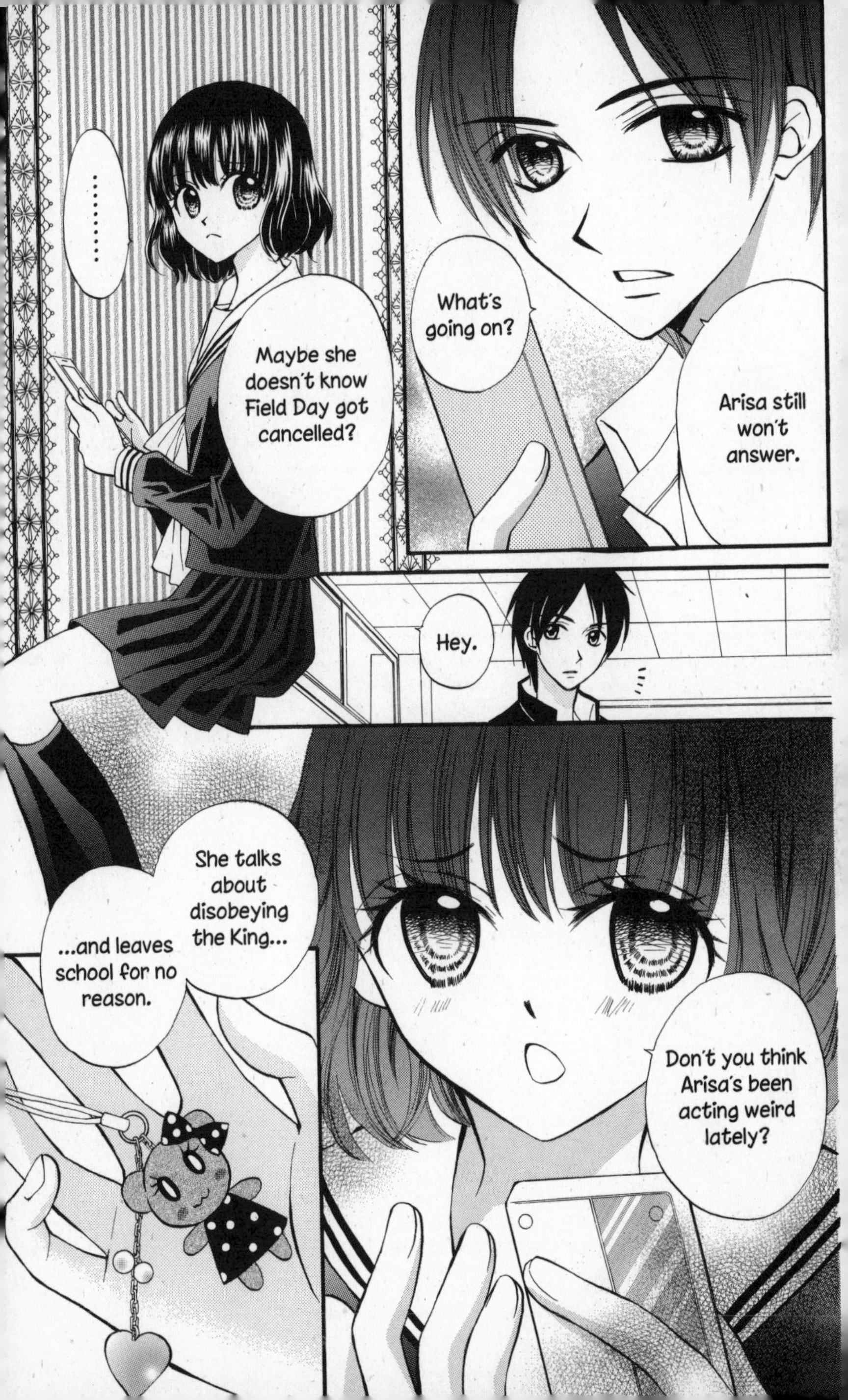

Arisa still won't answer.
What's going on?
Hey.
......
Maybe she doesn't know Field Day got cancelled?
Don't you think Arisa's been acting weird lately?
She talks about disobeying the King...
...and leaves school for no reason.

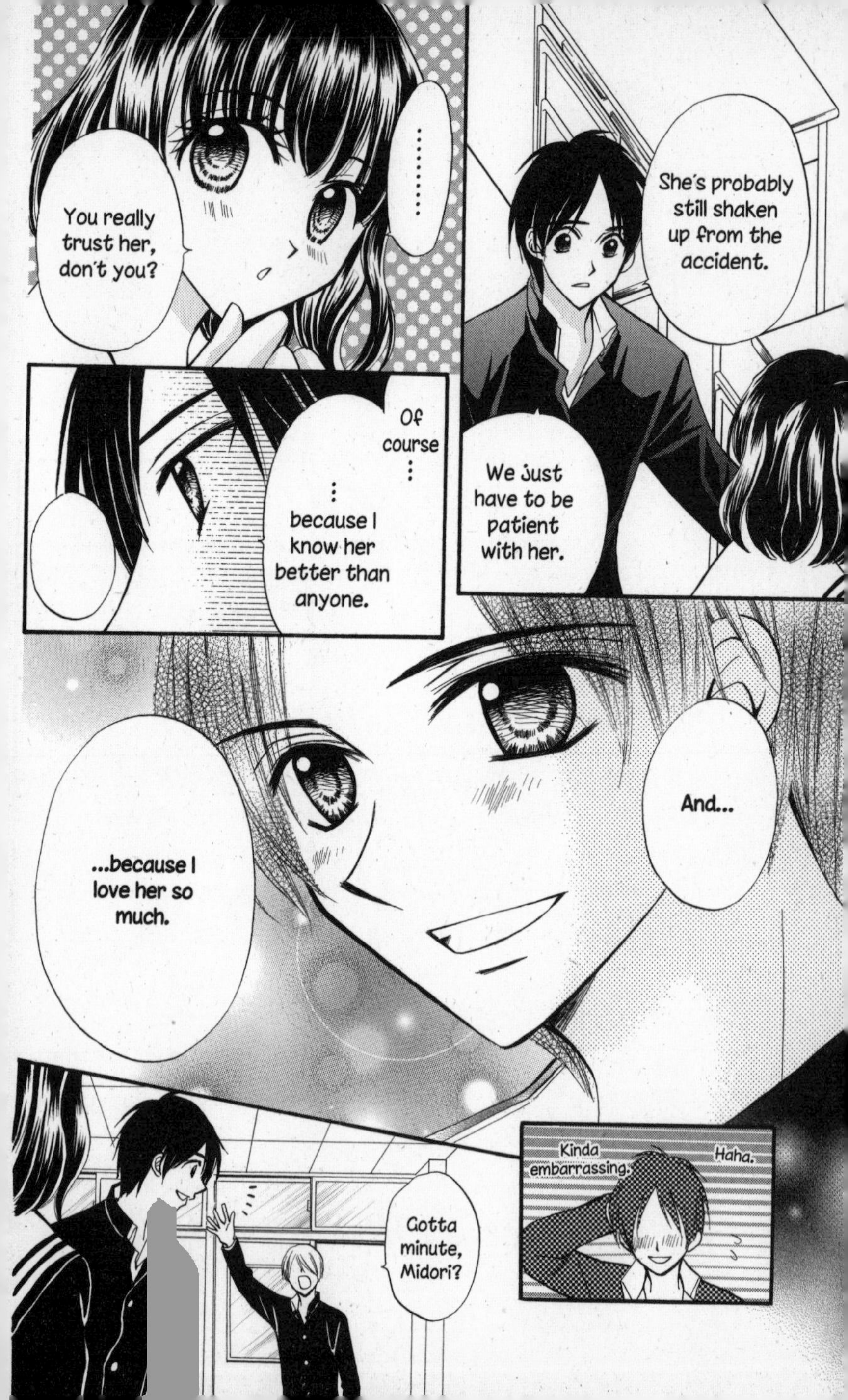
She's probably still shaken up from the accident.
We just have to be patient with her.
......
You really trust her, don't you?
Of course...
...because I know her better than anyone.
And...
...because I love her so much.
Kinda embarrassing.
Haha.
Gotta minute, Midori?

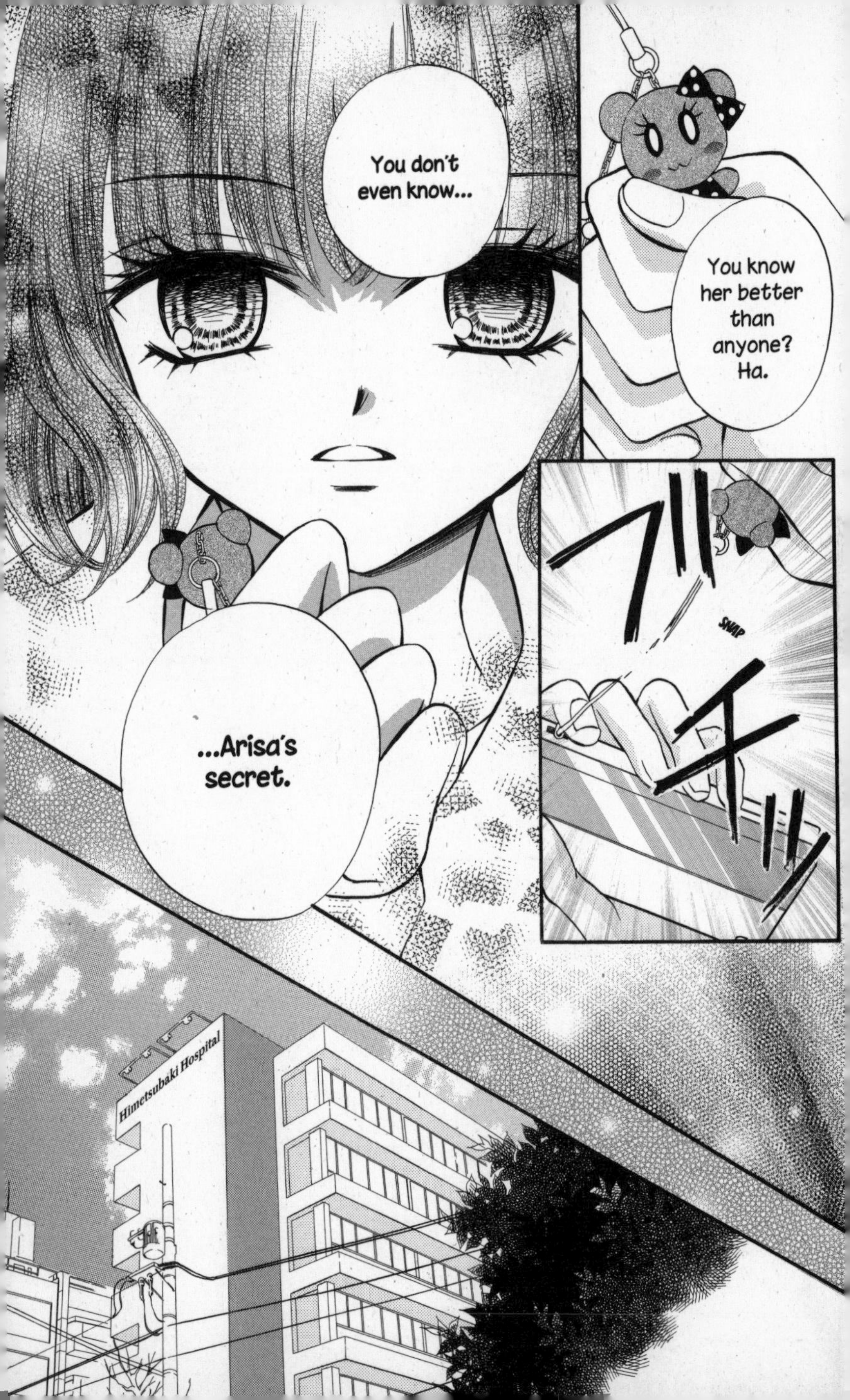
You know her better than anyone? Ha.
SNAP
You don't even know...
...Arisa's secret.
Himetsubaki Hospital

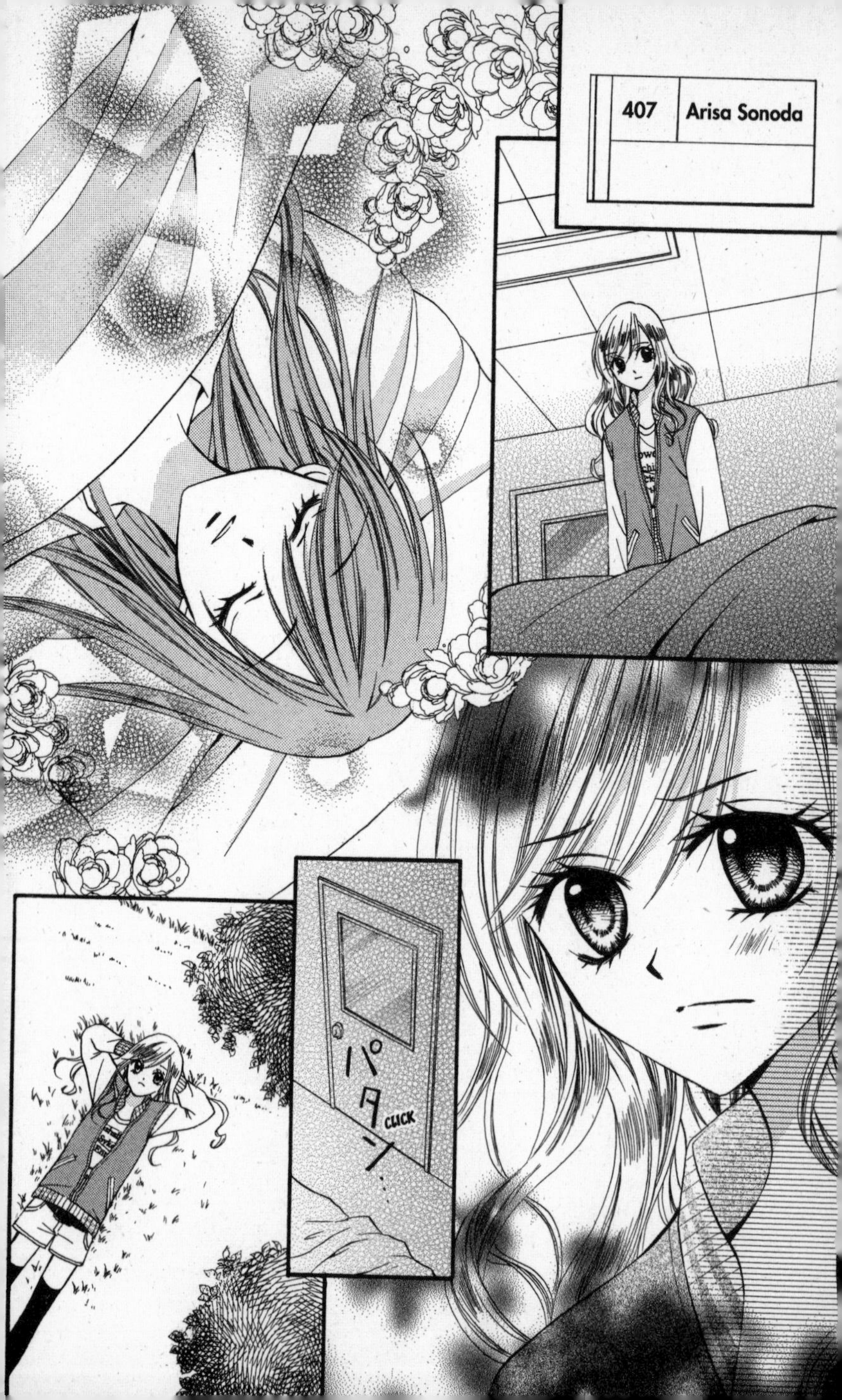
407
Arisa Sonoda
パタン
CLICK

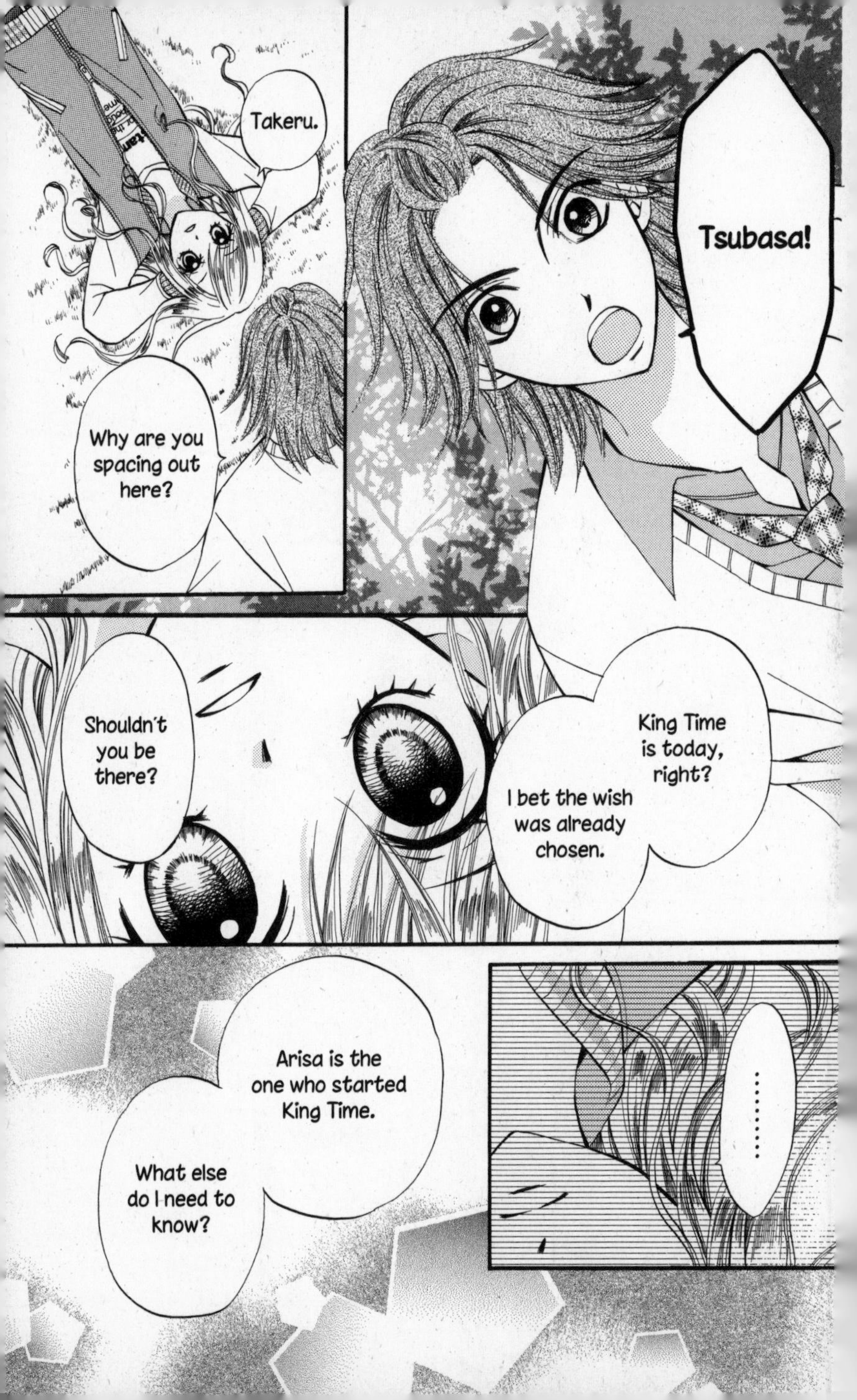
Tsubasa!
Takeru.
Why are you spacing out here?
King Time is today, right?
I bet the wish was already chosen.
Shouldn't you be there?
……
Arisa is the one who started King Time.
What else do I need to know?

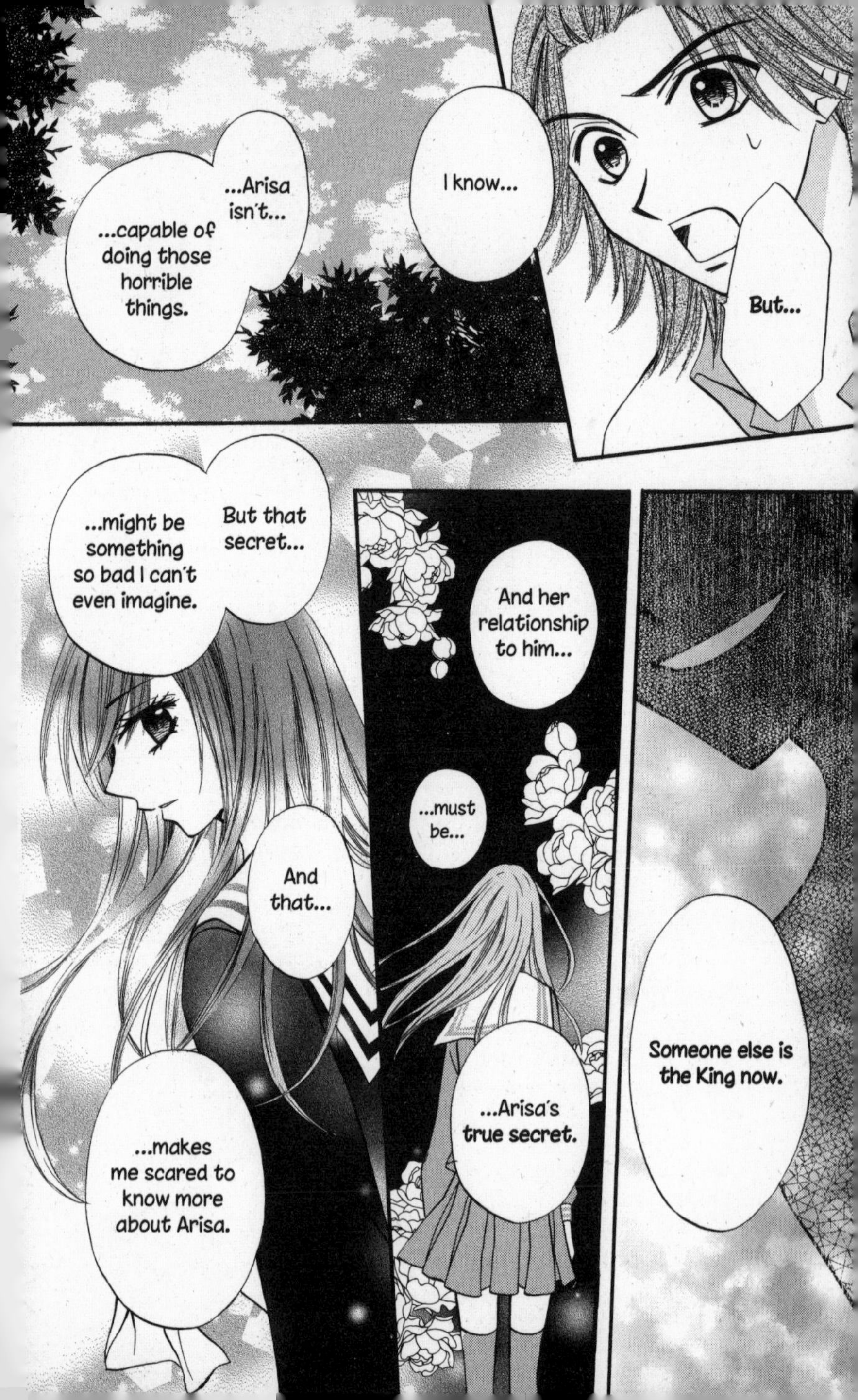
...Arisa isn't...
...capable of doing those horrible things.
I know...
But...
Someone else is the King now.
And her relationship to him...
...must be...
...Arisa's true secret.
But that secret...
...might be something so bad I can't even imagine.
And that...
...makes me scared to know more about Arisa.

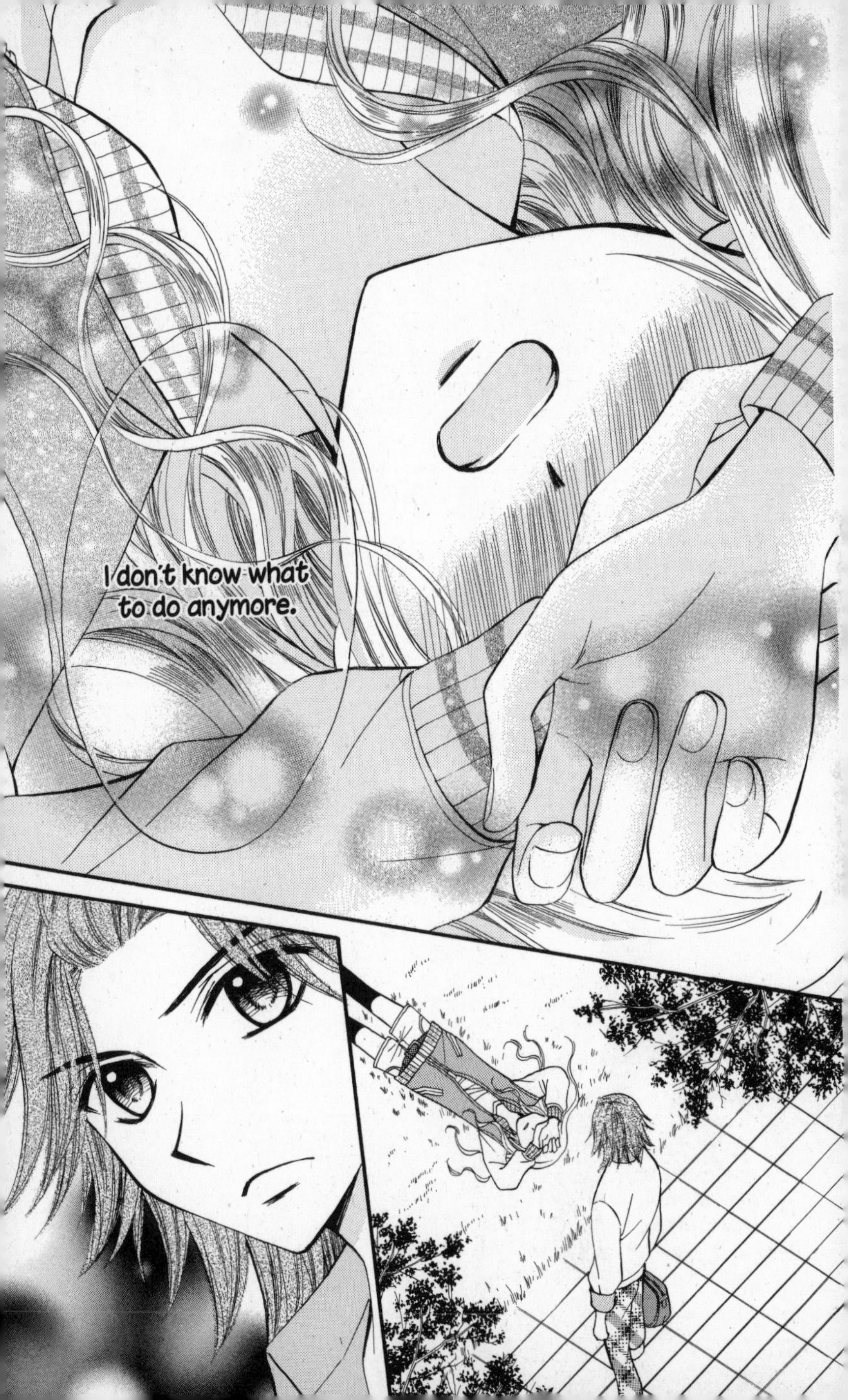
I don't know what to do anymore.

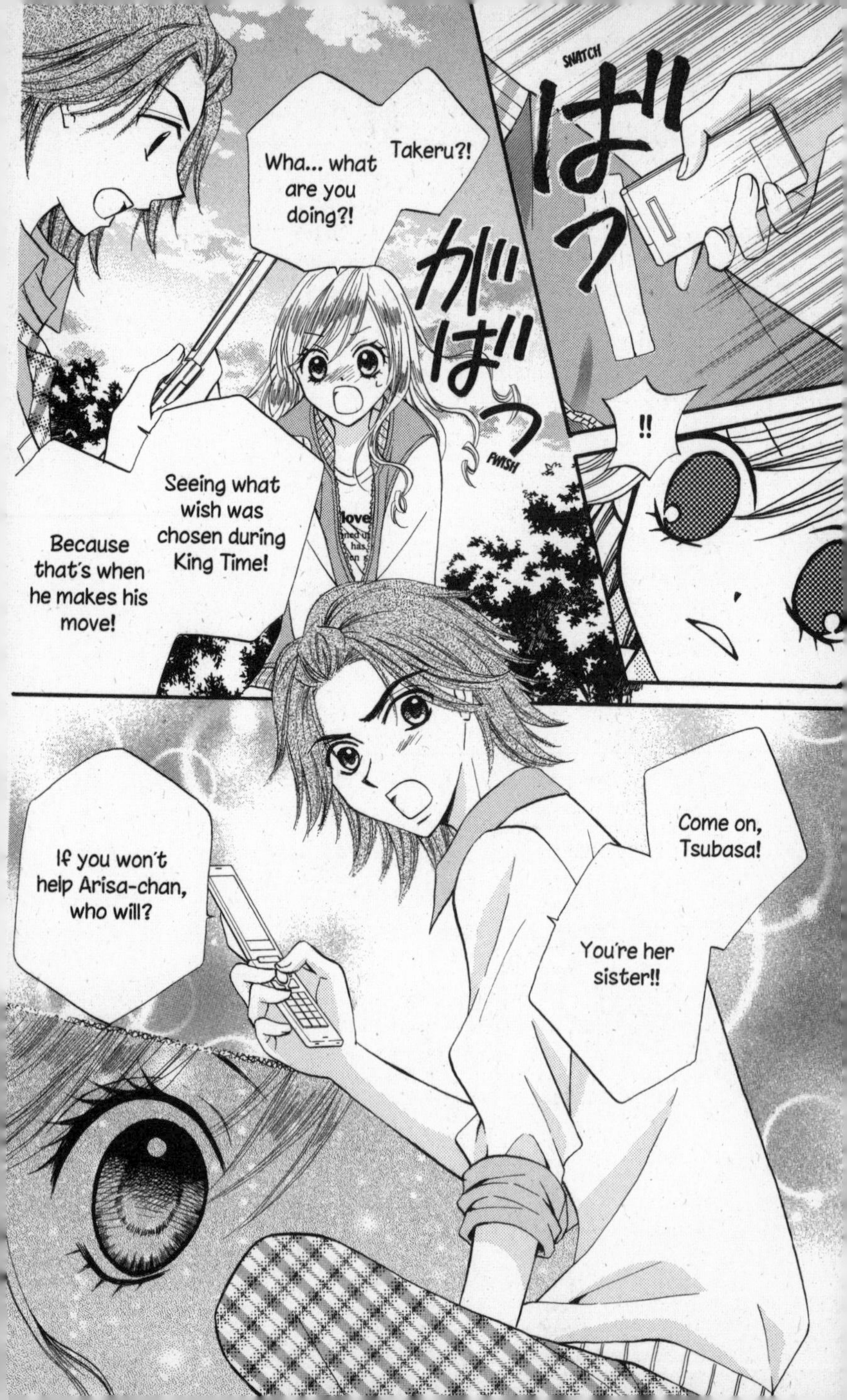
SNATCH
ばっ
!!
Takeru?!
Wha... what are you doing?!
がばっ
FWISH
Seeing what wish was chosen during King Time!
Because that's when he makes his move!
Come on, Tsubasa!
You're her sister!!
If you won't help Arisa-chan, who will?

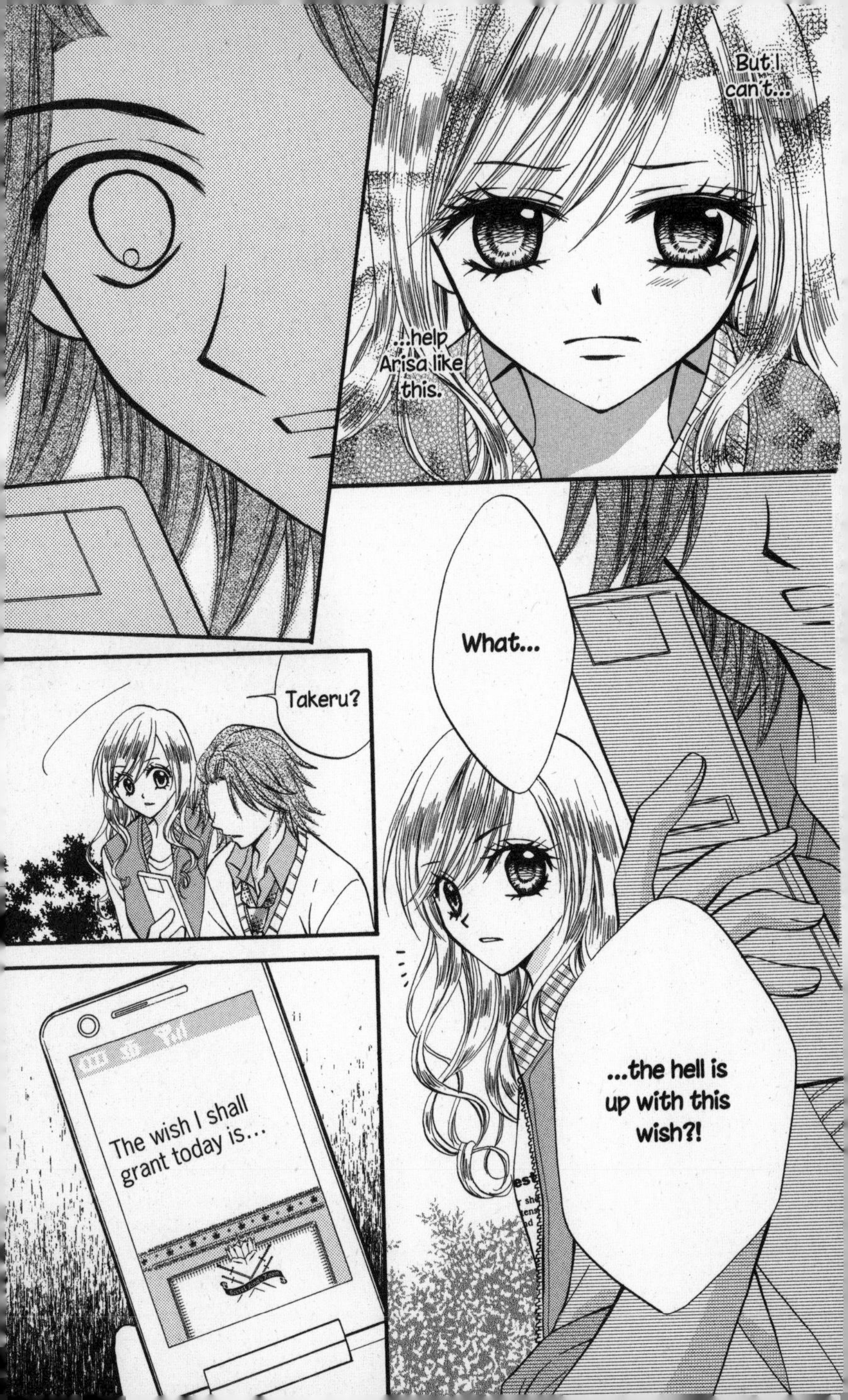
But I can't...
...help Arisa like this.
What...
...the hell is up with this wish?!
Takeru?
The wish I shall grant today is...

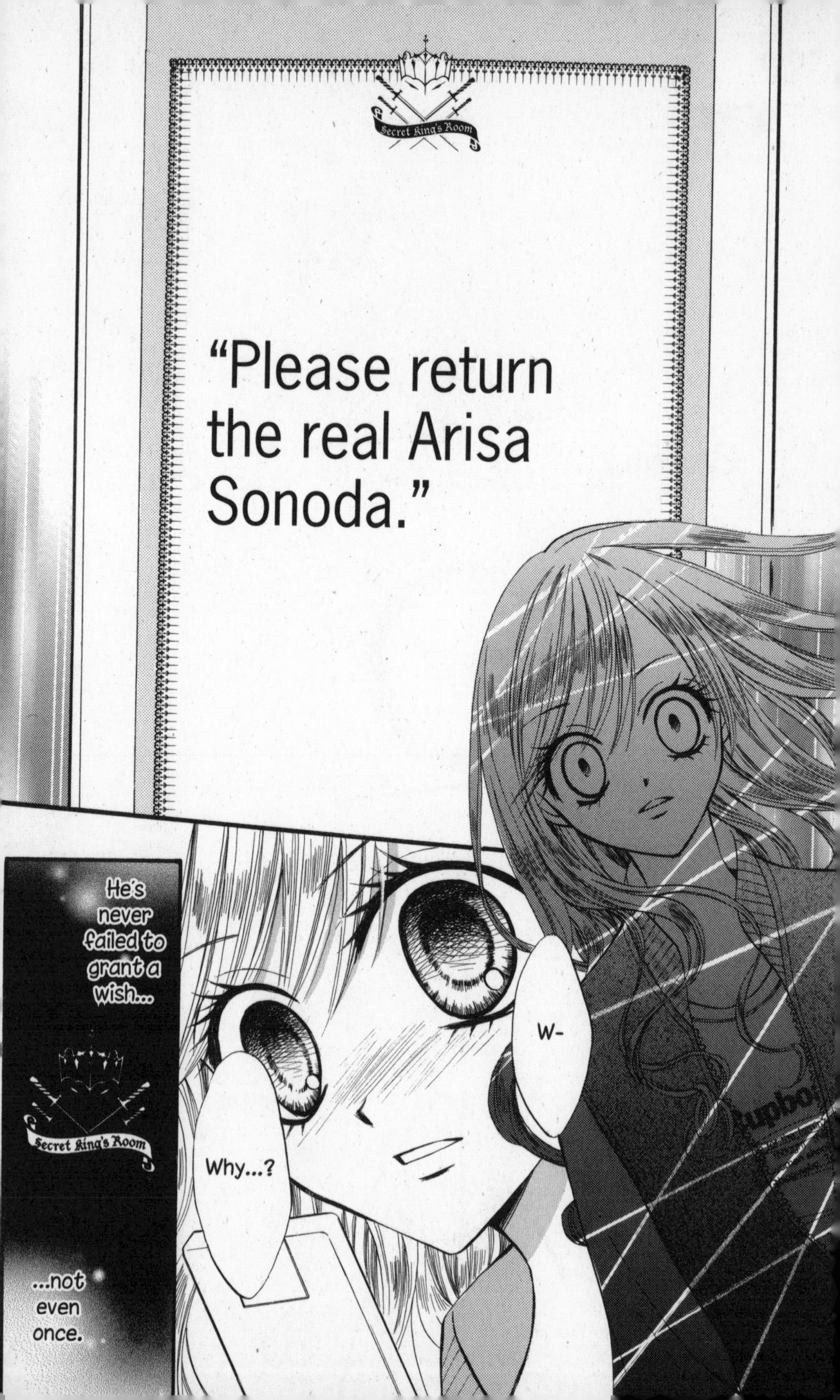
Secret King's Room
"Please return the real Arisa Sonoda."
W-
Why...?
He's never failed to grant a wish...
Secret King's Room
...not even once.

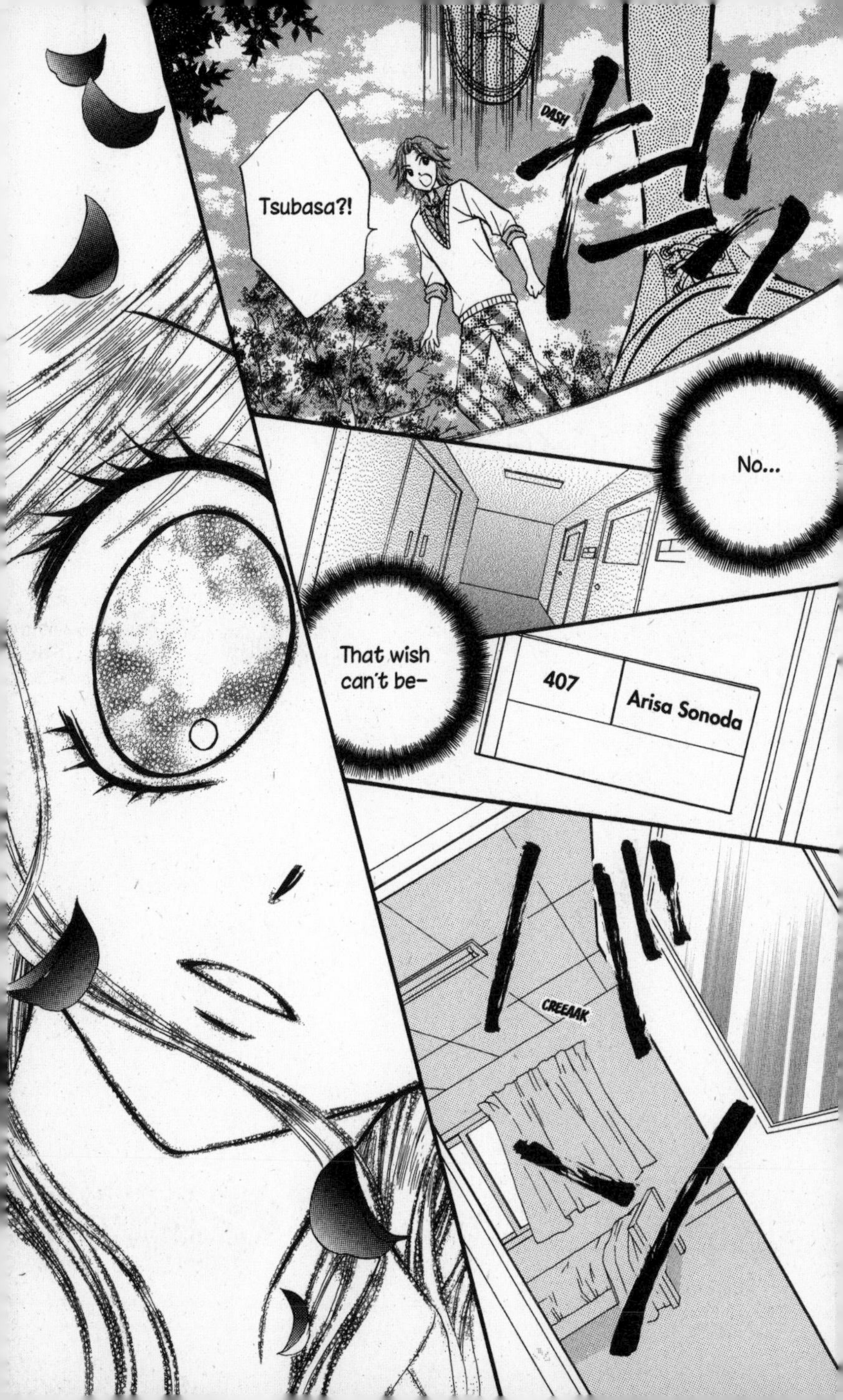
DASH
Tsubasa?!
No...
That wish can't be-
407
Arisa Sonoda
CREEAAK

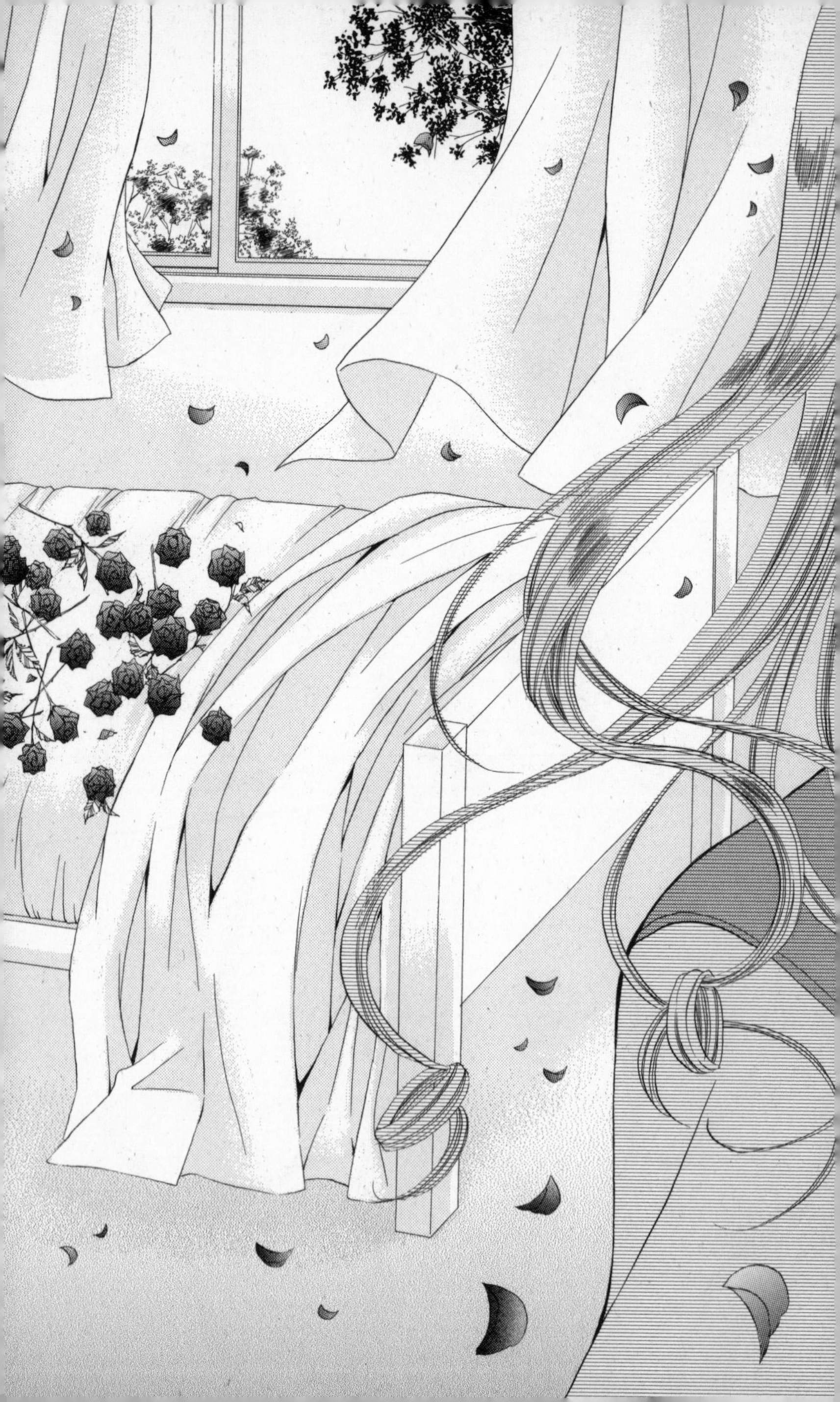

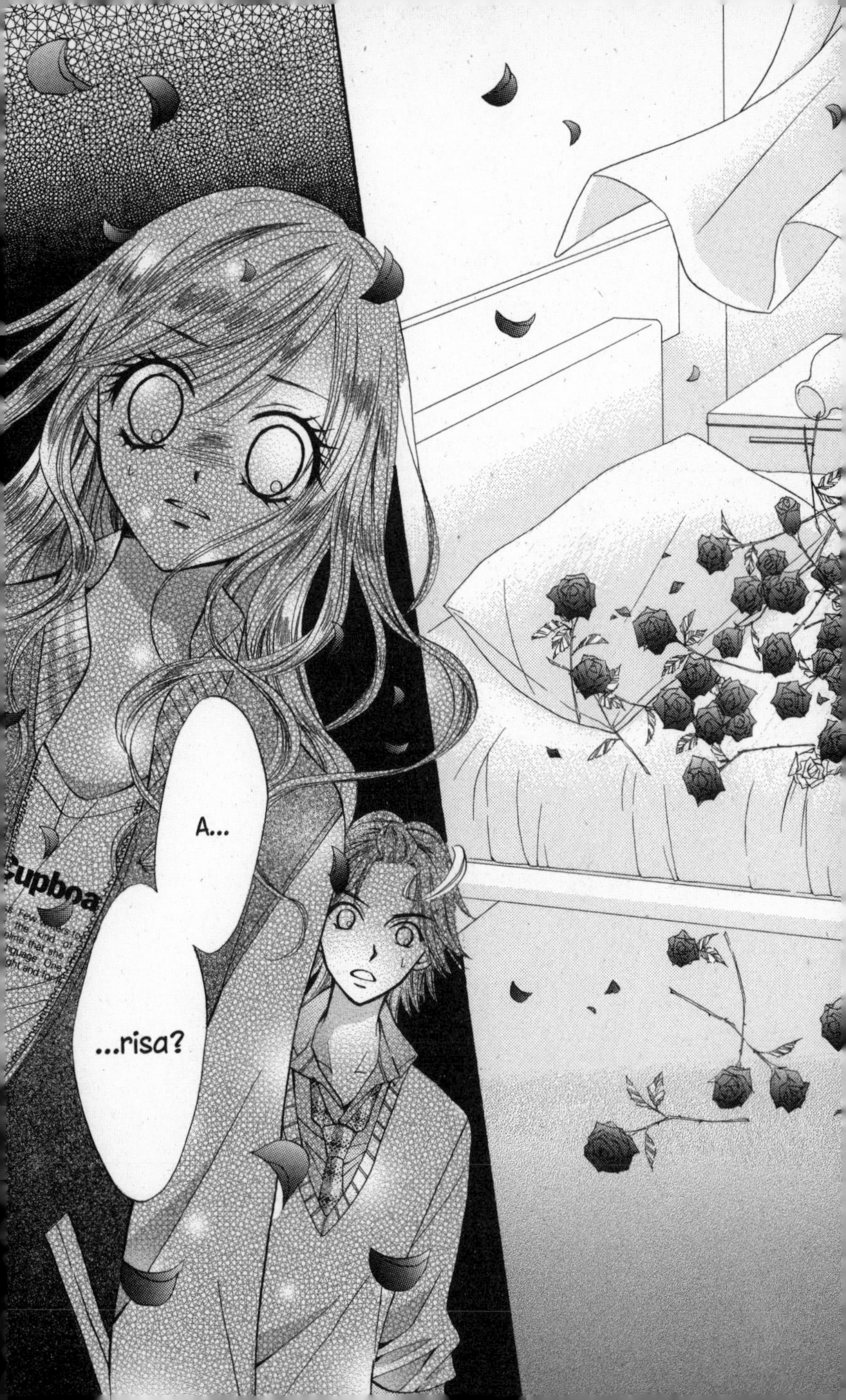
A...
...risa?

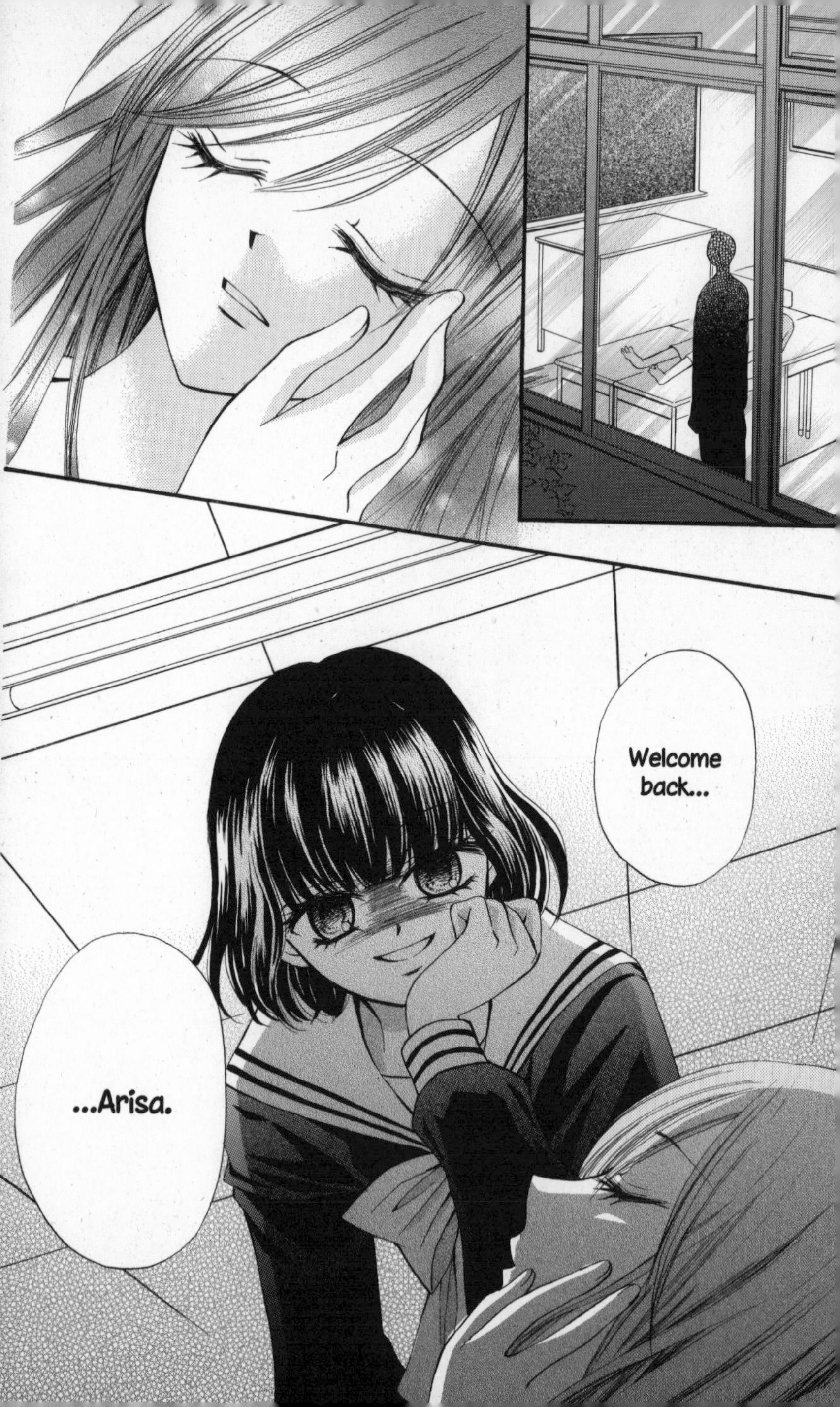
Welcome back...
...Arisa.

ARISA

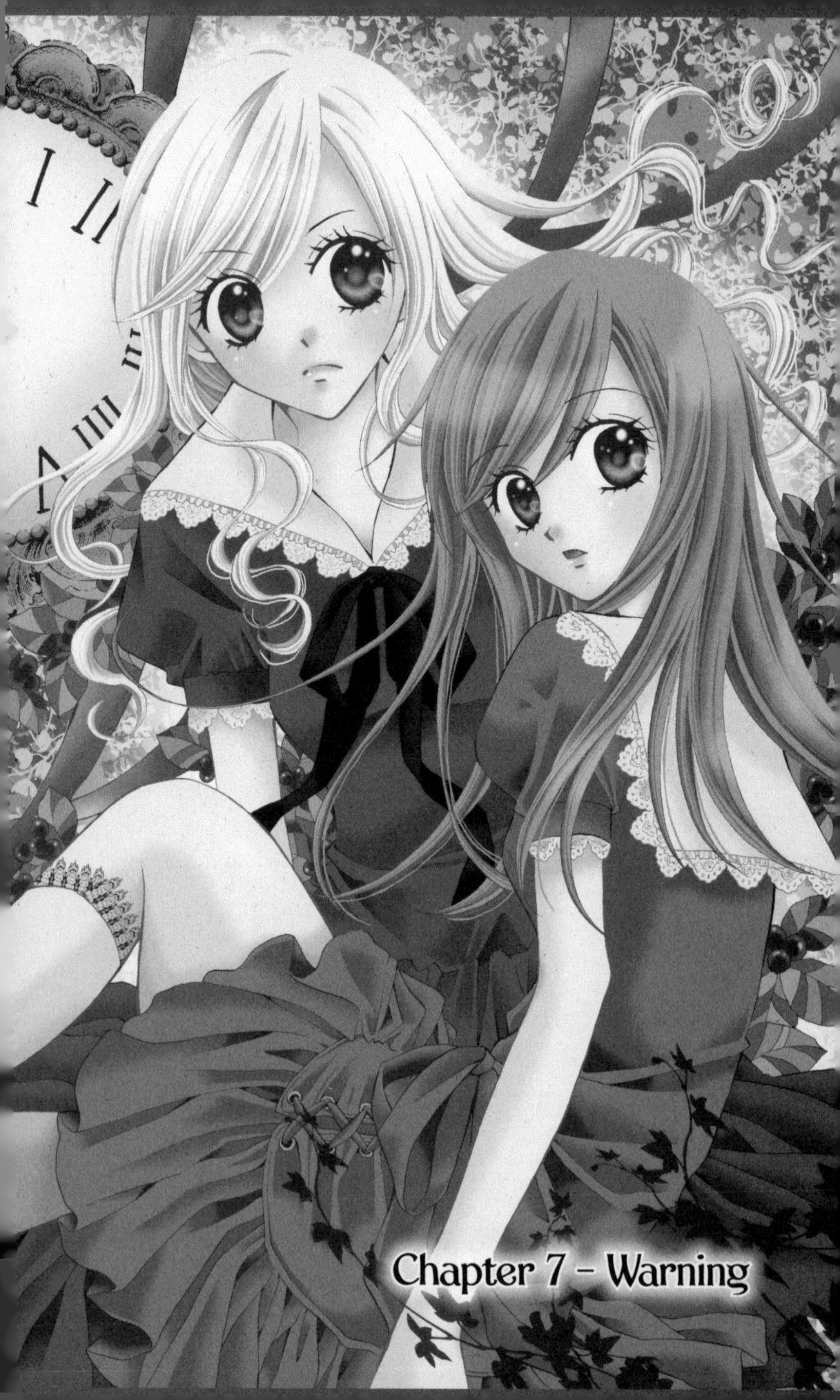
Chapter 7 - Warning

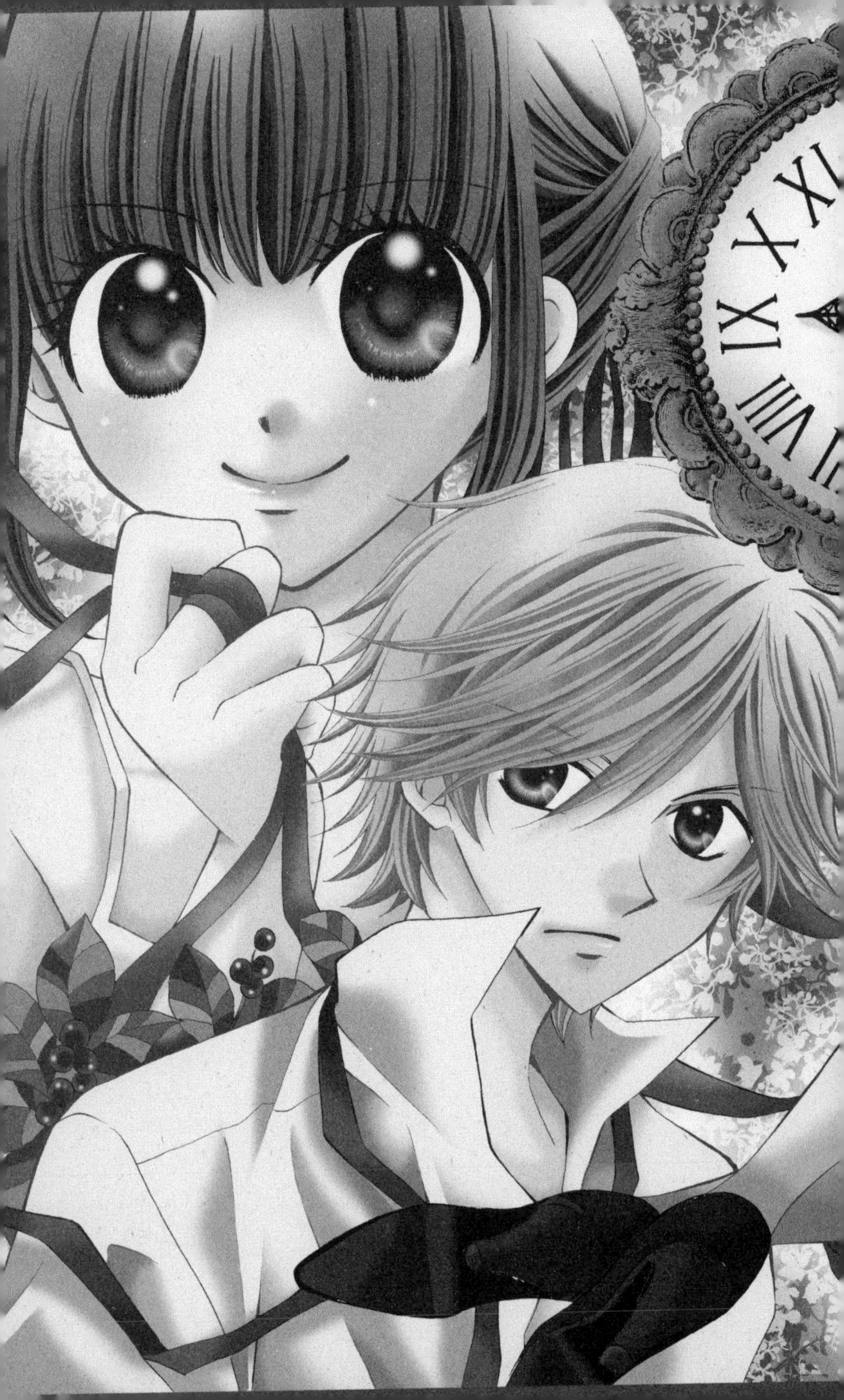

ARISA

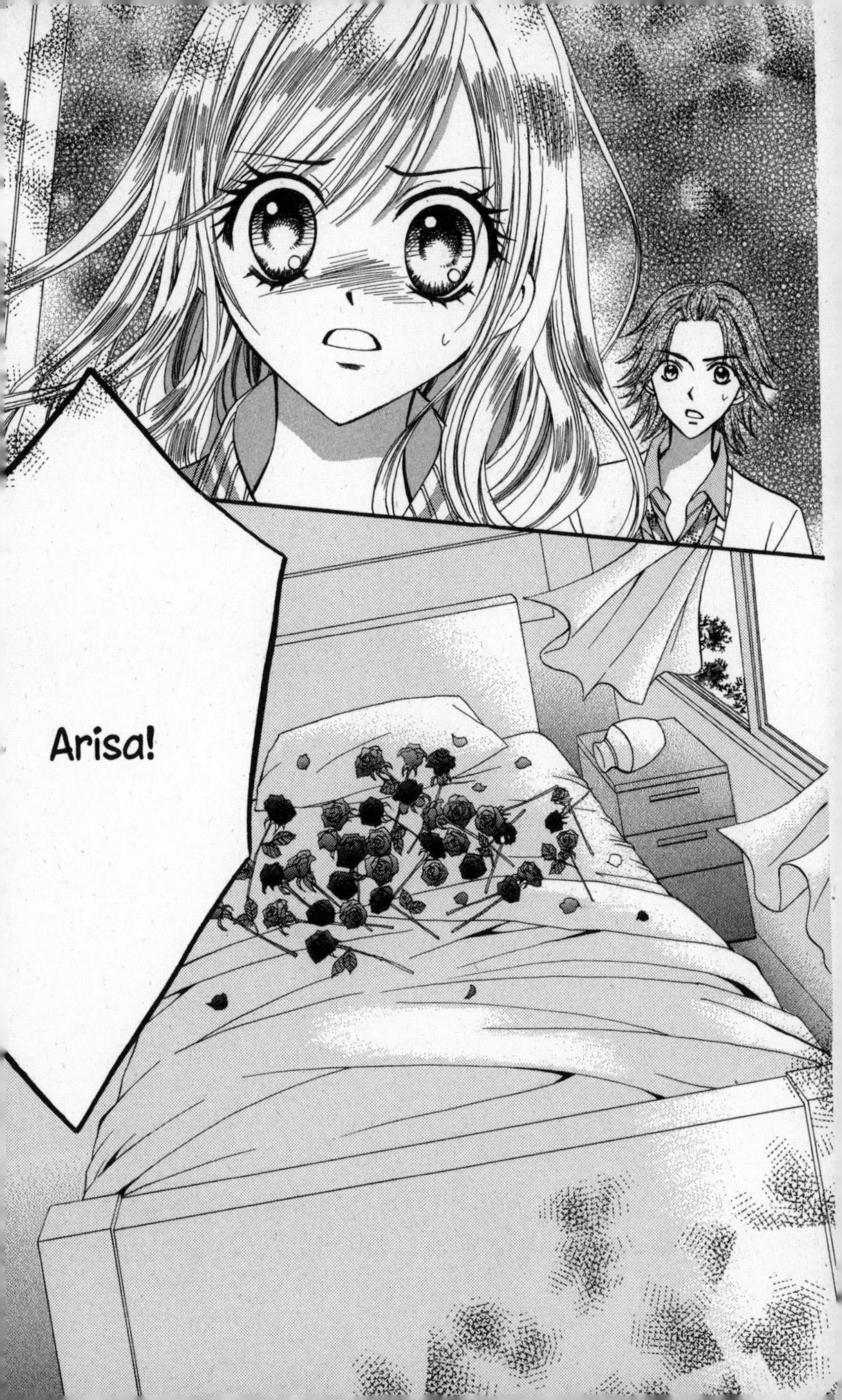
Arisa!

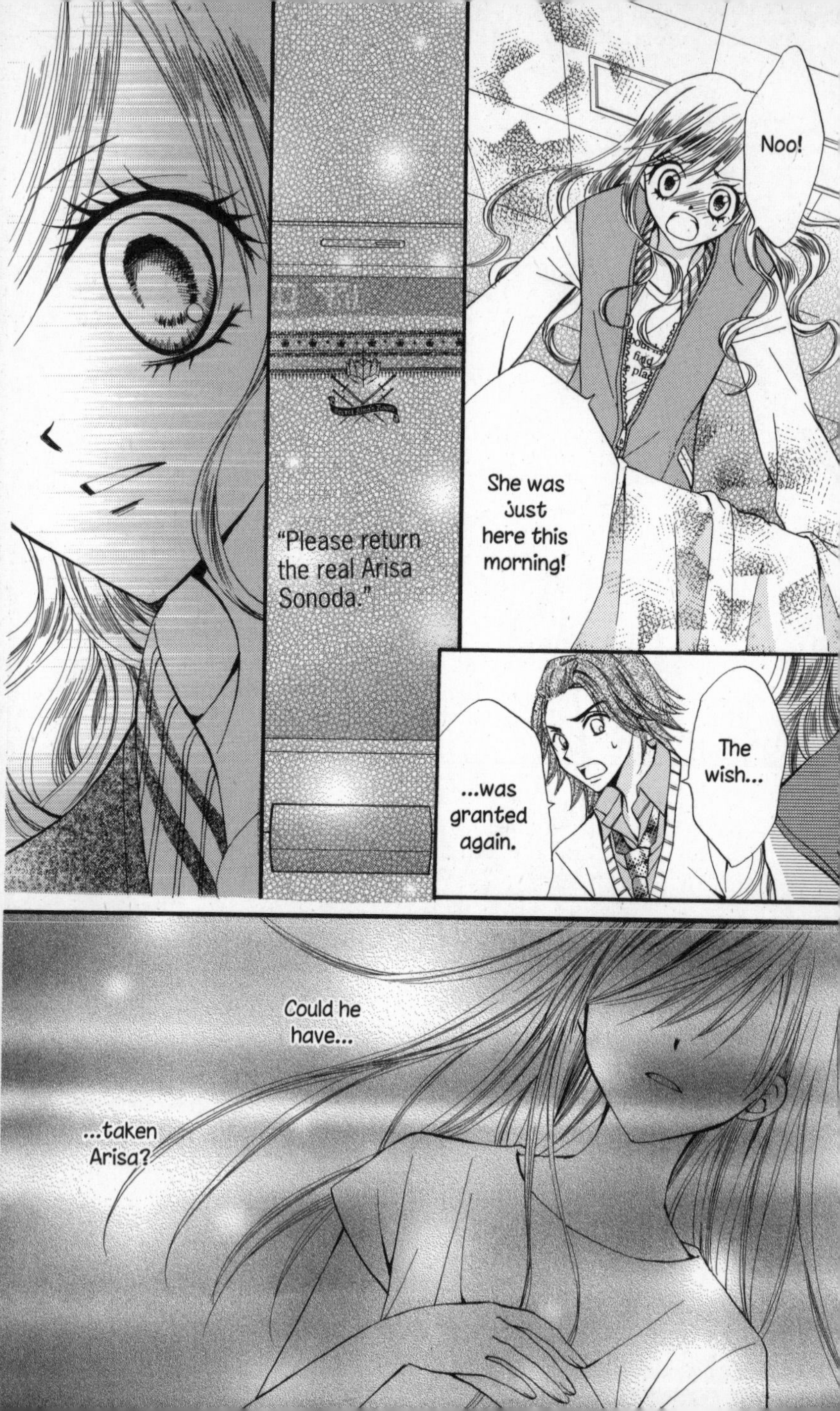
Noo!
She was just here this morning!
The wish...
...was granted again.
"Please return the real Arisa Sonoda."
Could he have...
...taken Arisa?

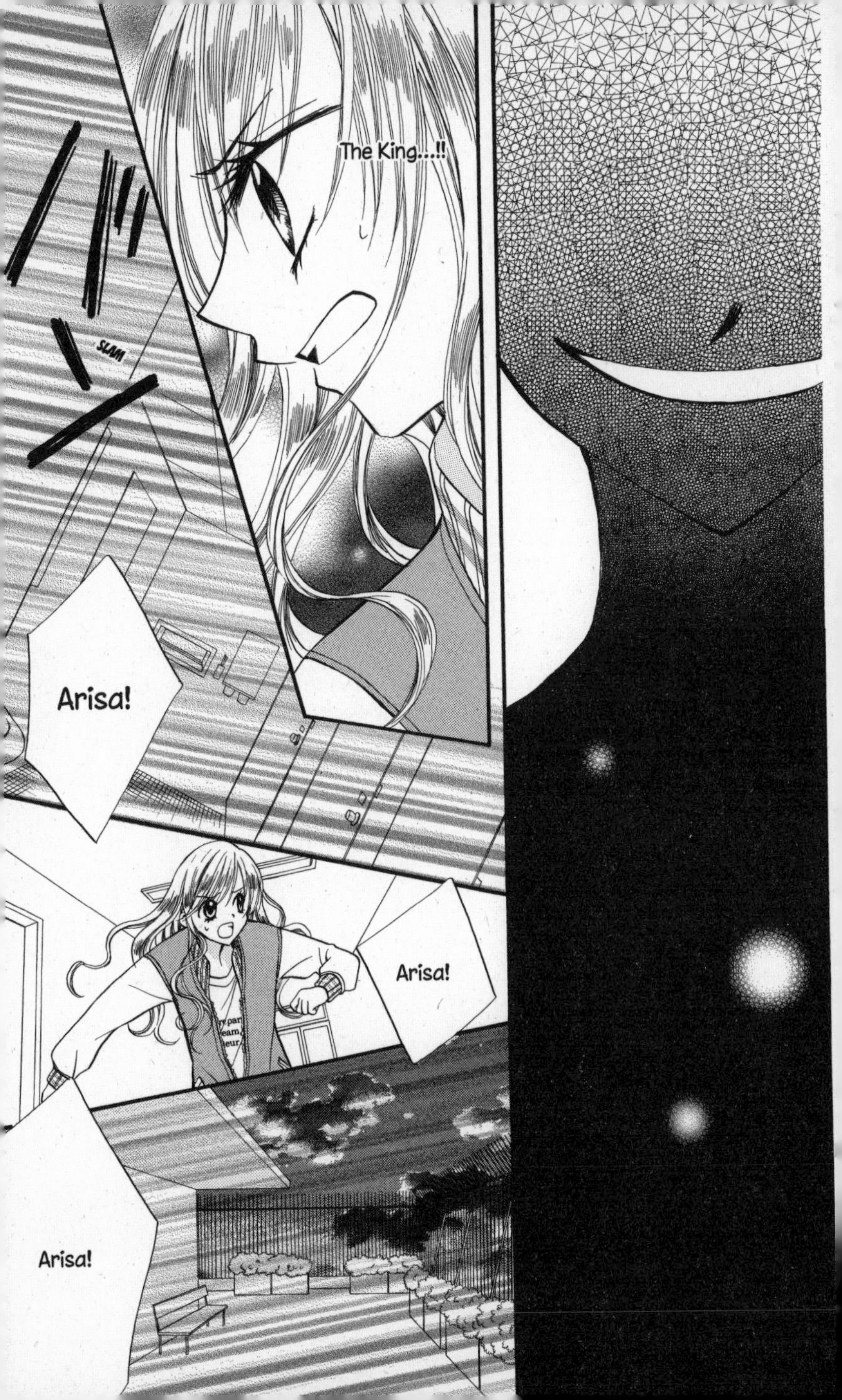
The King...!!
SLAM
Arisa!
Arisa!
Arisa!

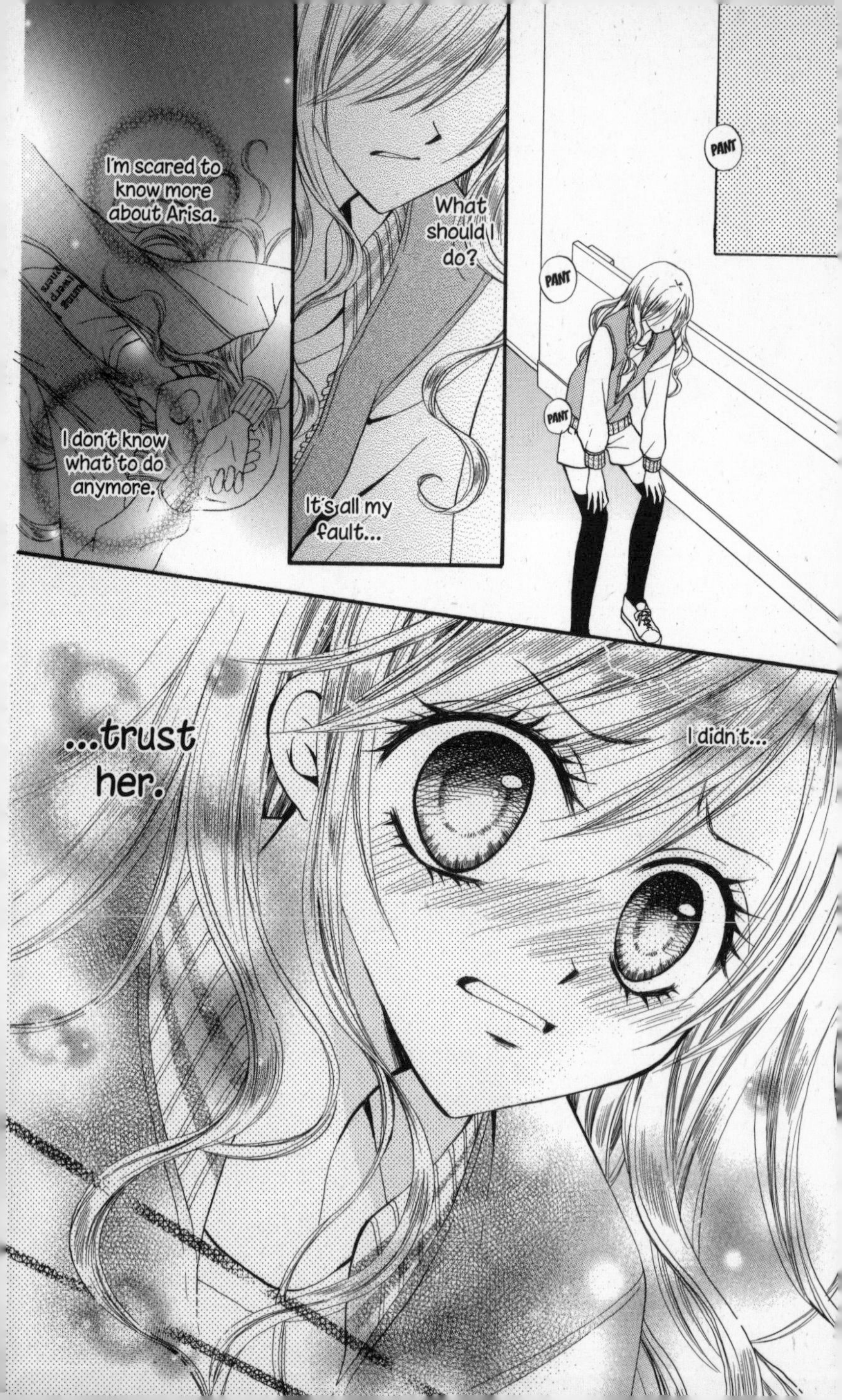
PANT
PANT
PANT
What should I do?
It's all my fault...
I'm scared to know more about Arisa.
I don't know what to do anymore.
I didn't...
...trust her.

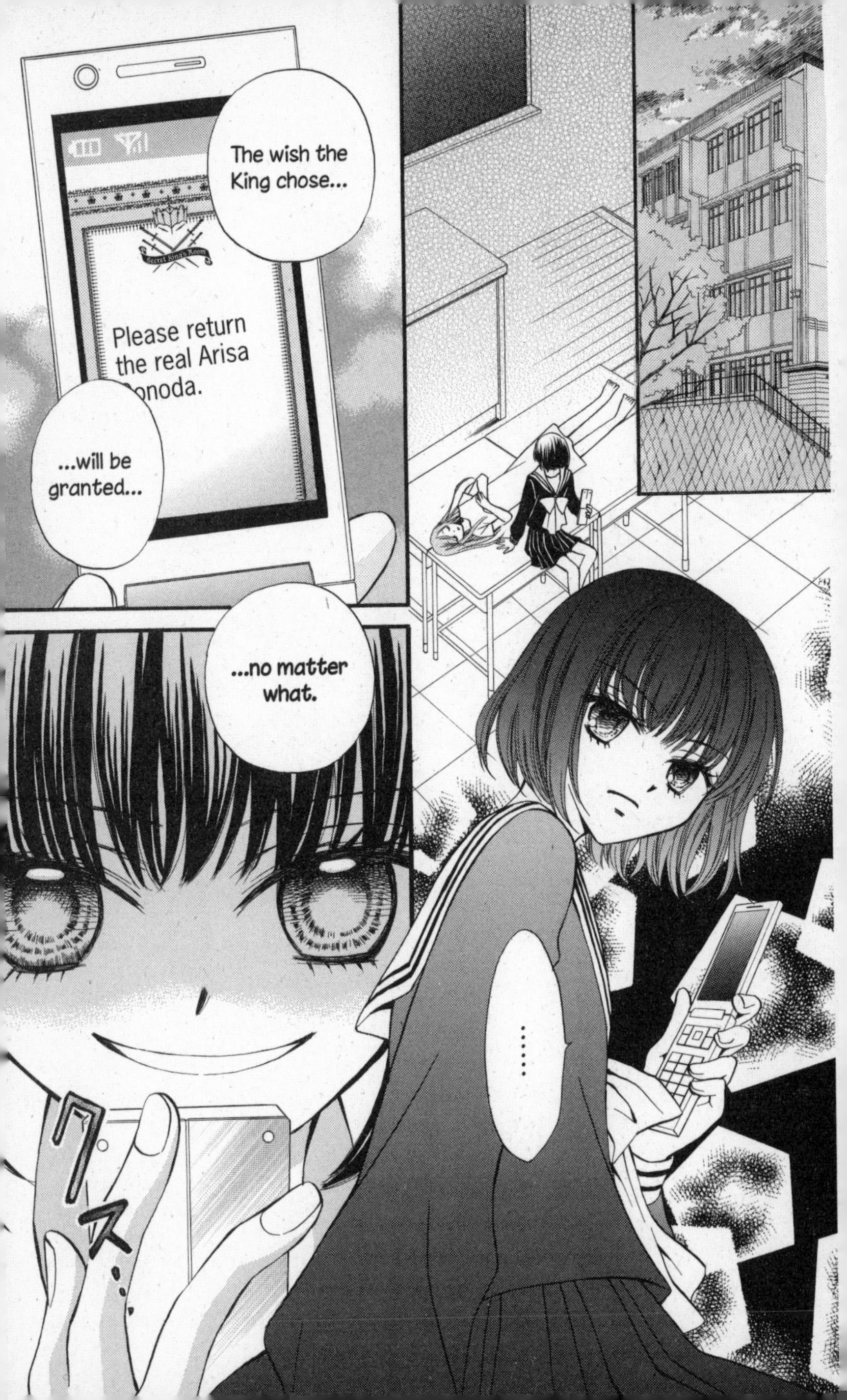
......
The wish the King chose...
Secret King's Room
Please return the real Arisa Sonoda.
...will be granted...
...no matter what.
クス…

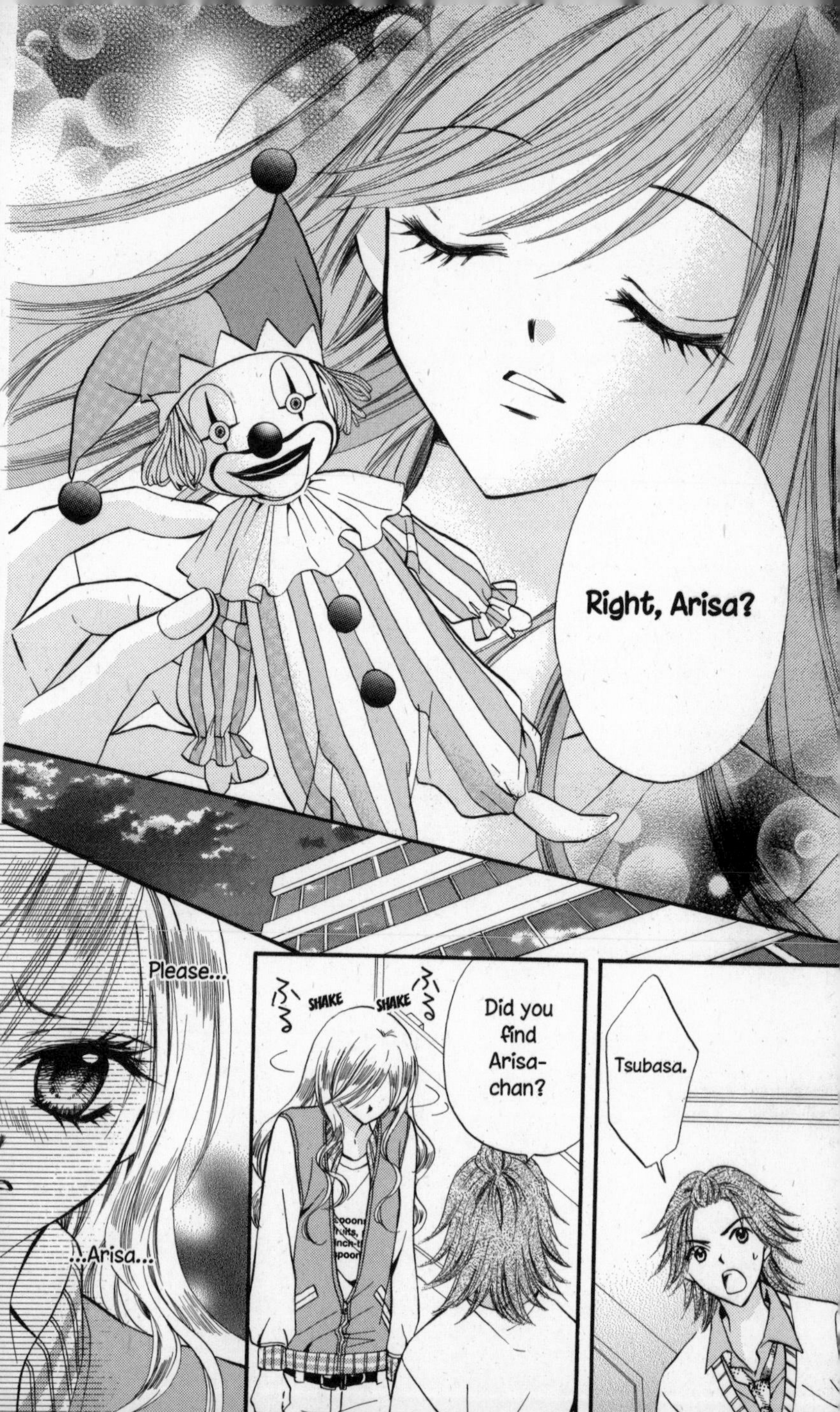
Right, Arisa?
Tsubasa.
Did you find Arisa-chan?
ふる
SHAKE
ふる
SHAKE
Please...
...Arisa...

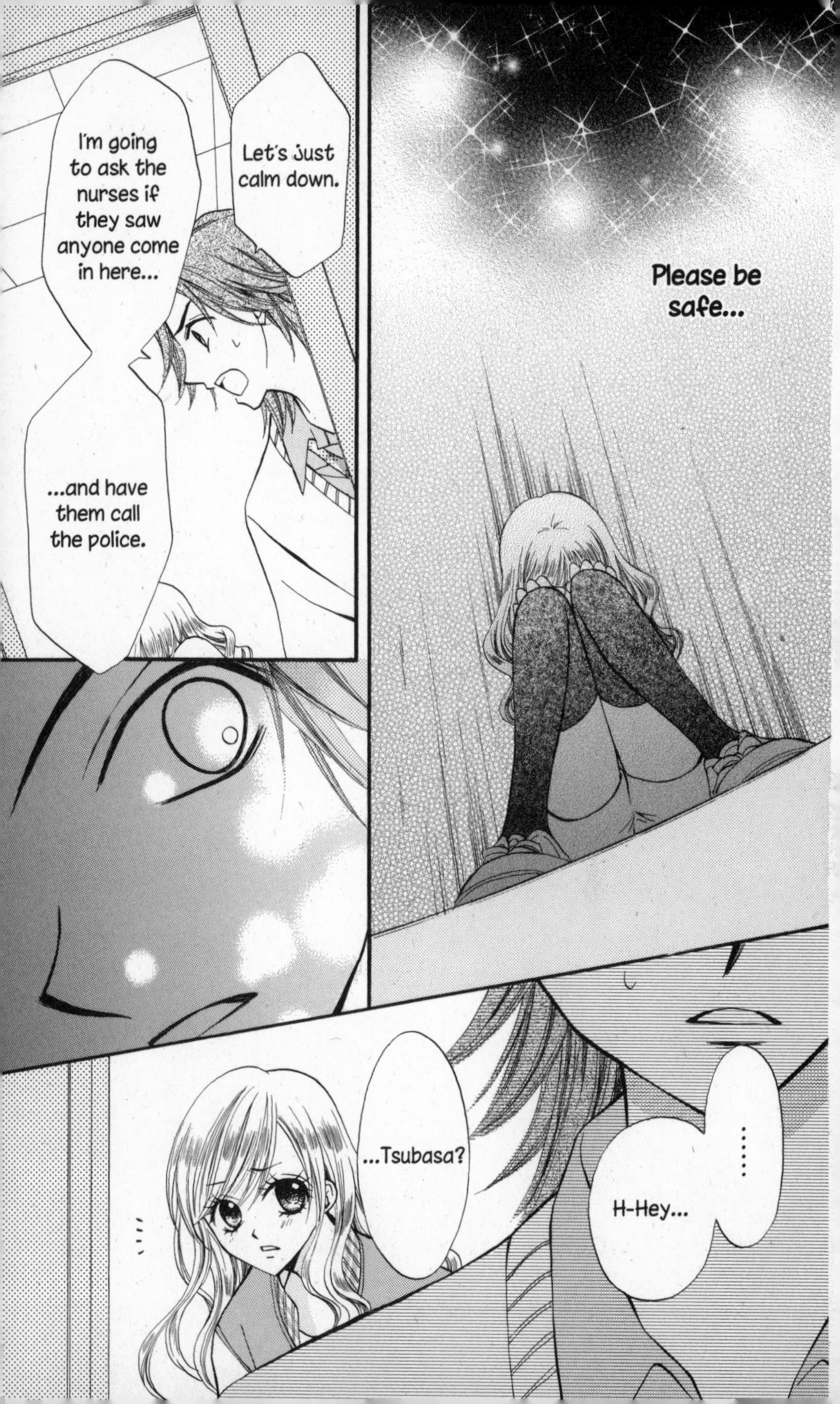
Please be safe...
Let's just calm down.
I'm going to ask the nurses if they saw anyone come in here...
...and have them call the police.
......
H-Hey...
...Tsubasa?

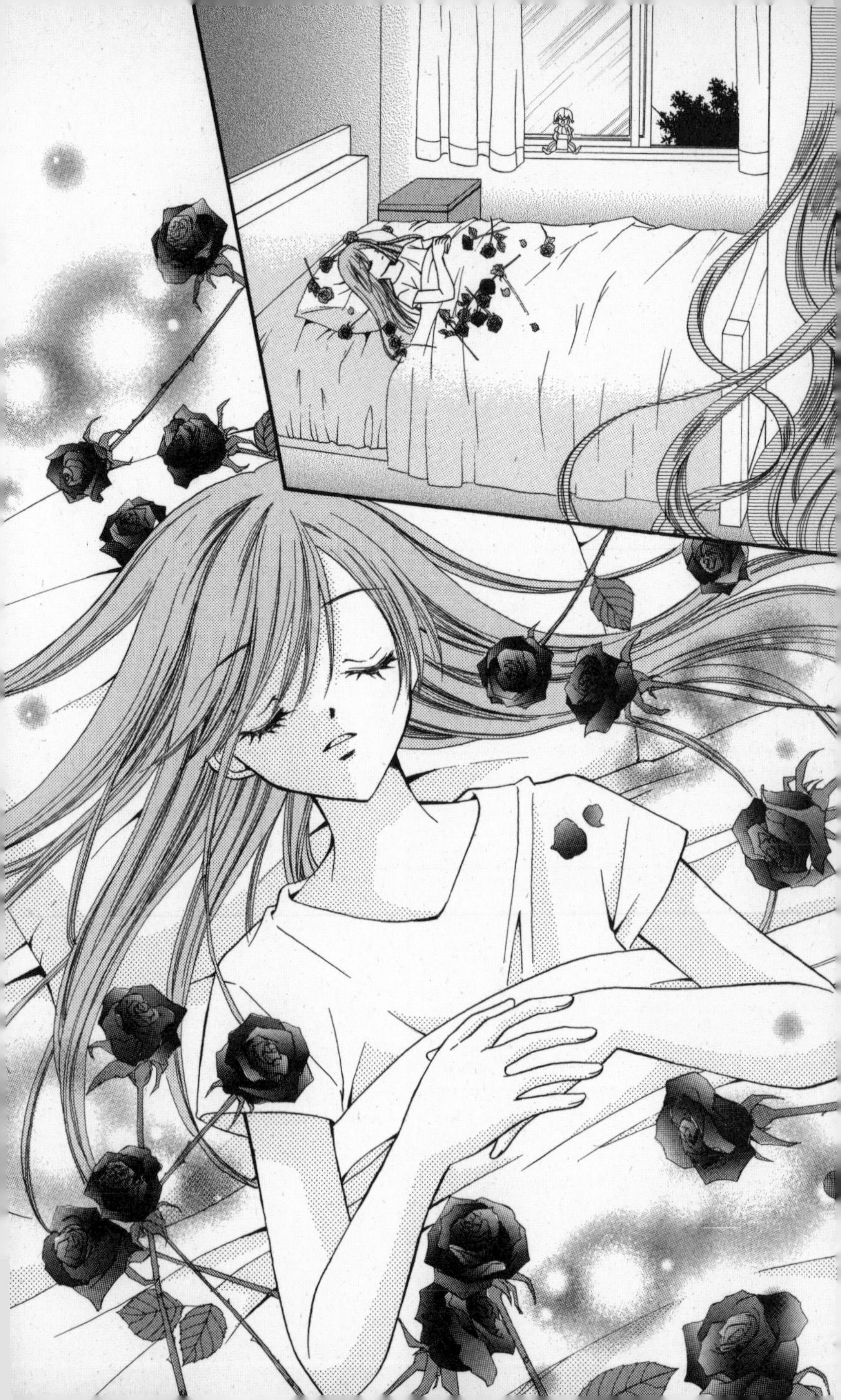

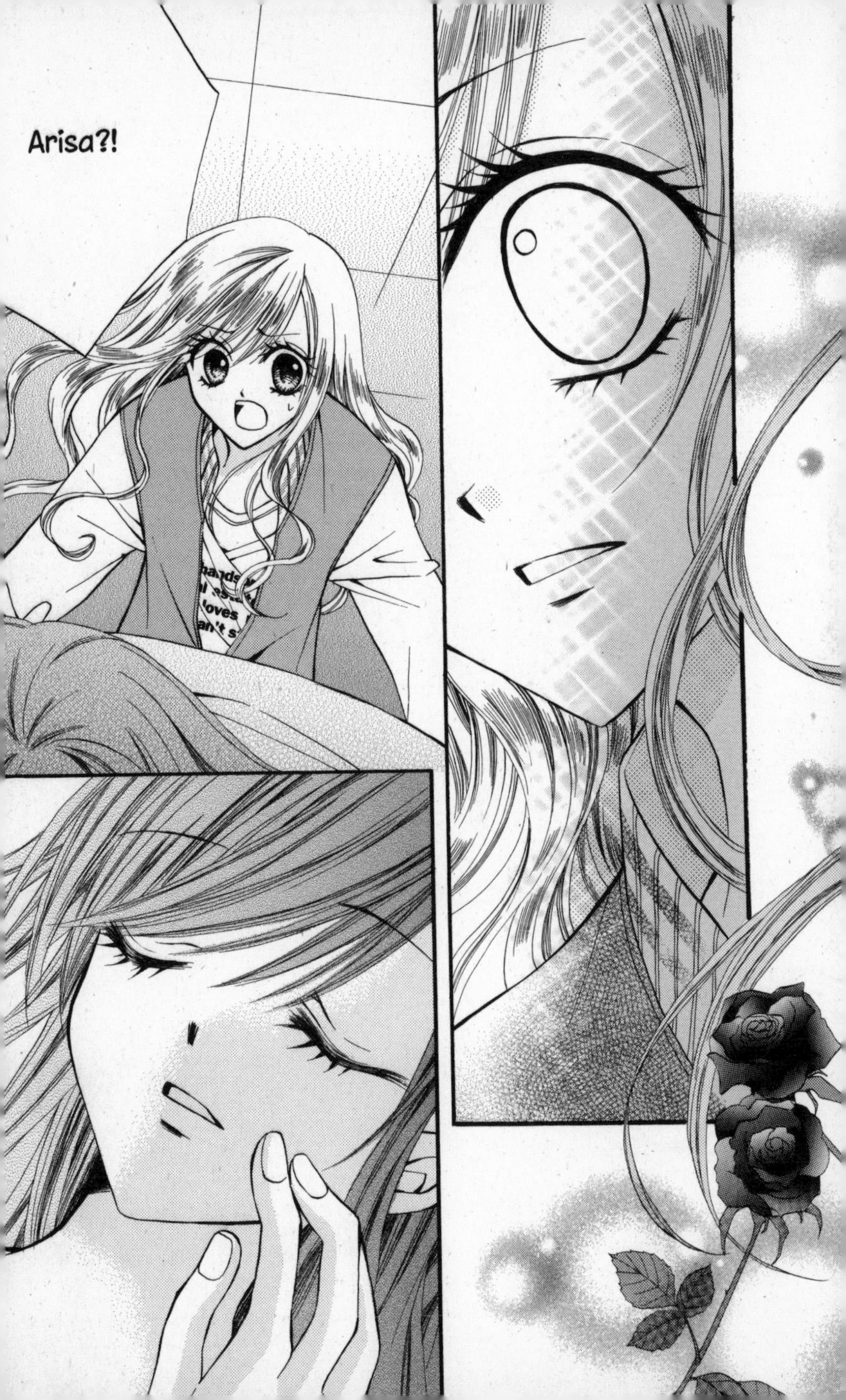
Arisa?!

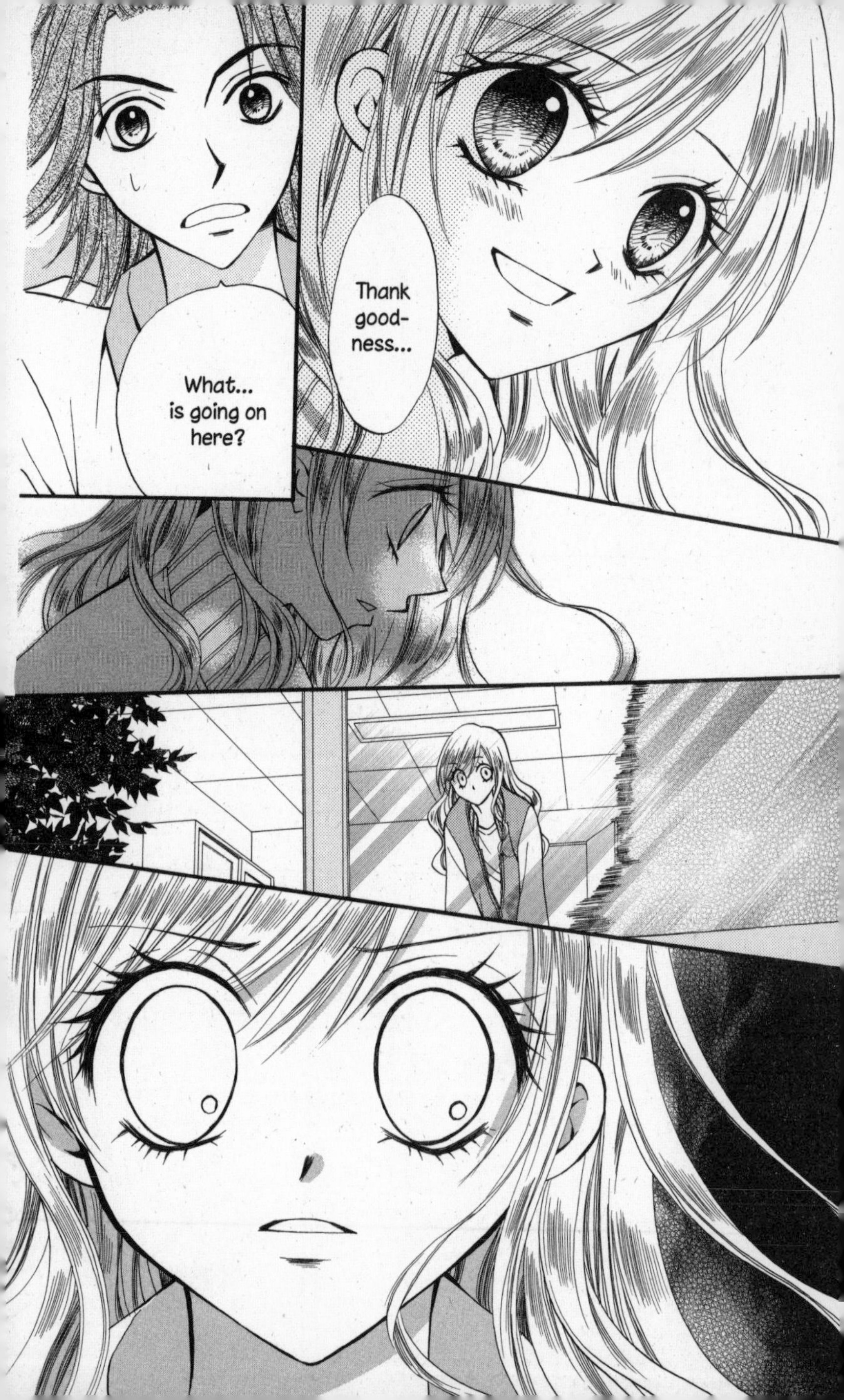
Thank good-ness...
What... is going on here?

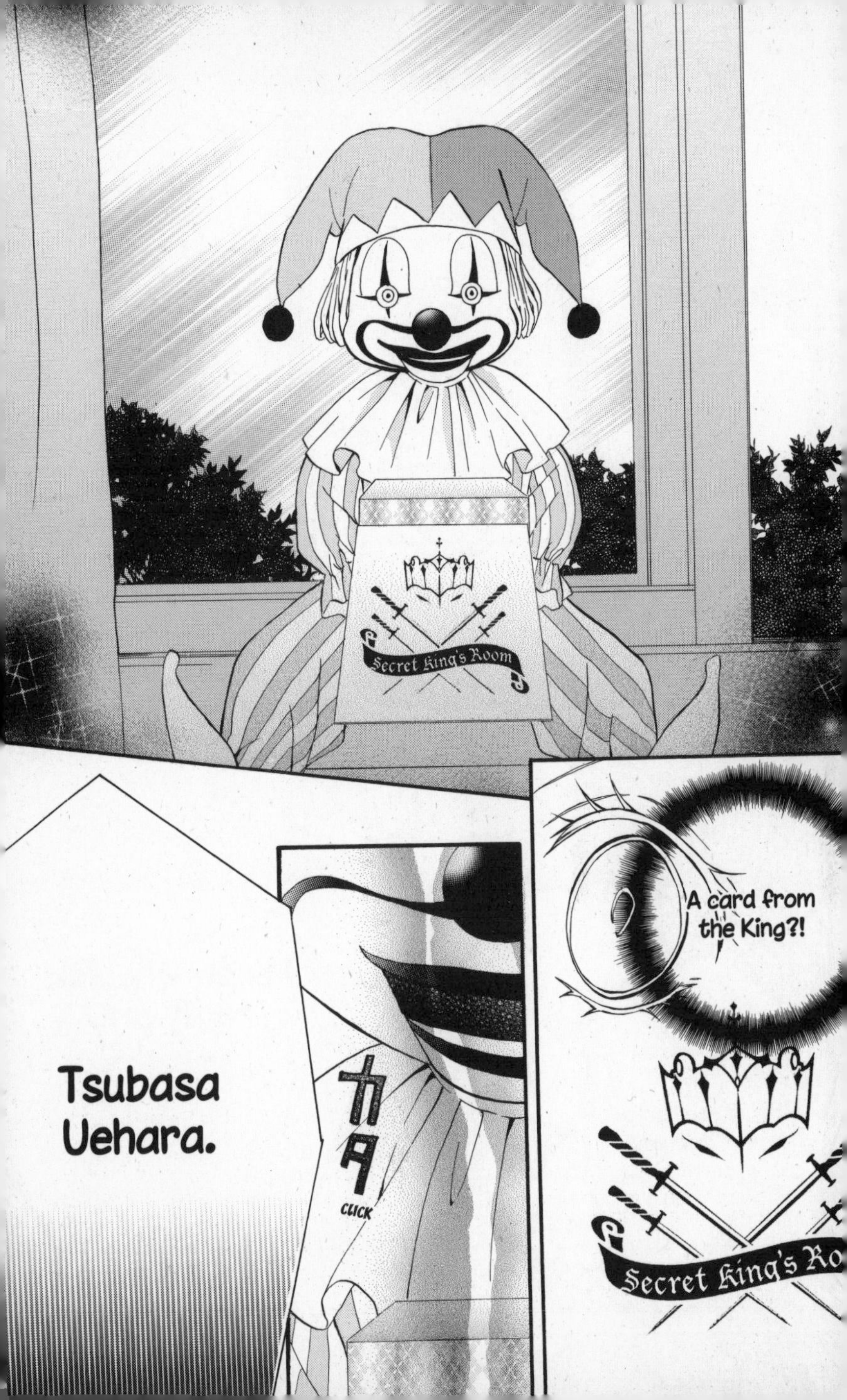
Secret King's Room
A card from the King?!
Secret King's Ro
カタ
CLICK
Tsubasa Uehara.

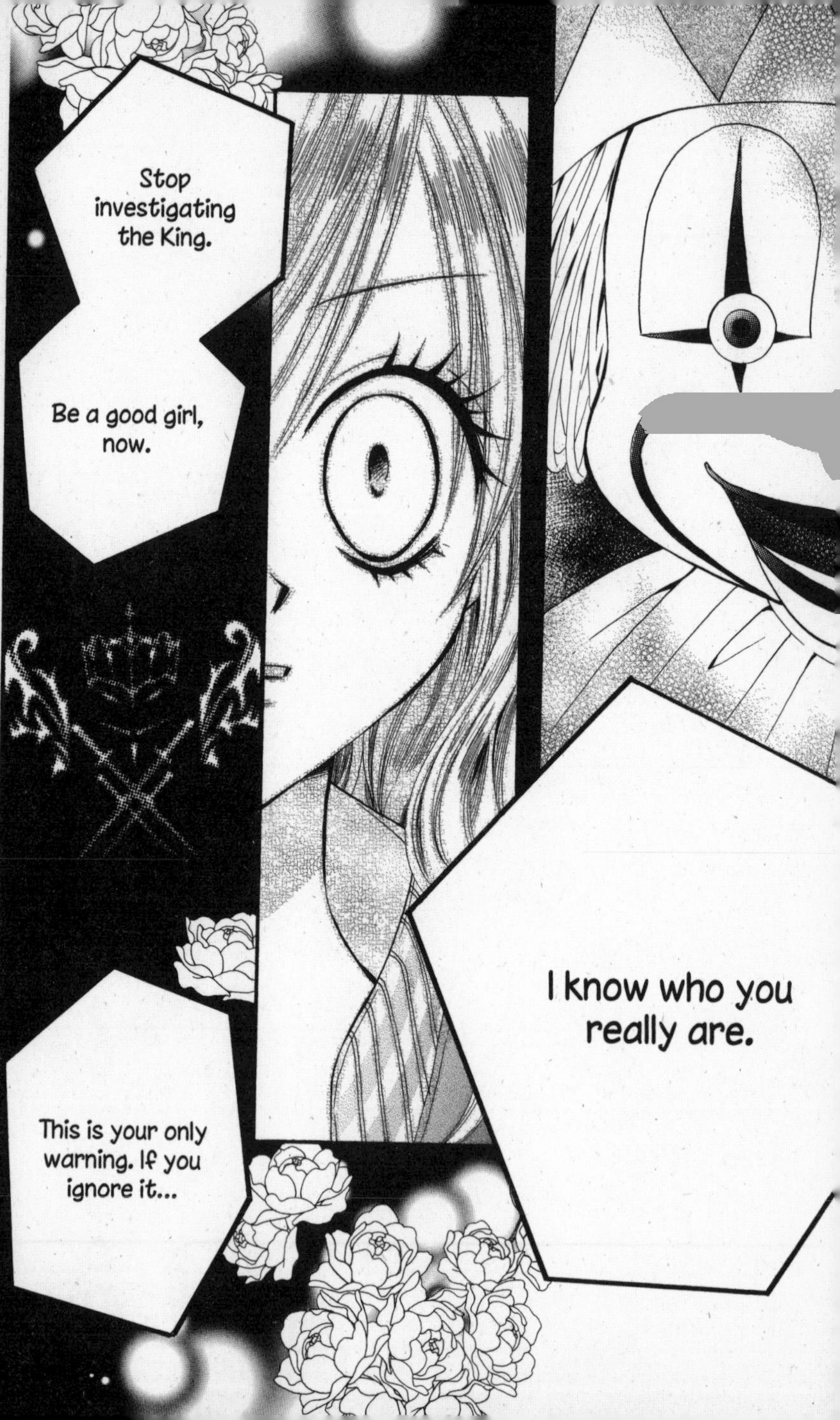

I know who you really are.
Stop investigating the King.
Be a good girl, now.
This is your only warning. If you ignore it...

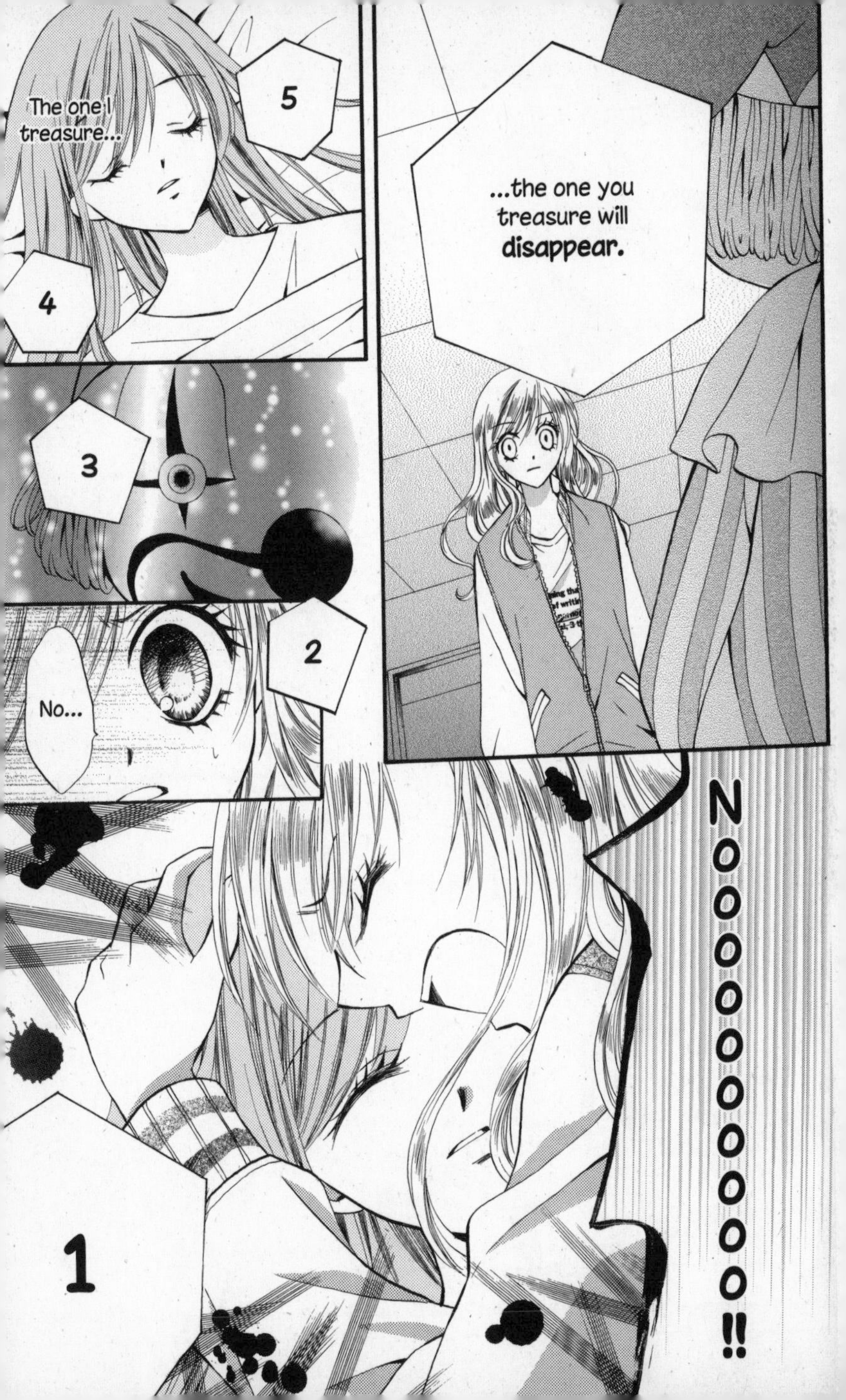
...the one you treasure will **disappear.**
5
The one I treasure...
4
3
2
No...
1
NOOOOOOOOOOOO!!

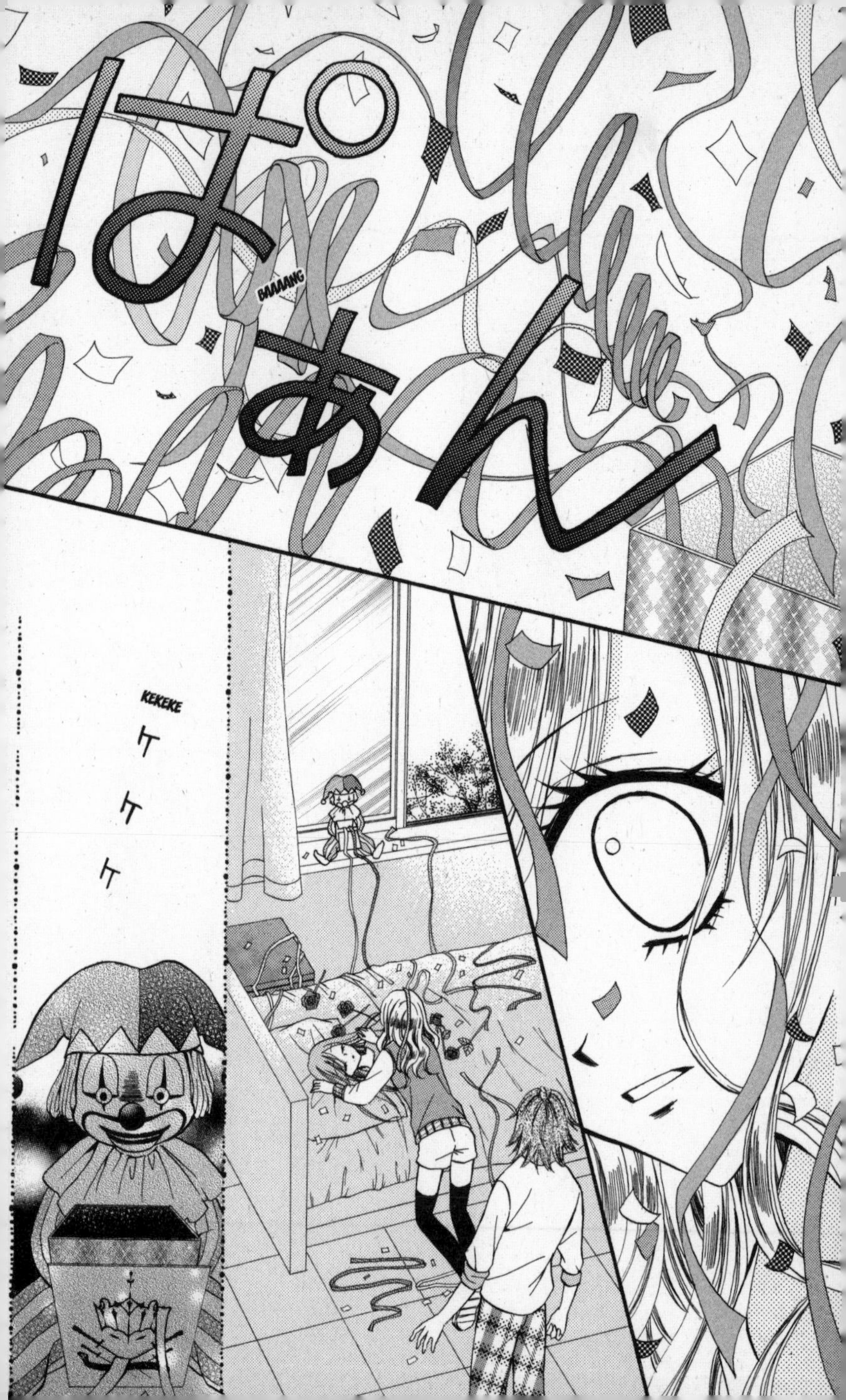

ぱあん
BAAAANG
ケケケ
KEKEKE

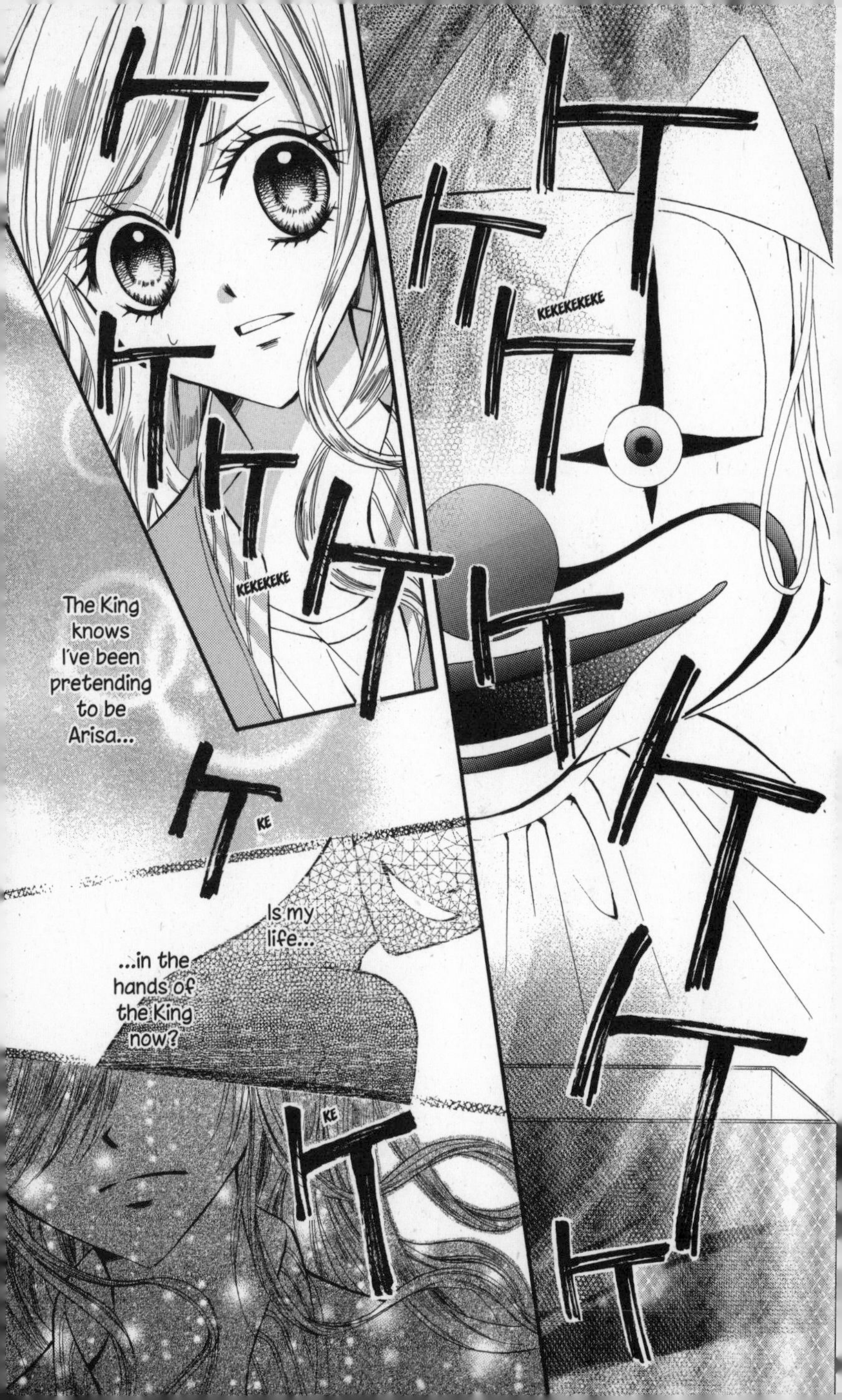

KEKEKEKEKE
KEKEKEKE
The King knows I've been pretending to be Arisa...
KE
Is my life...
...in the hands of the King now?
KE

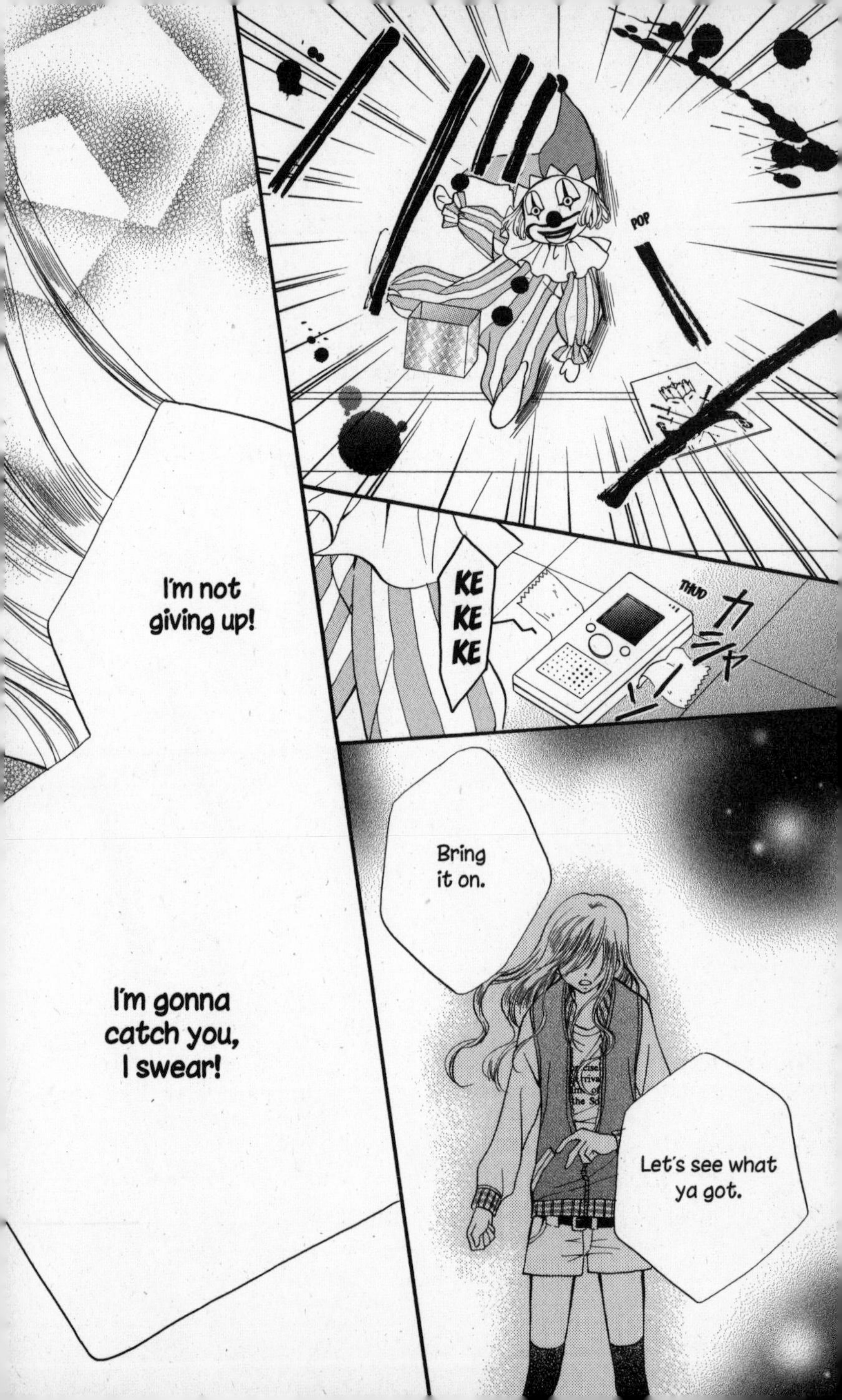
POP
KE KE KE
THUD
カシャン
Bring it on.
Let's see what ya got.
I'm not giving up!
I'm gonna catch you, I swear!

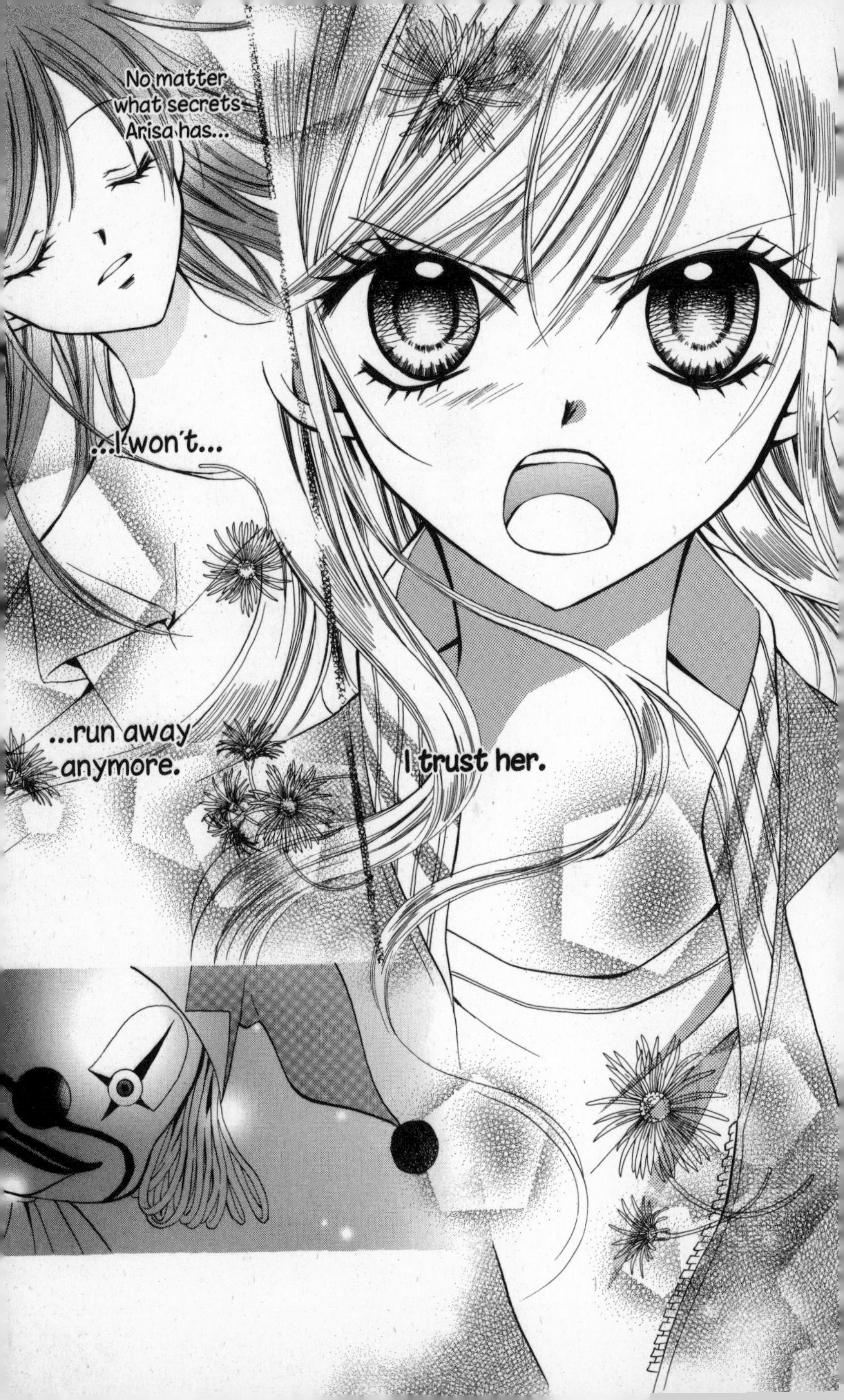
No matter what secrets Arisa has...
I trust her.
...I won't...
...run away anymore.

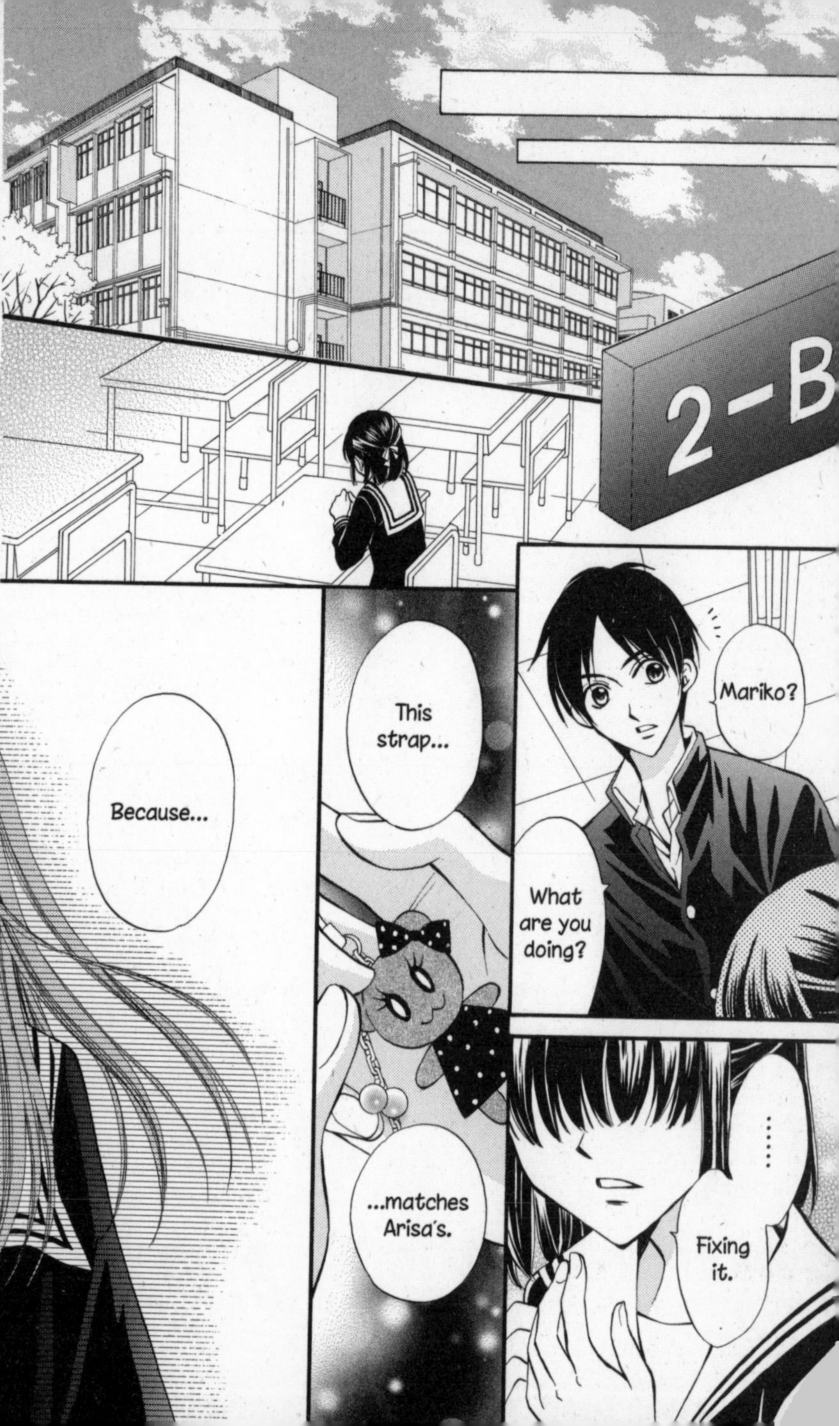
2-B
Mariko?
What are you doing?
......
Fixing it.
This strap...
...matches Arisa's.
Because...

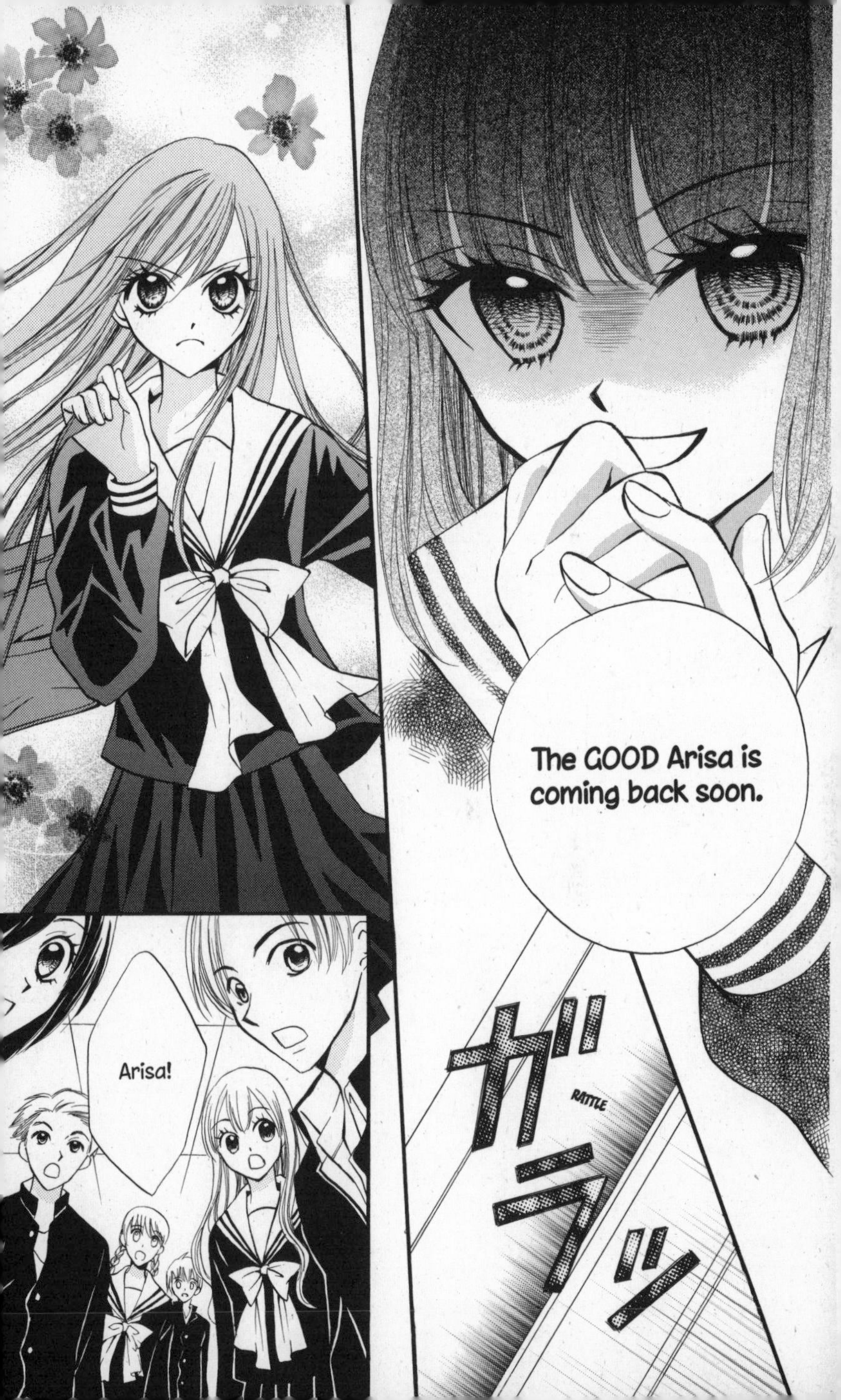
The GOOD Arisa is coming back soon.
ガラッ
RATTLE
Arisa!

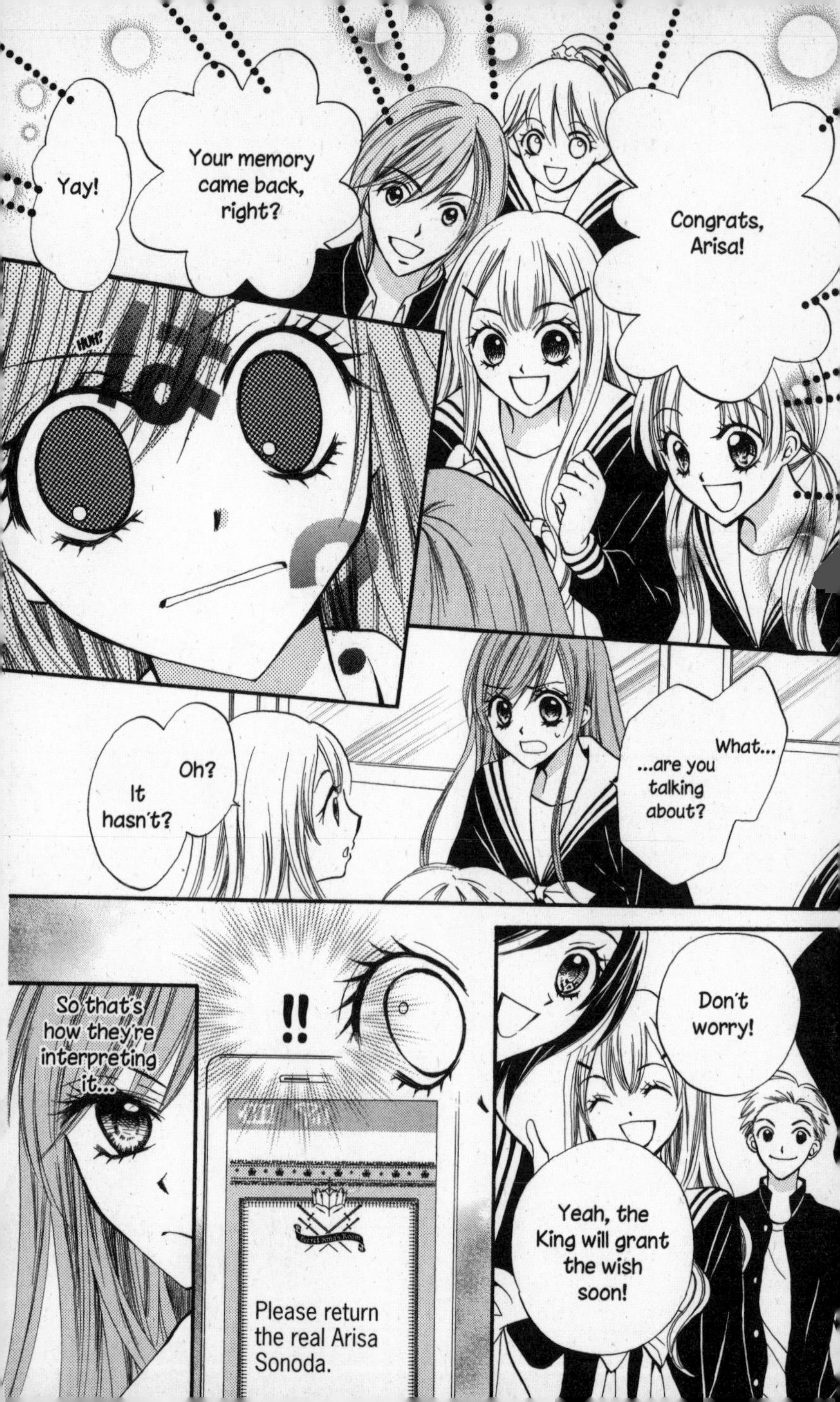
Congrats, Arisa!
Your memory came back, right?
Yay!
HUH?
What... ...are you talking about?
Oh? It hasn't?
Don't worry!
Yeah, the King will grant the wish soon!
!!
Please return the real Arisa Sonoda.
So that's how they're interpreting it...

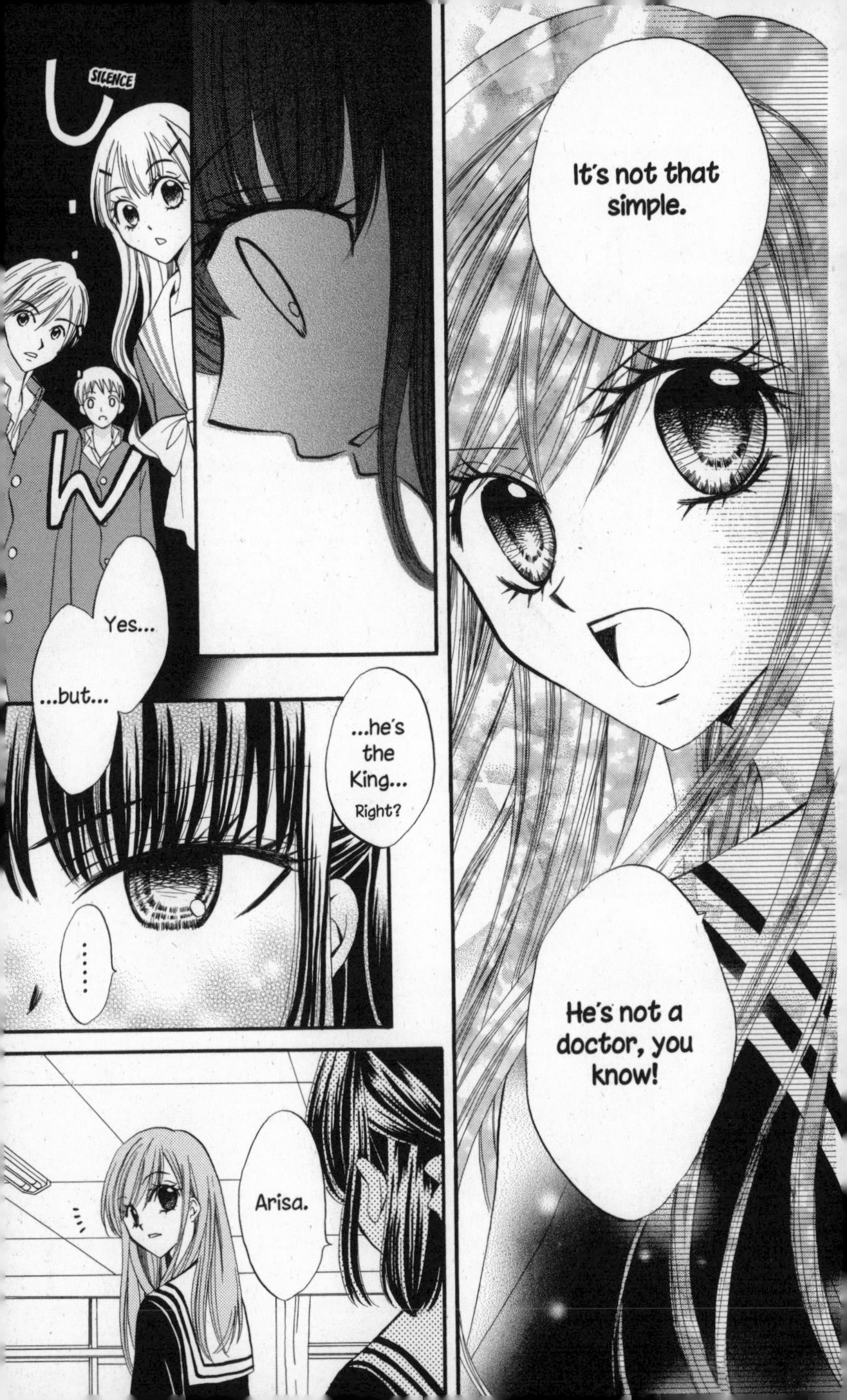
It's not that simple.
He's not a doctor, you know!
SILENCE
Yes...
...but...
...he's the King...
Right?
......
Arisa.

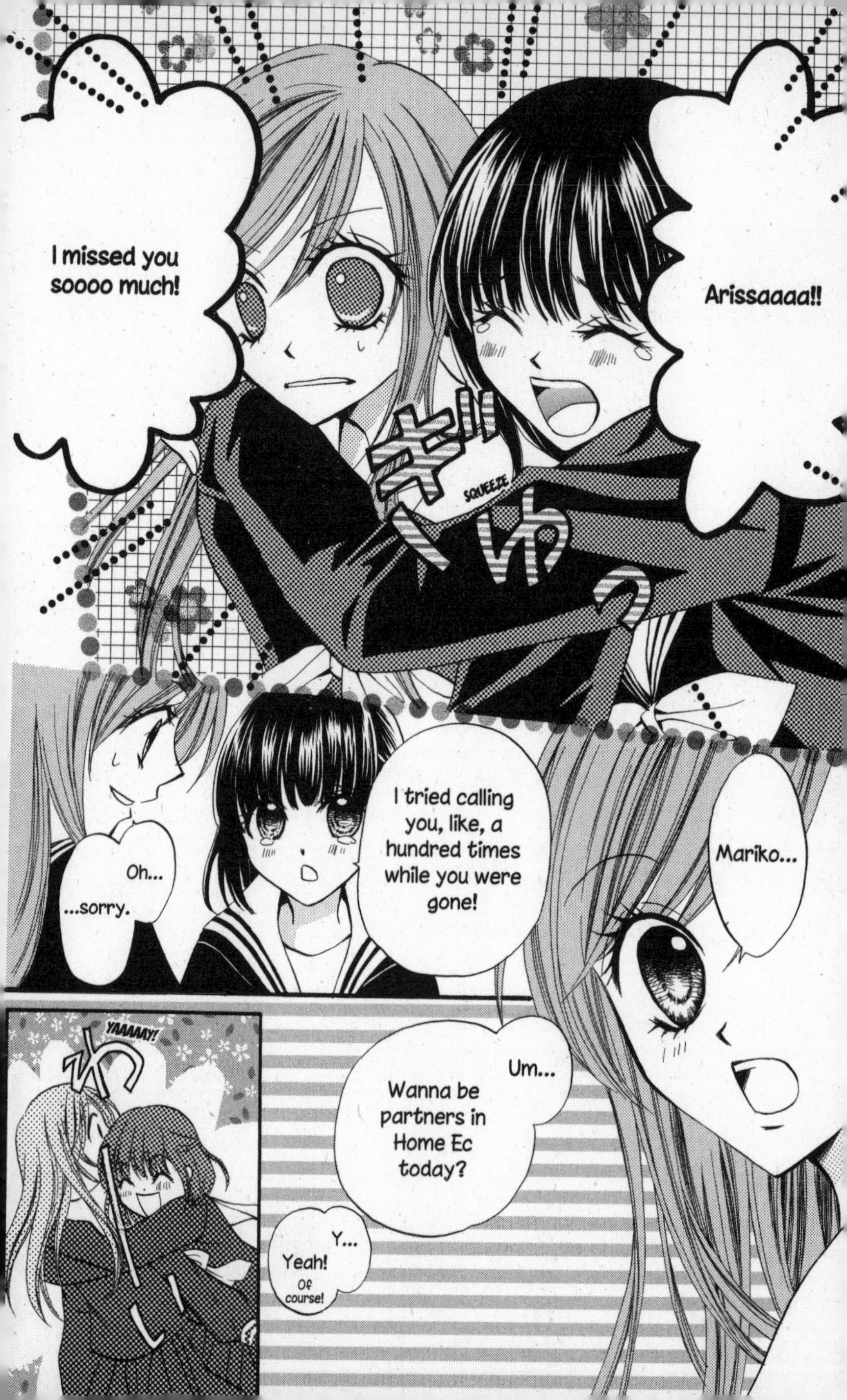

Arissaaaa!!
SQUEEZE
I missed you soooo much!
Mariko...
Um...
Wanna be partners in Home Ec today?
I tried calling you, like, a hundred times while you were gone!
Oh...
...sorry.
YAAAAAY!
Y...
Yeah!
Of course!

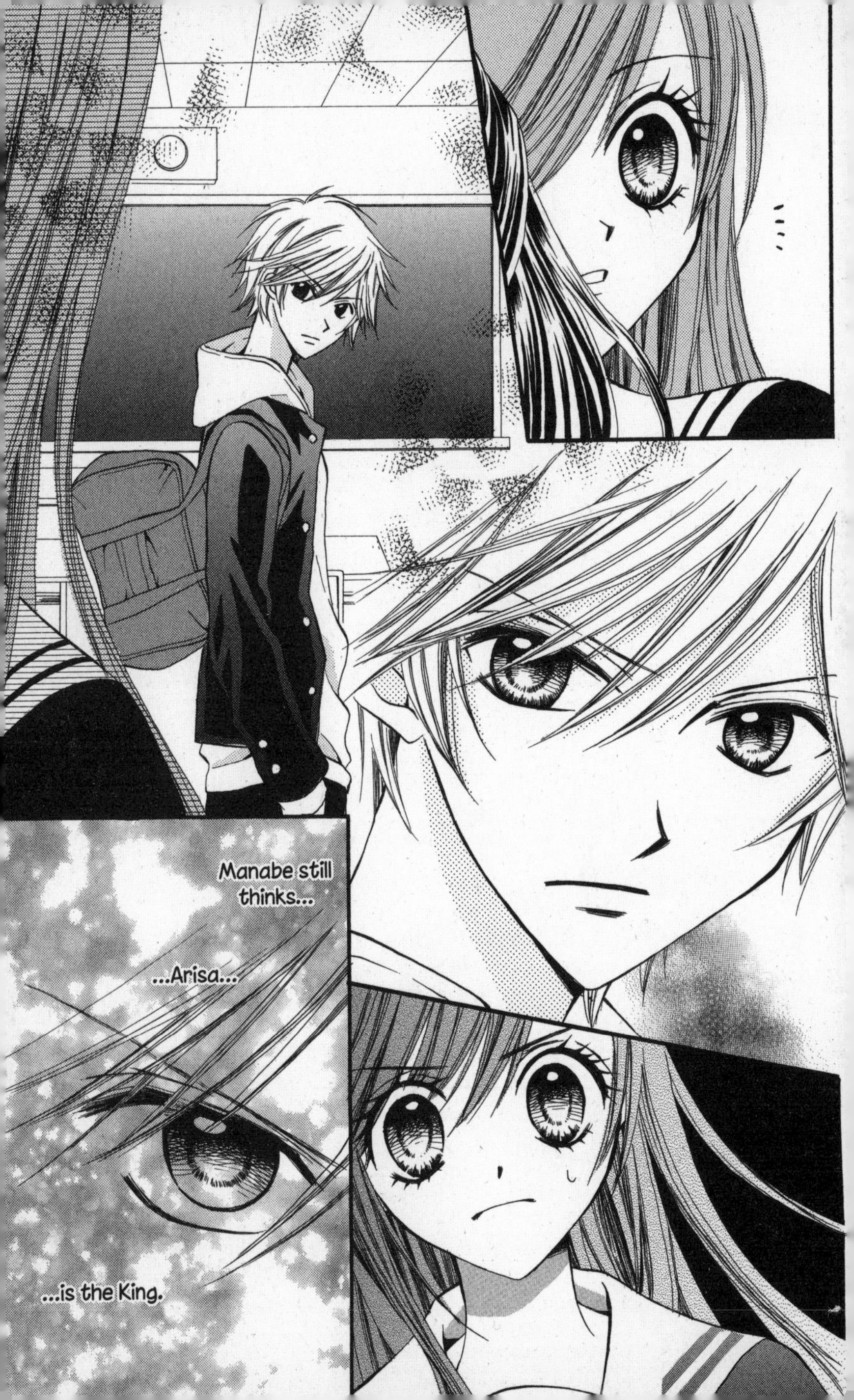
Manabe still thinks...
...Arisa...
...is the King.

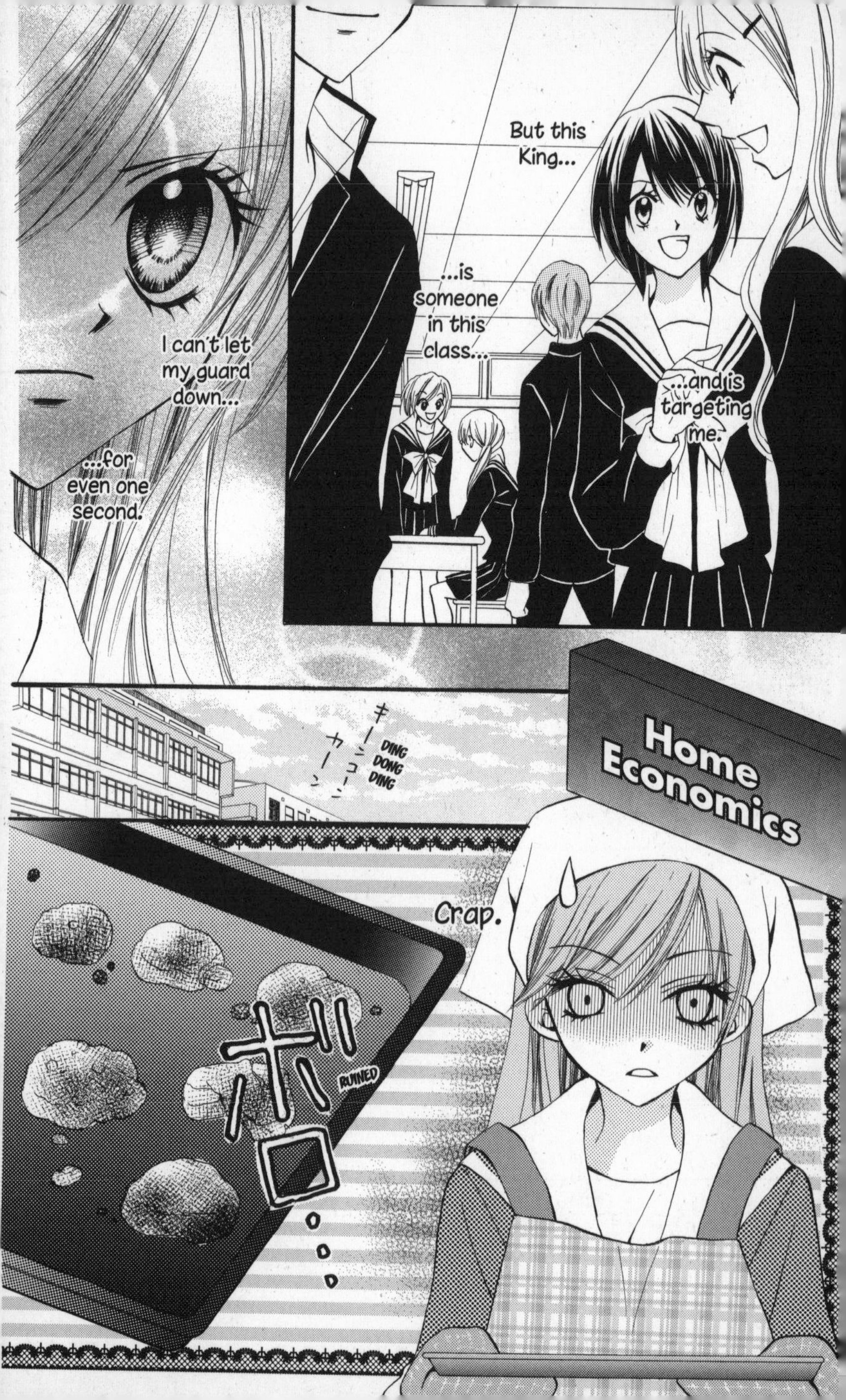
But this King...
...is someone in this class...
...and is targeting me.
I can't let my guard down...
...for even one second.
Home Economics
キーンコーンカーンコーン
DING DONG DING
Crap.
ボロ
RUINED

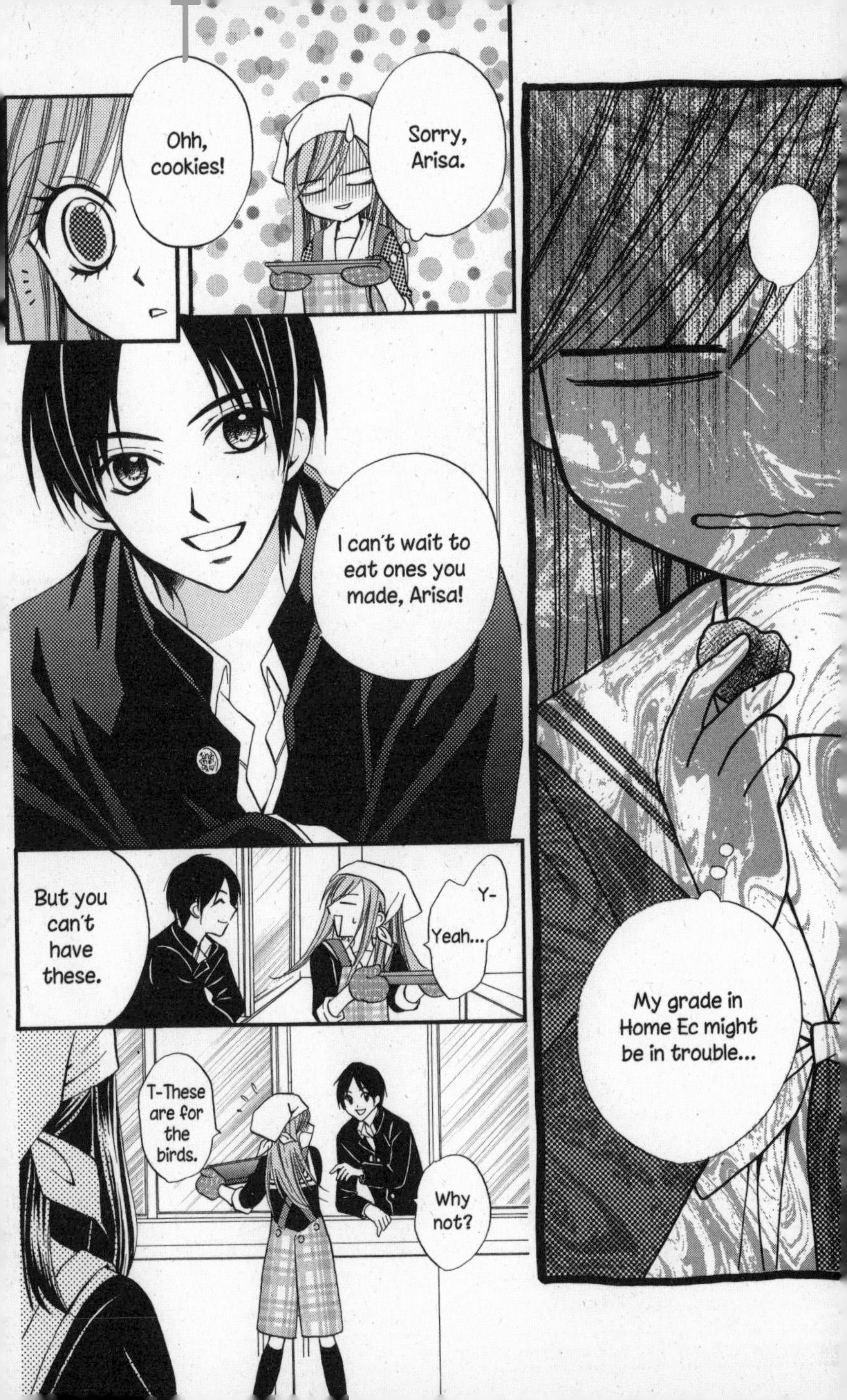
Sorry, Arisa.
Ohh, cookies!
I can't wait to eat ones you made, Arisa!
Y- Yeah...
But you can't have these.
Why not?
T-These are for the birds.
My grade in Home Ec might be in trouble...

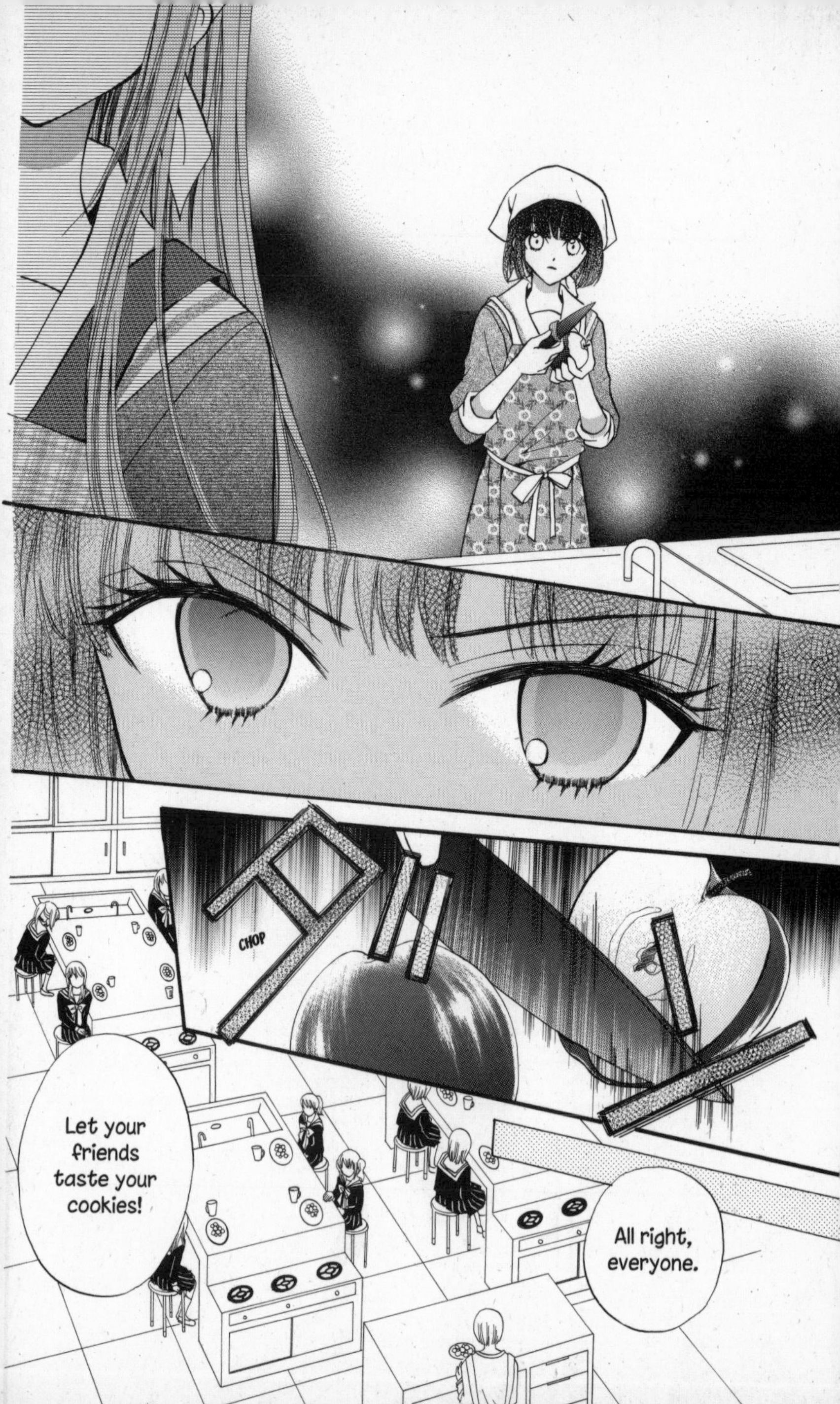
CHOP
All right, everyone.
Let your friends taste your cookies!

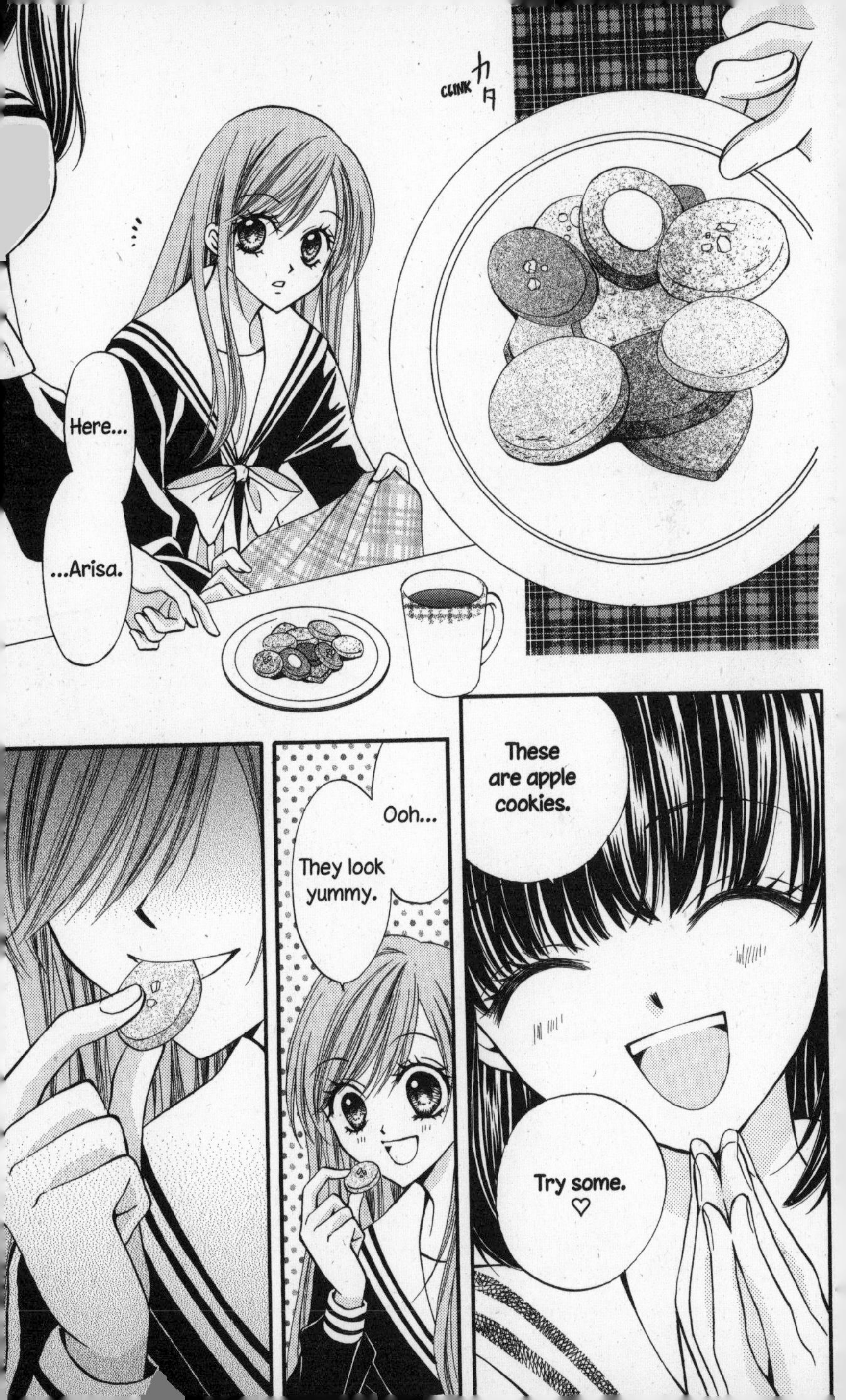
CLINK カタ
Here...
...Arisa.
These are apple cookies.
Try some. ♡
Ooh...
They look yummy.

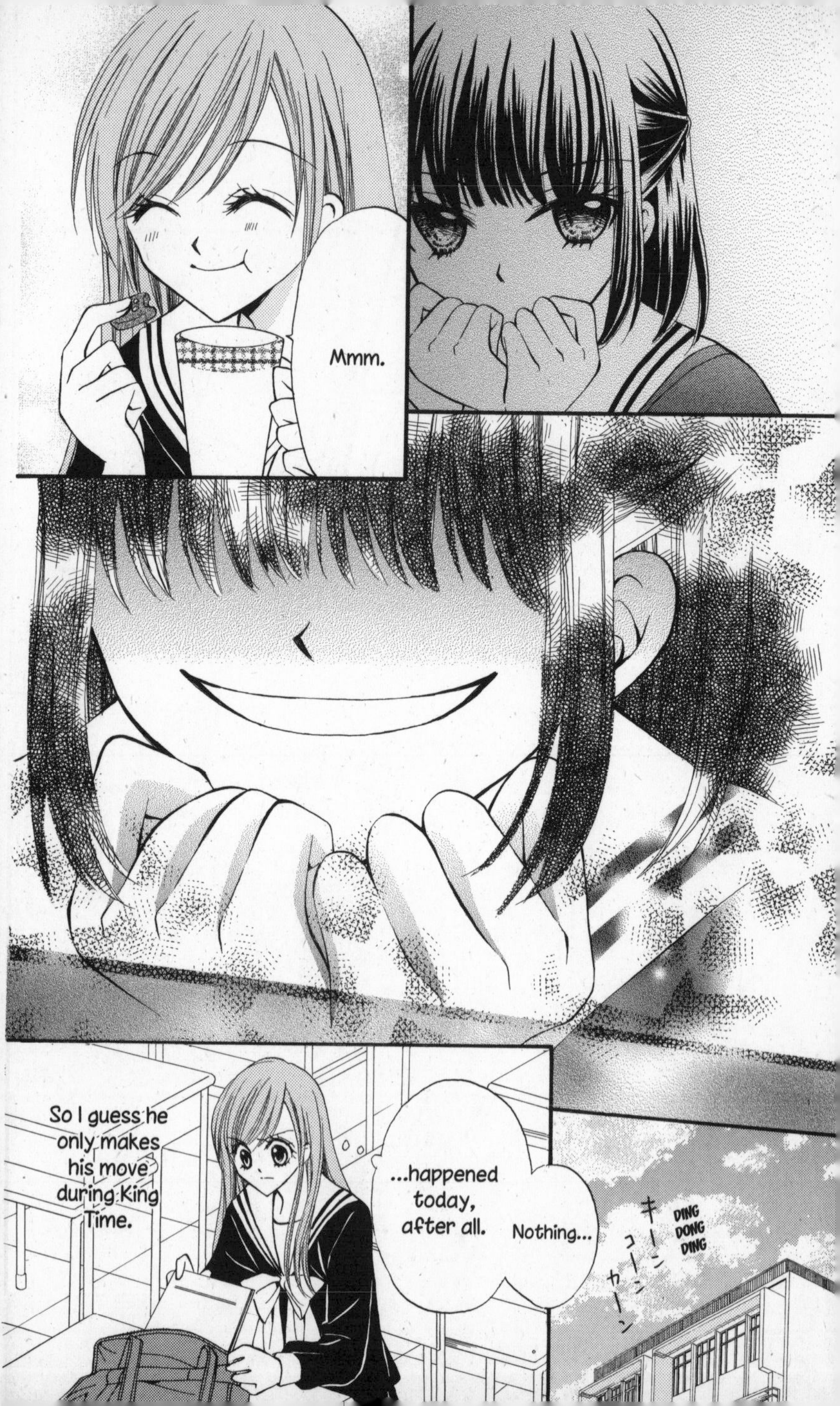
Mmm.
キーン コーン カーン
DING DONG DING
Nothing...
...happened today, after all.
So I guess he only makes his move during King Time.

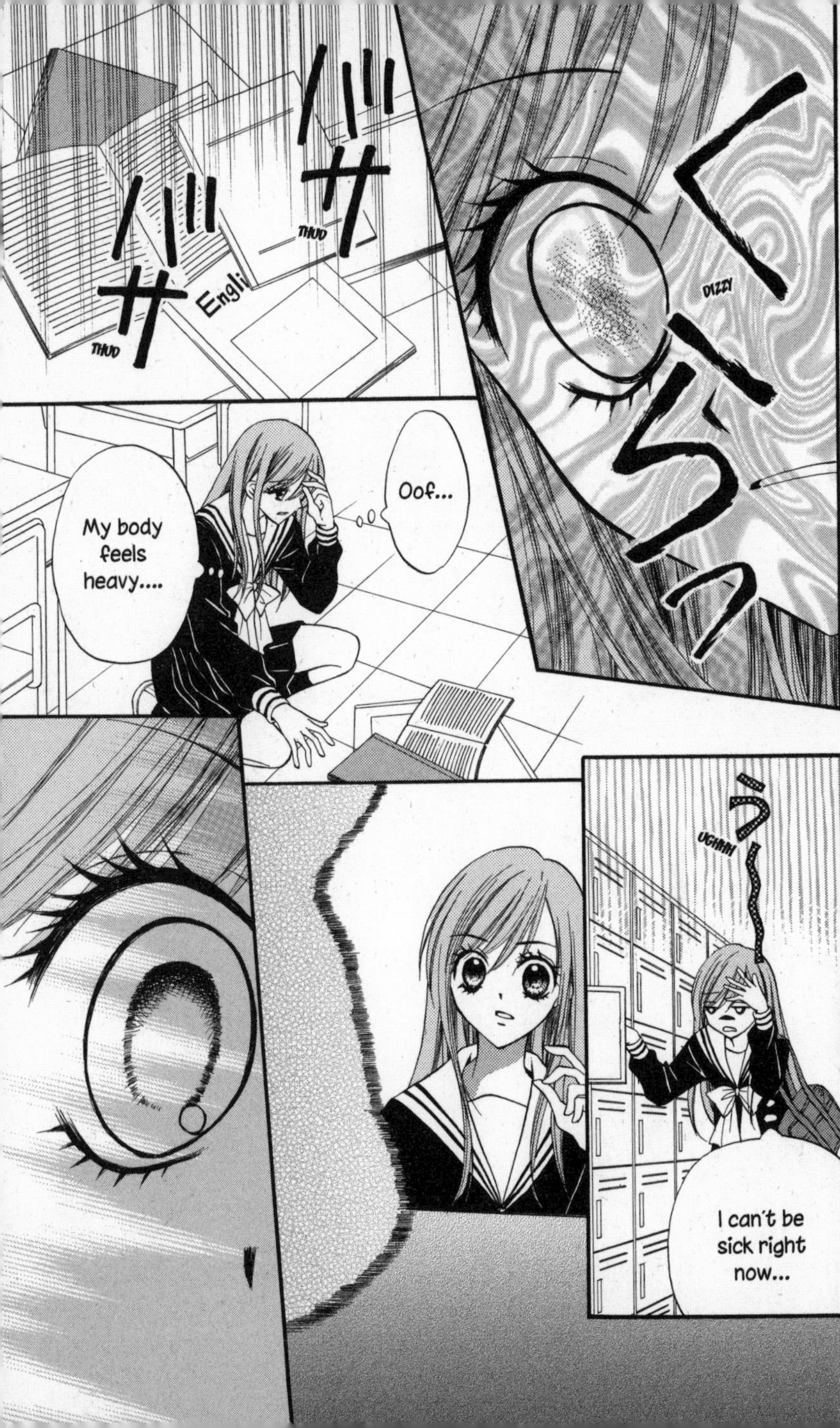
DIZZY
THUD
Engli
THUD
Oof...
My body feels heavy....
UGHHH
I can't be sick right now...

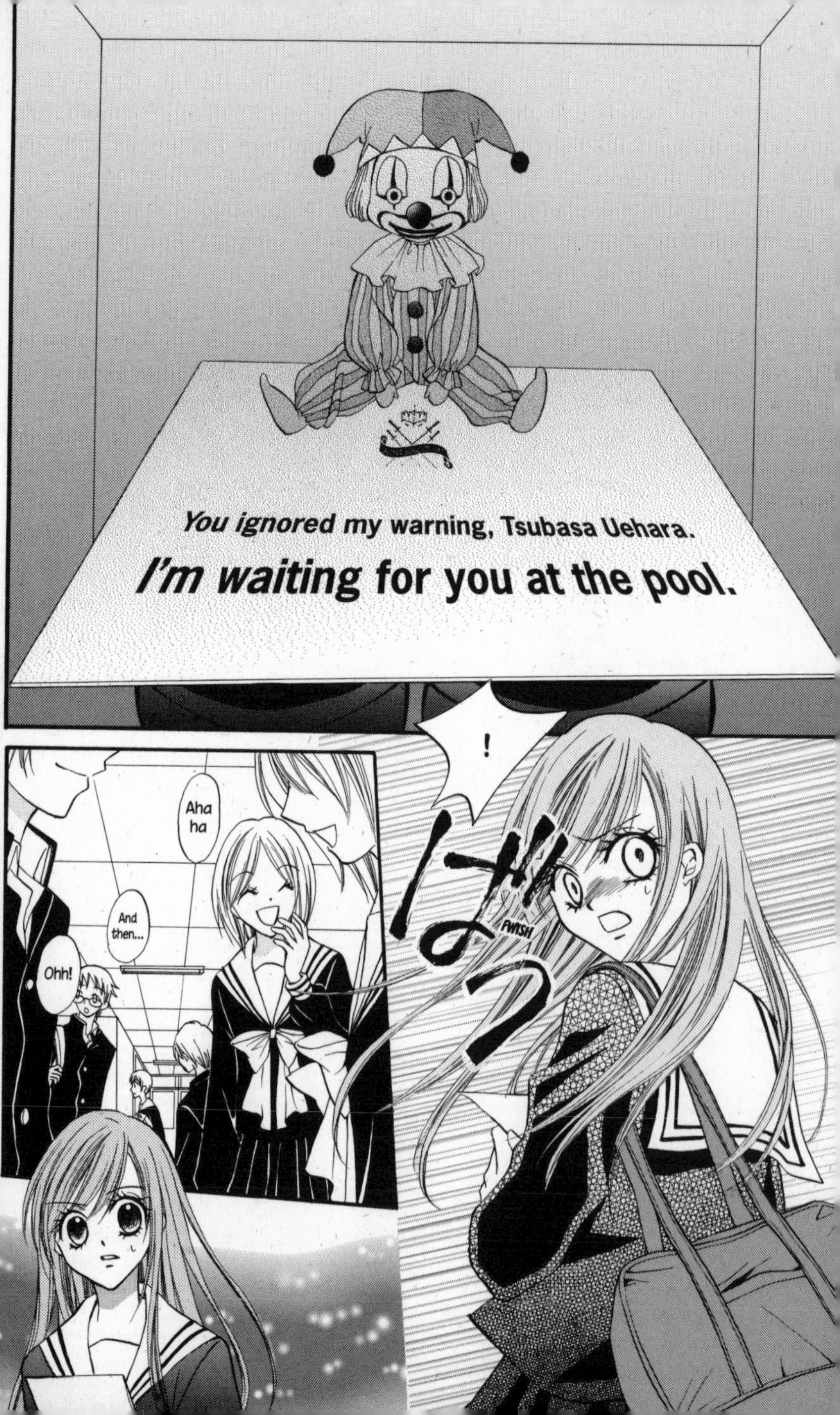
You ignored my warning, Tsubasa Uehara.
I'm waiting for you at the pool.
!
はっ
FWISH
Aha ha
And then...
Ohh!

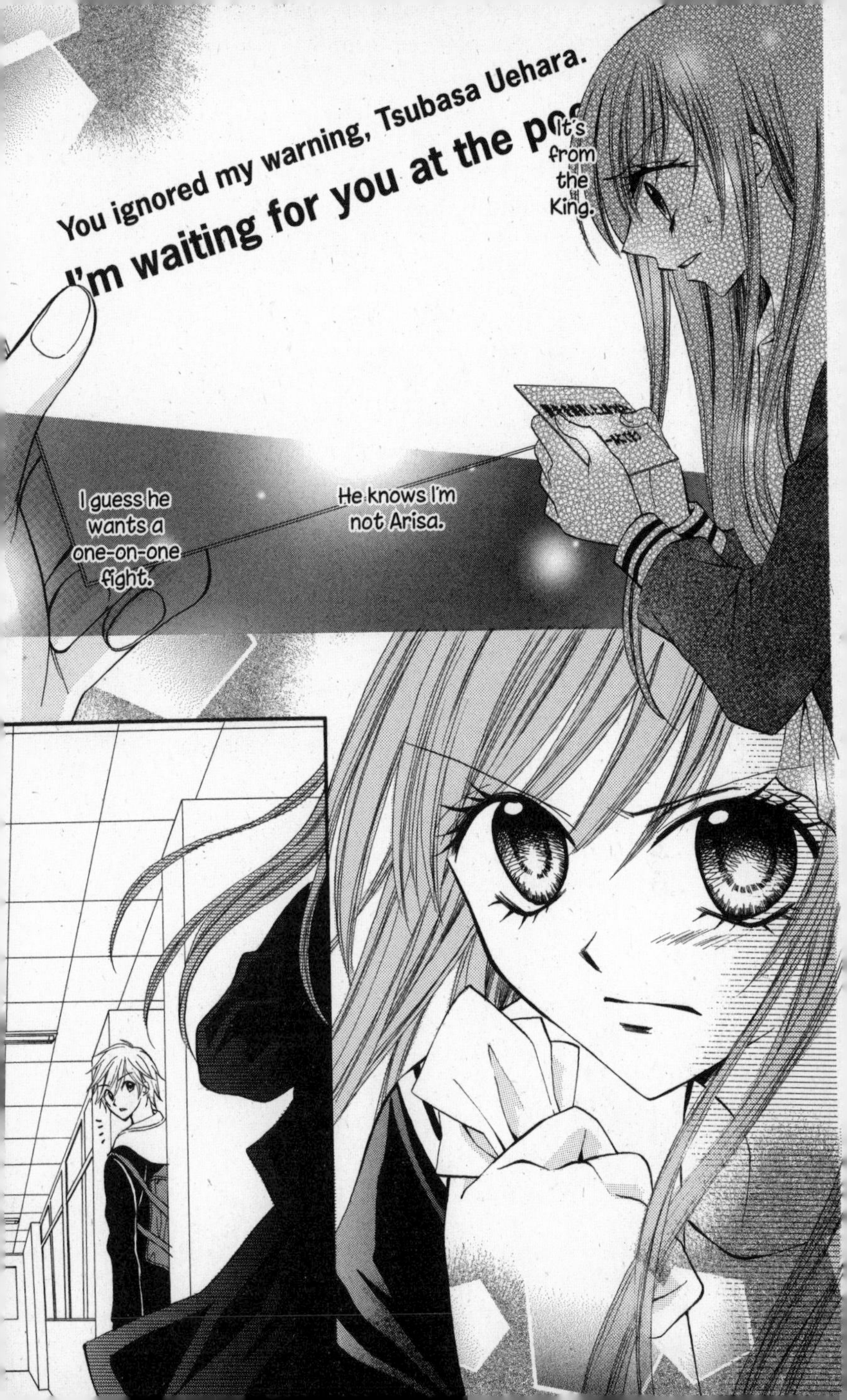
You ignored my warning, Tsubasa Uehara.
I'm waiting for you at the po
It's from the King.
He knows I'm not Arisa.
I guess he wants a one-on-one fight.

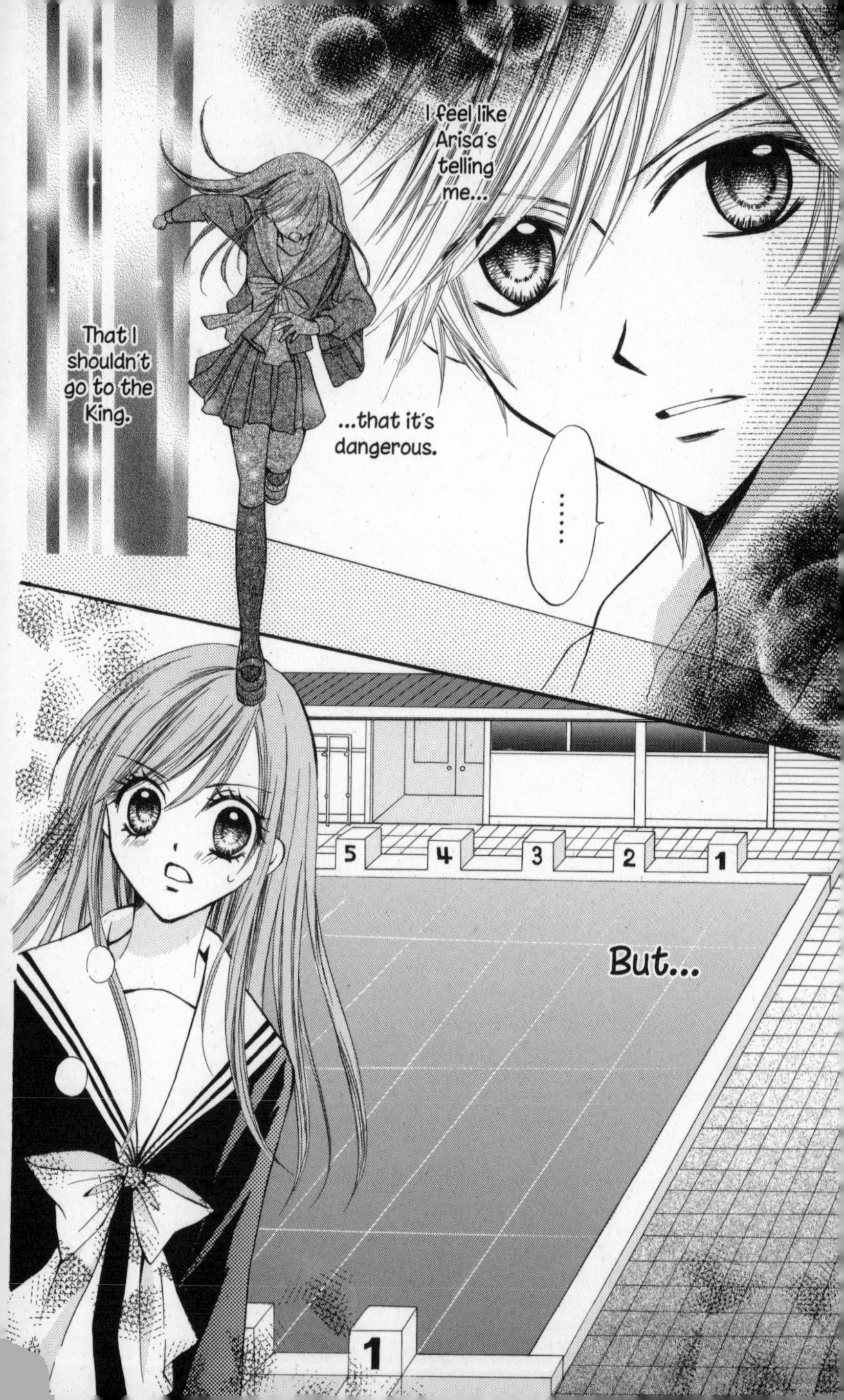
I feel like Arisa's telling me...
......
...that it's dangerous.
That I shouldn't go to the King.
But...

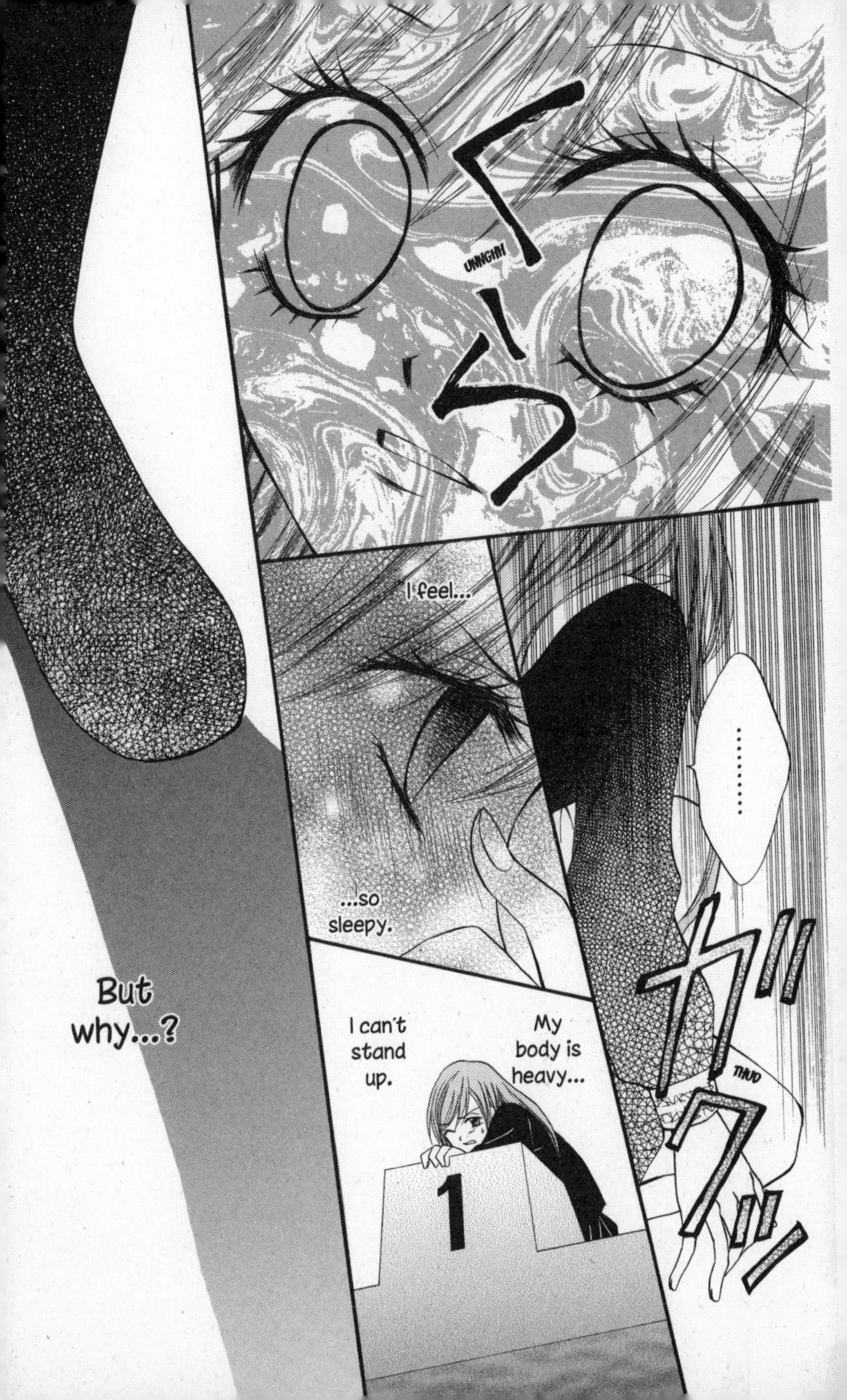
UNNGHH
......
THUD
I feel...
...so sleepy.
My body is heavy...
I can't stand up.
1
But why...?

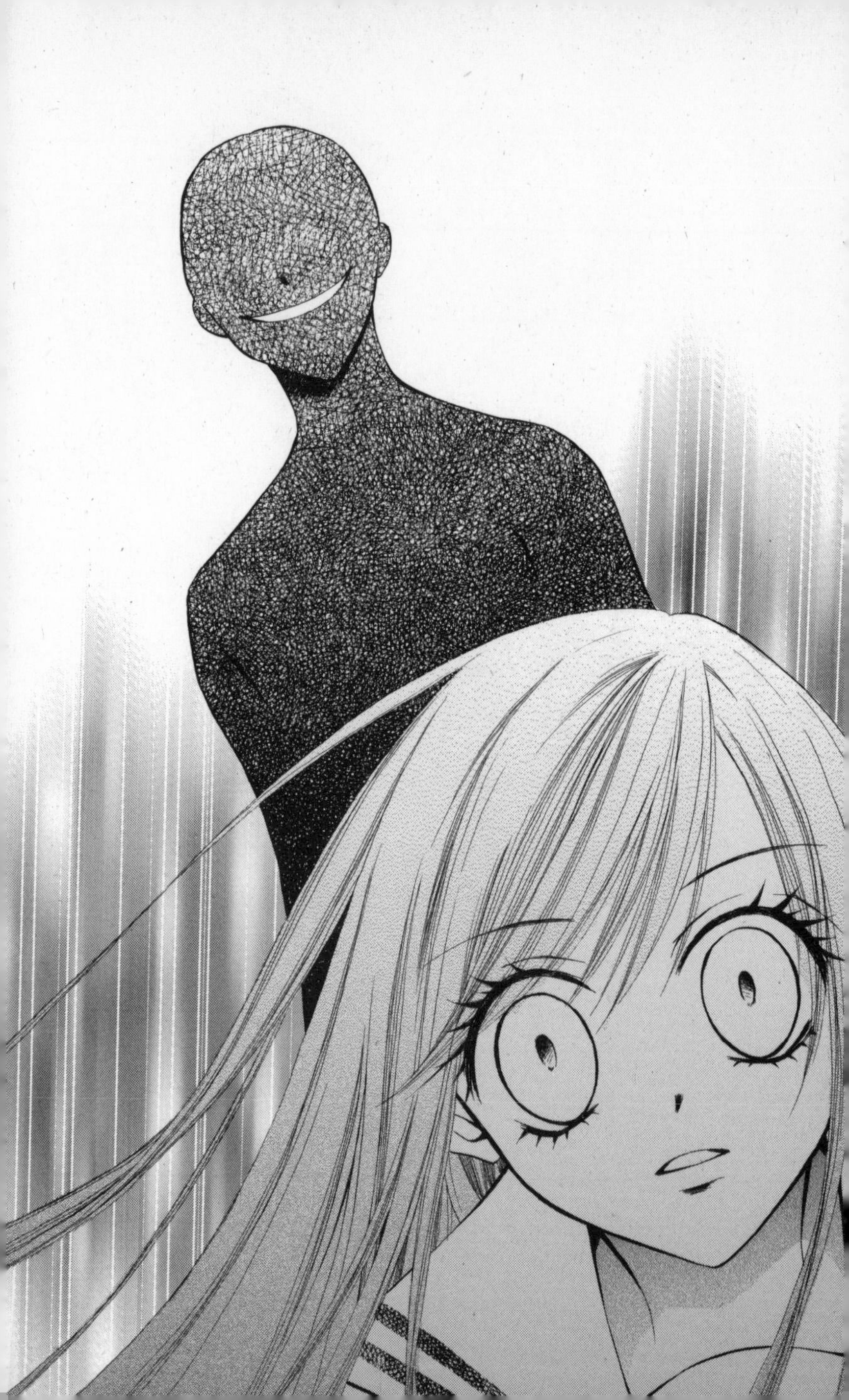

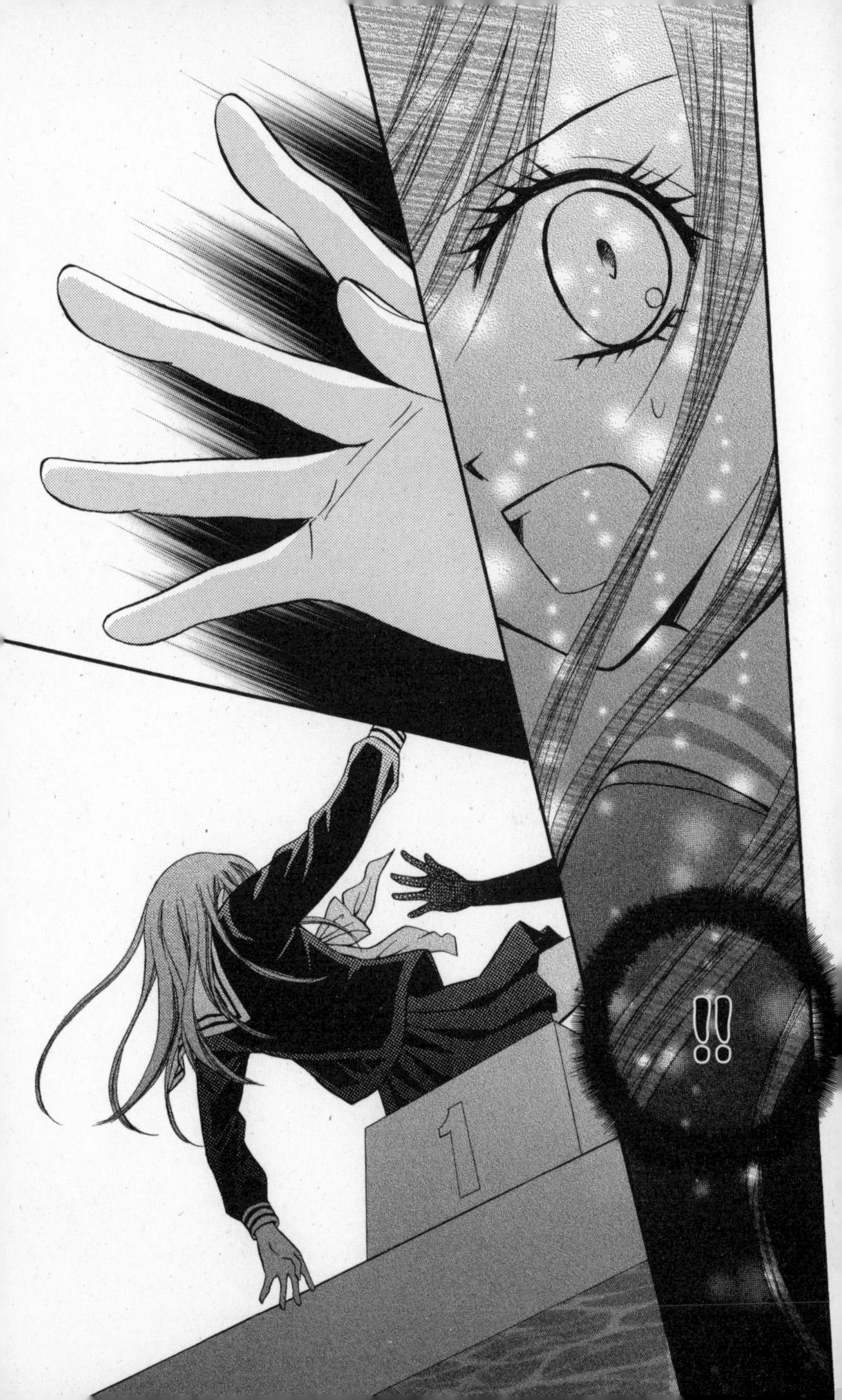
!!

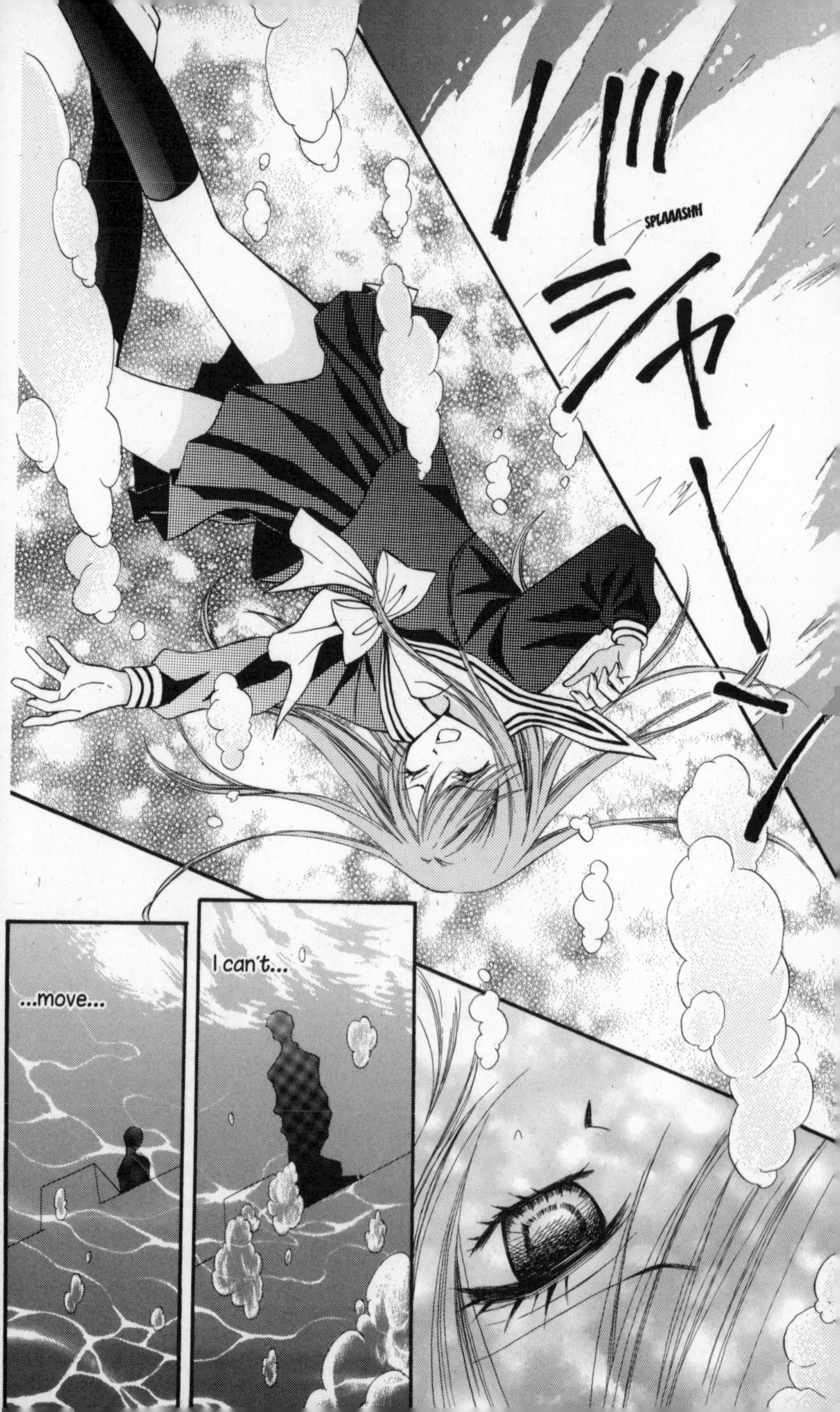
SPLAAASHH
I can't...
...move...

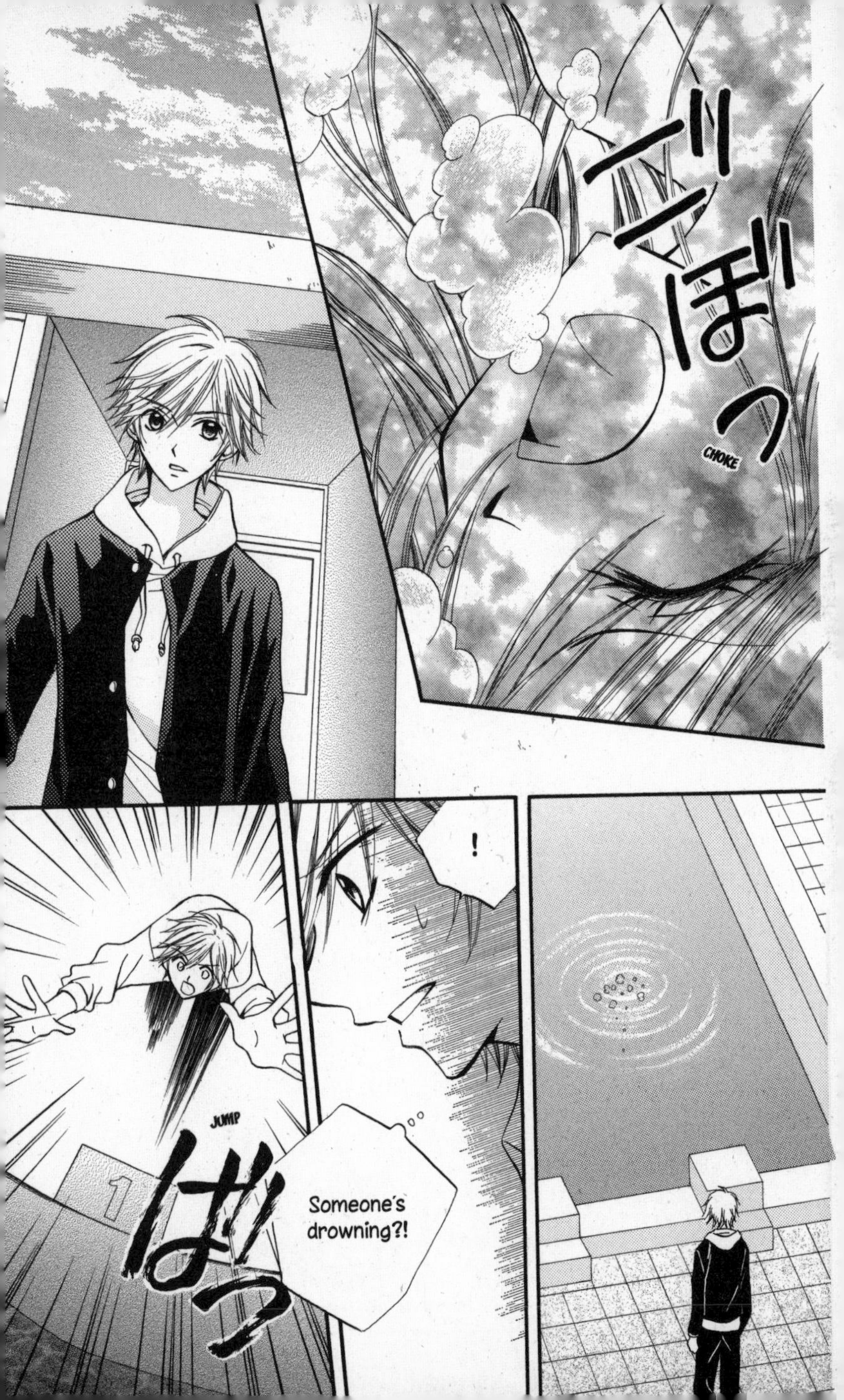

ごぼっ
CHOKE
!
Someone's drowning?!
はっ
JUMP

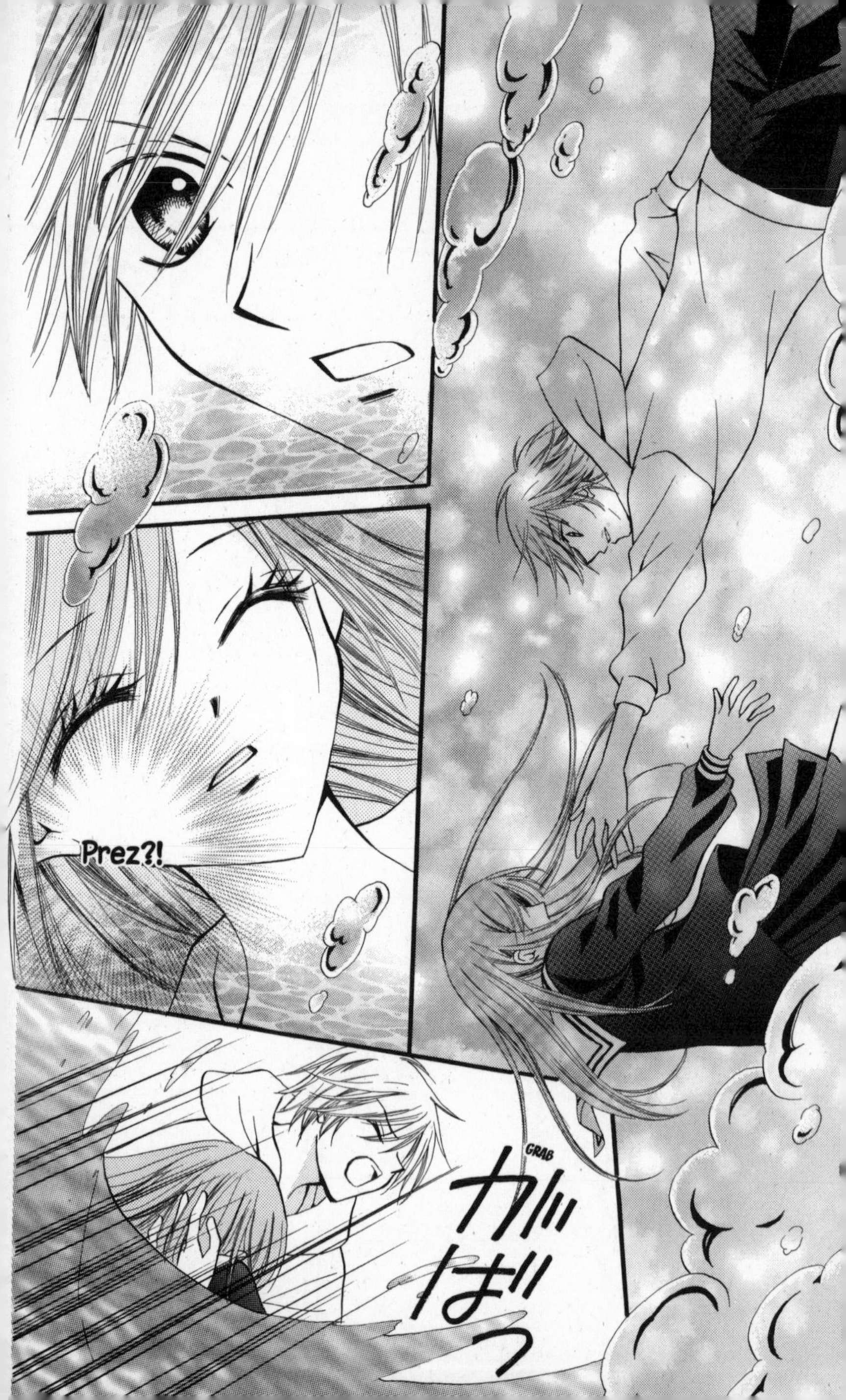
Prez?!
GRAB
がばっ

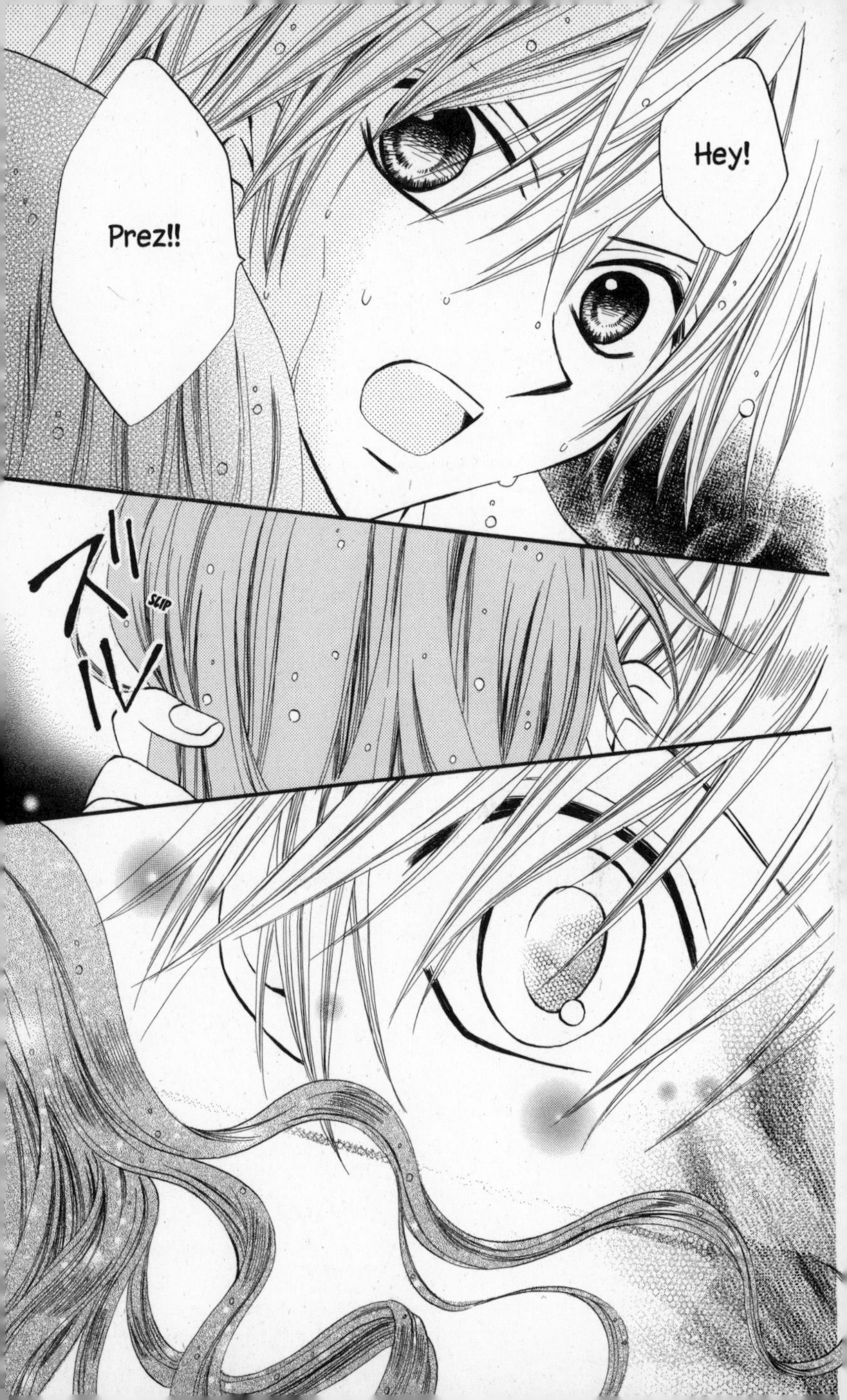

Hey!
Prez!!
ズル
SLIP

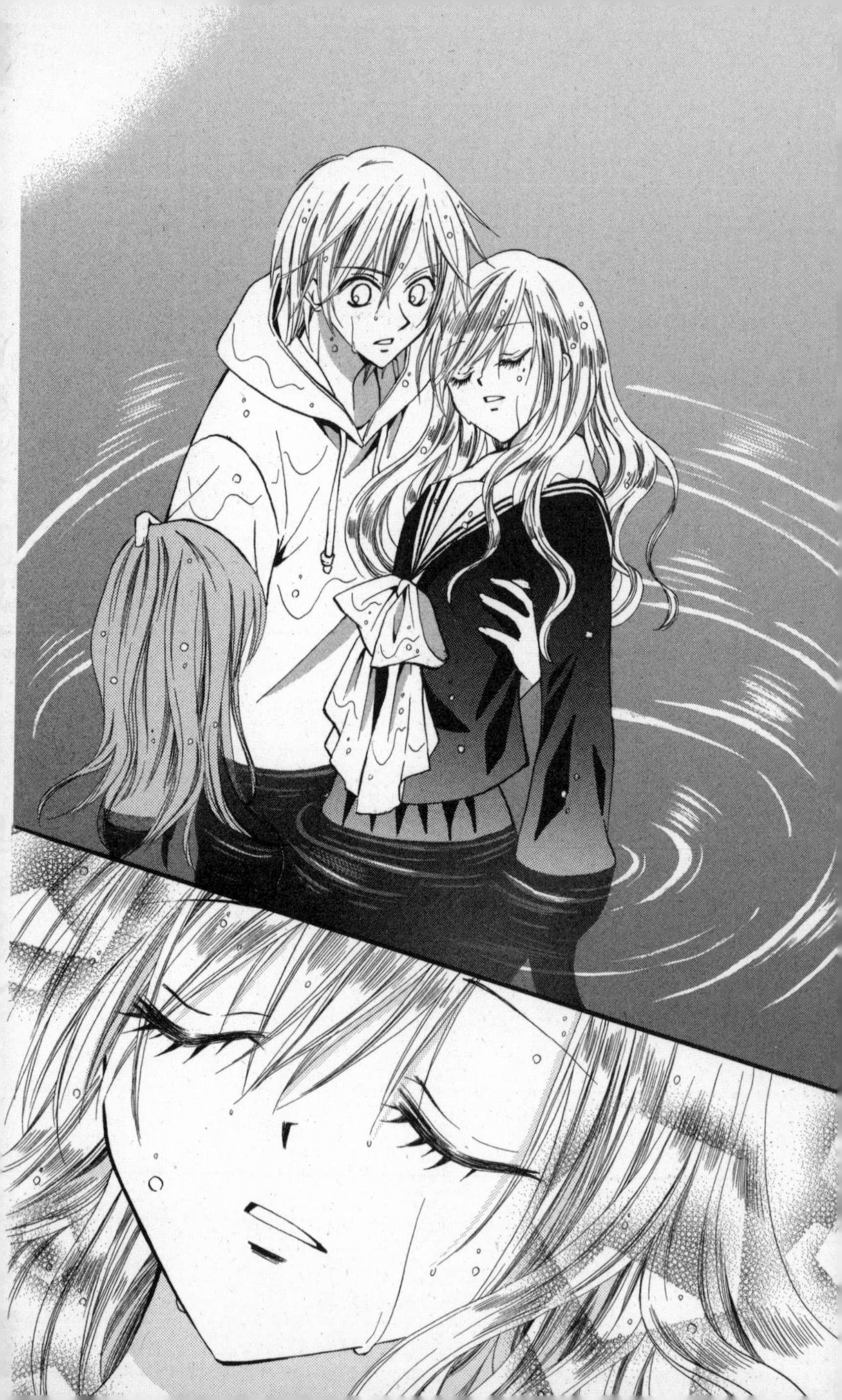

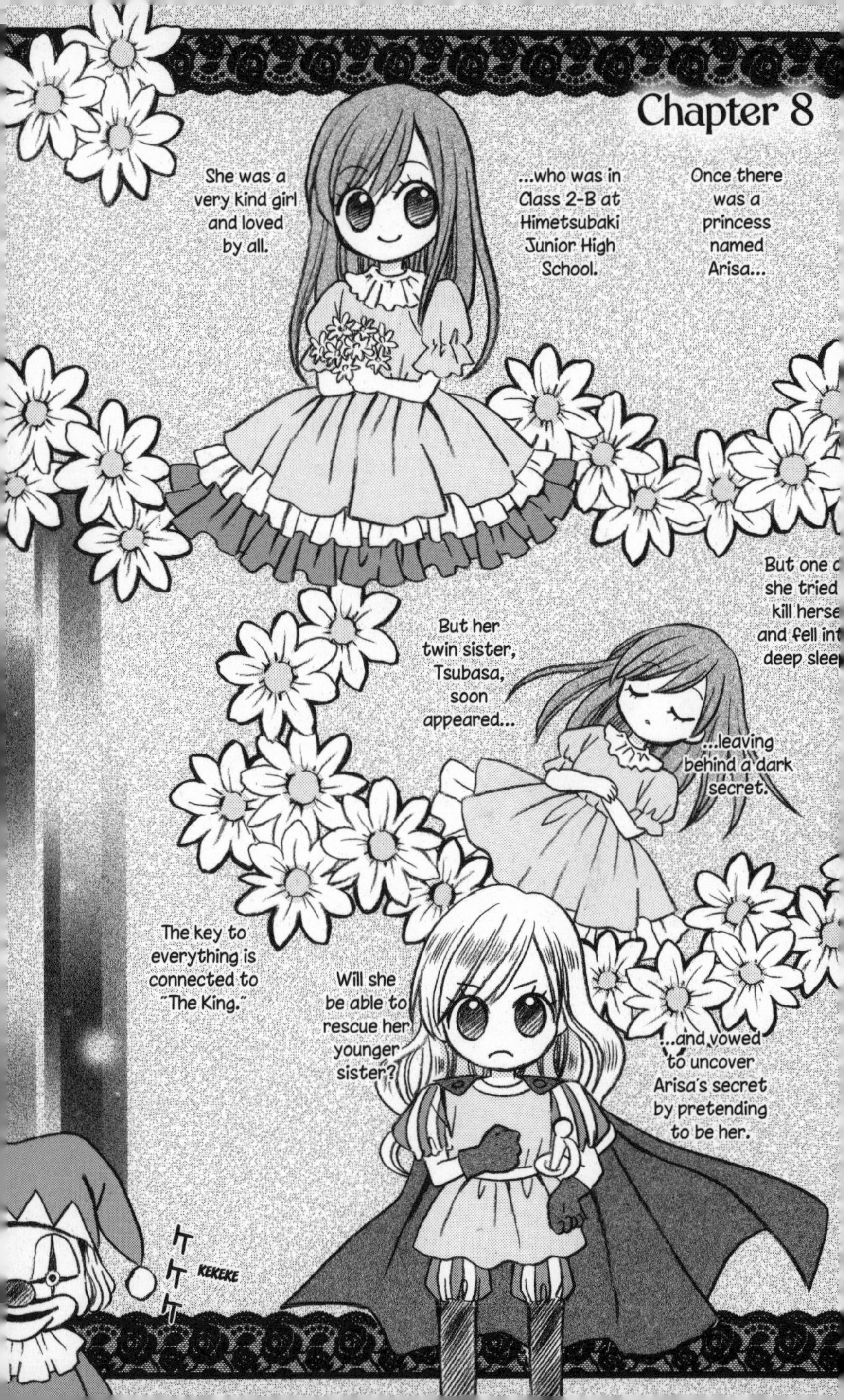
Chapter 8
Once there was a princess named Arisa...
...who was in Class 2-B at Himetsubaki Junior High School.
She was a very kind girl and loved by all.
But one d she tried kill herse and fell int deep slee
...leaving behind a dark secret.
But her twin sister, Tsubasa, soon appeared...
...and vowed to uncover Arisa's secret by pretending to be her.
Will she be able to rescue her younger sister?
The key to everything is connected to "The King."
KEKEKE

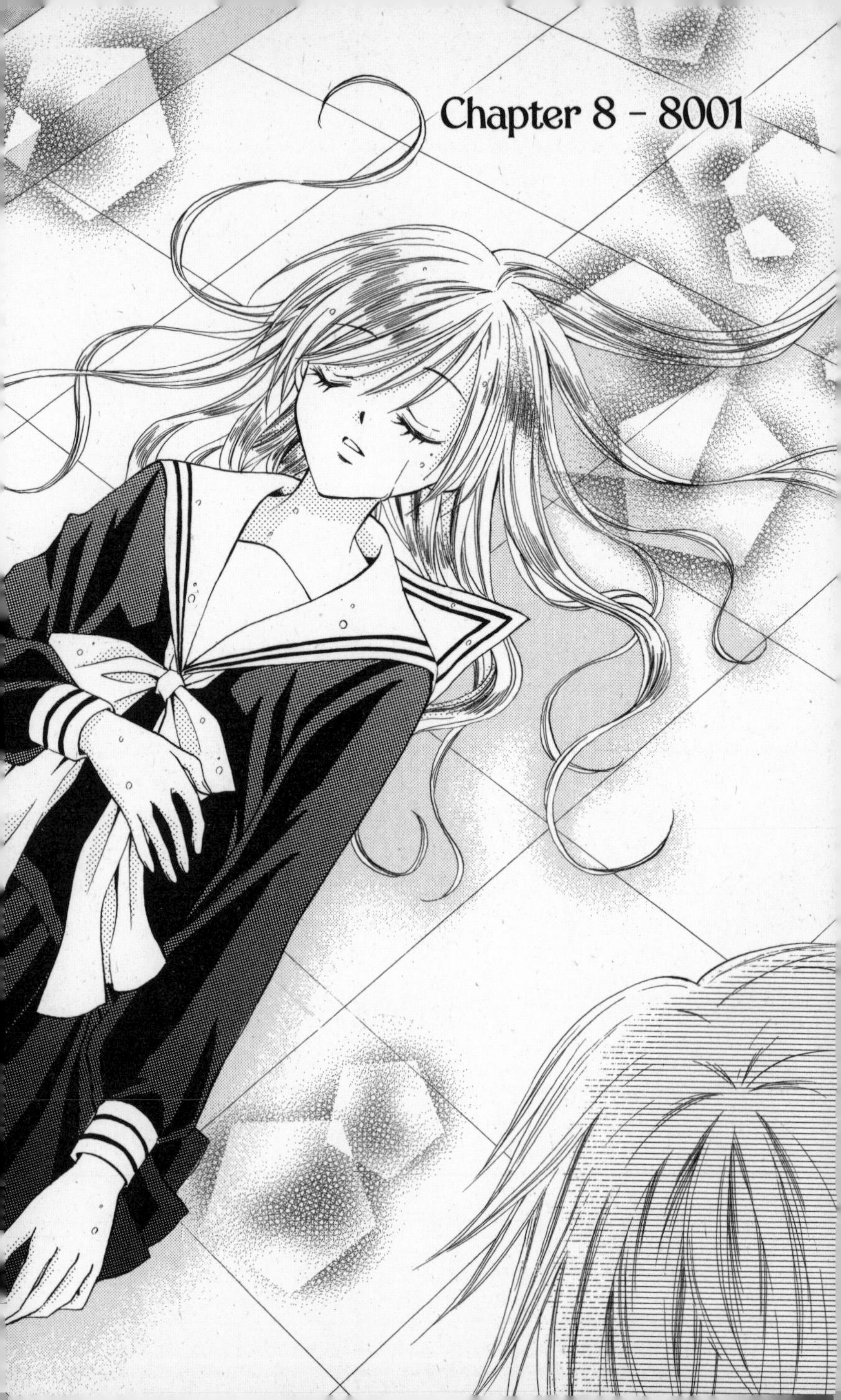
Chapter 8 - 8001

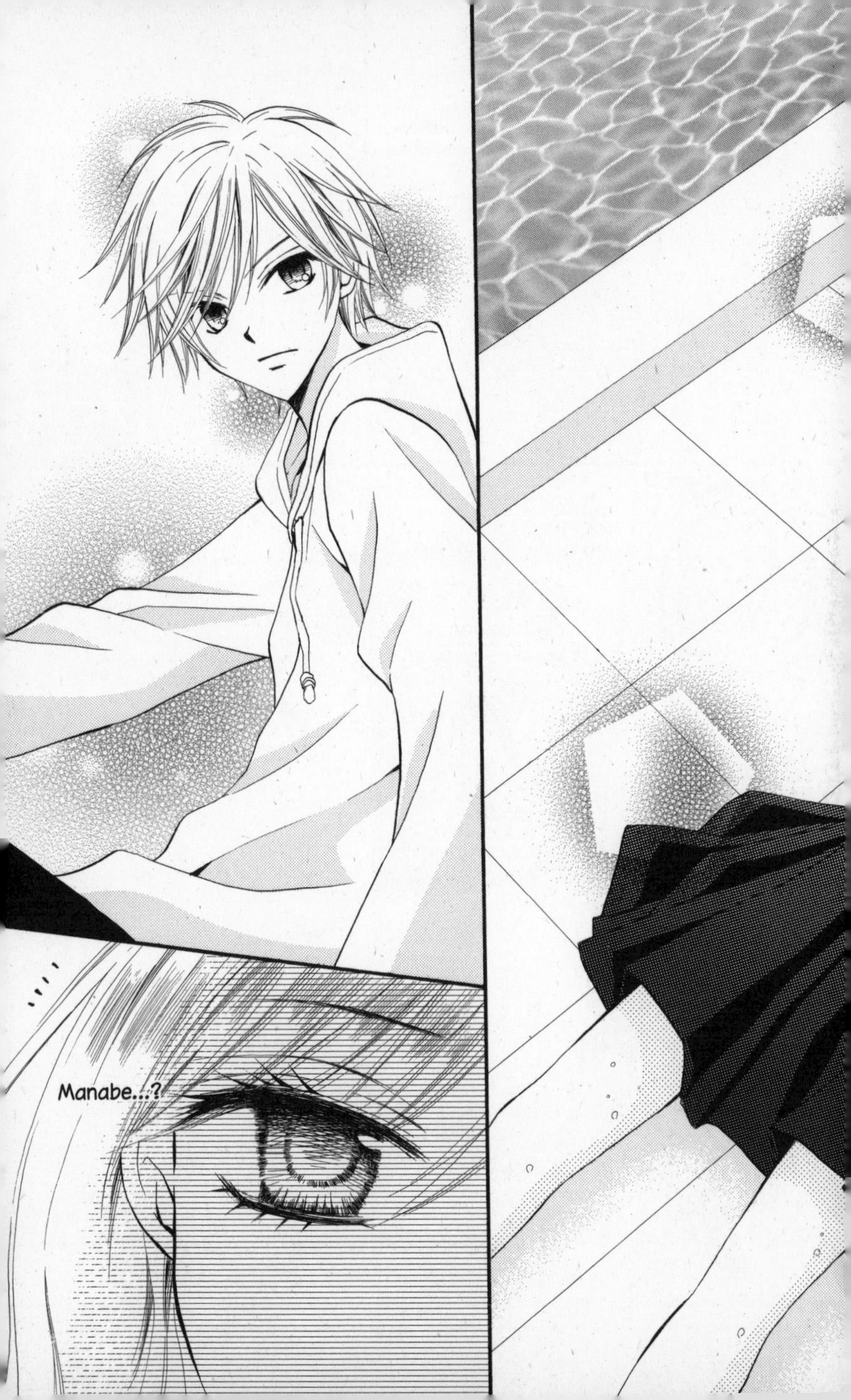

...
Manabe...?

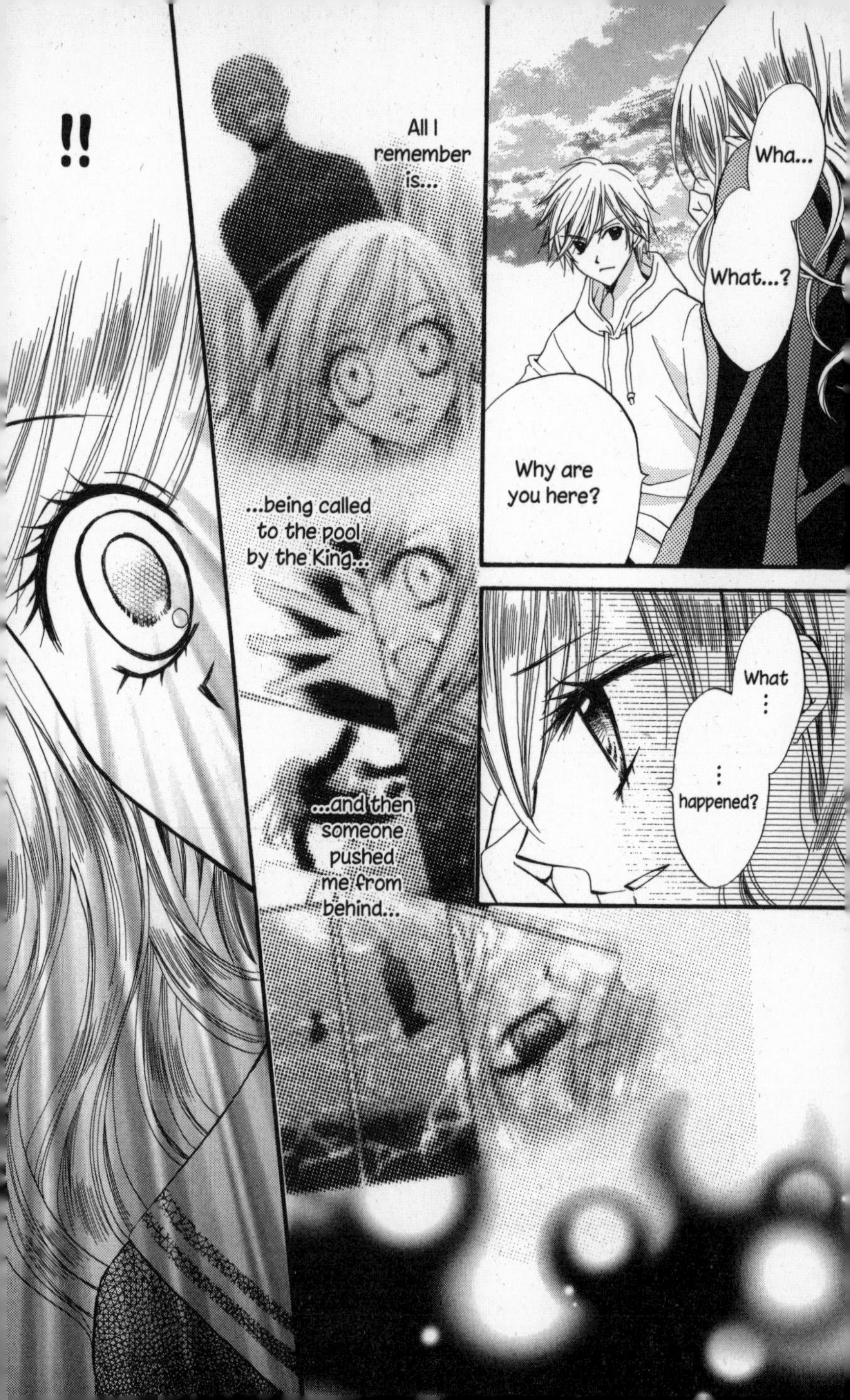
Wha...
What...?
Why are you here?
What ... ... happened?
All I remember is...
...being called to the pool by the King...
...and then someone pushed me from behind...
!!

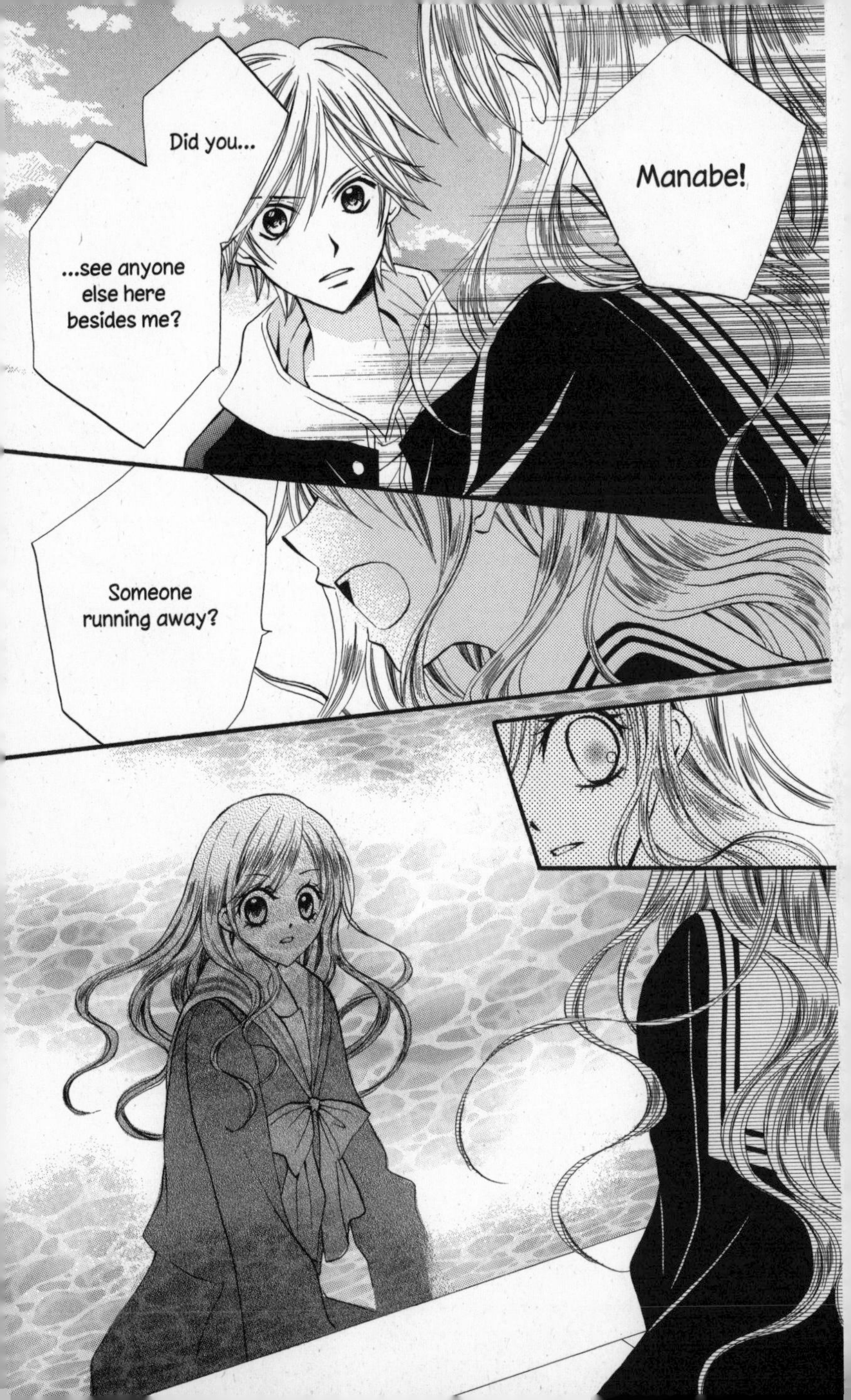
Manabe!
Did you...
...see anyone else here besides me?
Someone running away?

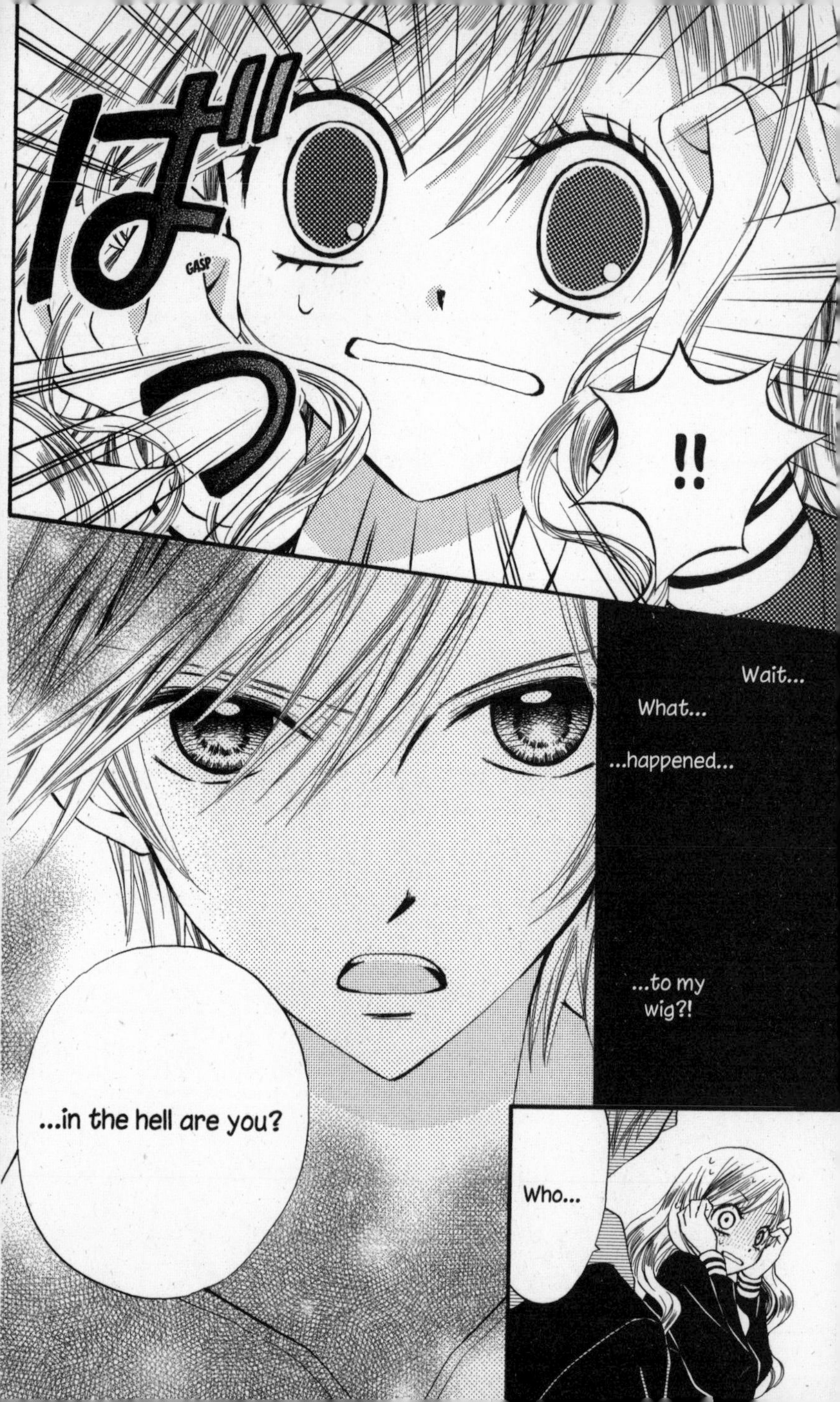
!!
ばっ
GASP
Wait...
What...
...happened...
...to my wig?!
Who...
...in the hell are you?

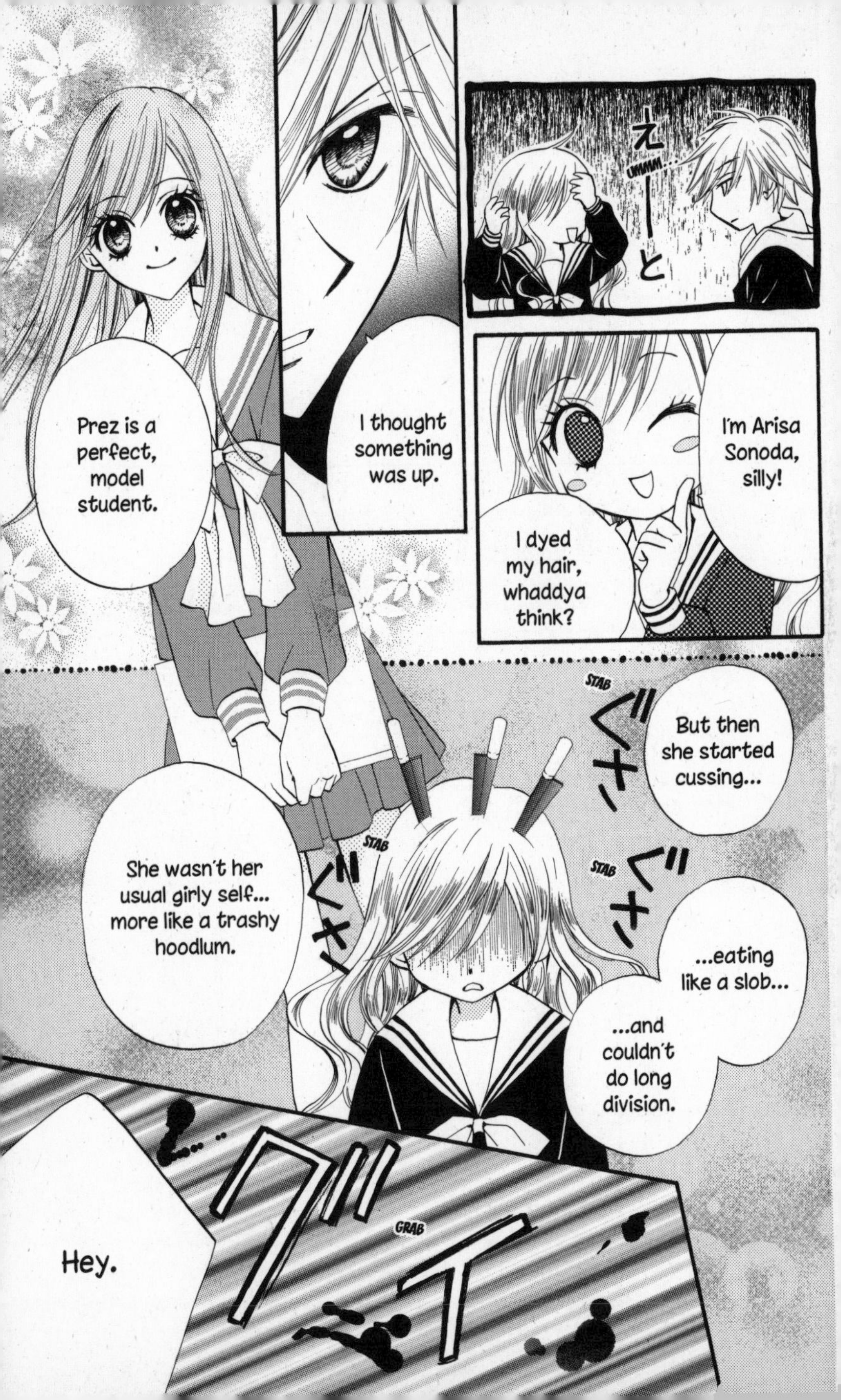
えーと
UMMM...
I'm Arisa Sonoda, silly!
I dyed my hair, whaddya think?
I thought something was up.
Prez is a perfect, model student.
STAB
ぐさ
But then she started cussing...
STAB
ぐさ
...eating like a slob...
...and couldn't do long division.
STAB
ぐさ
She wasn't her usual girly self... more like a trashy hoodlum.
GRAB
グイ
Hey.

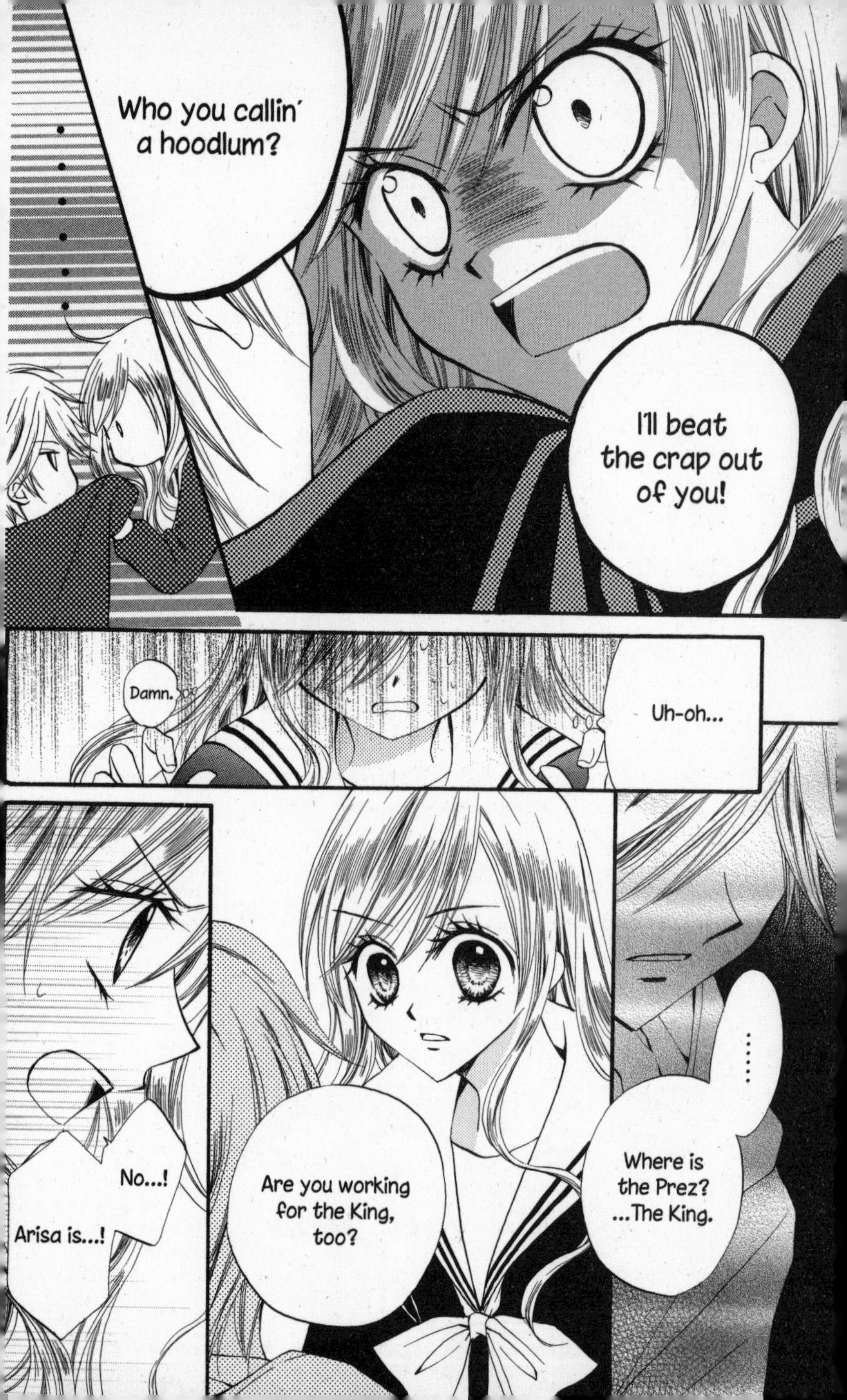
Who you callin' a hoodlum?
I'll beat the crap out of you!
Uh-oh...
Damn.
......
Where is the Prez? ...The King.
Are you working for the King, too?
No...!
Arisa is...!

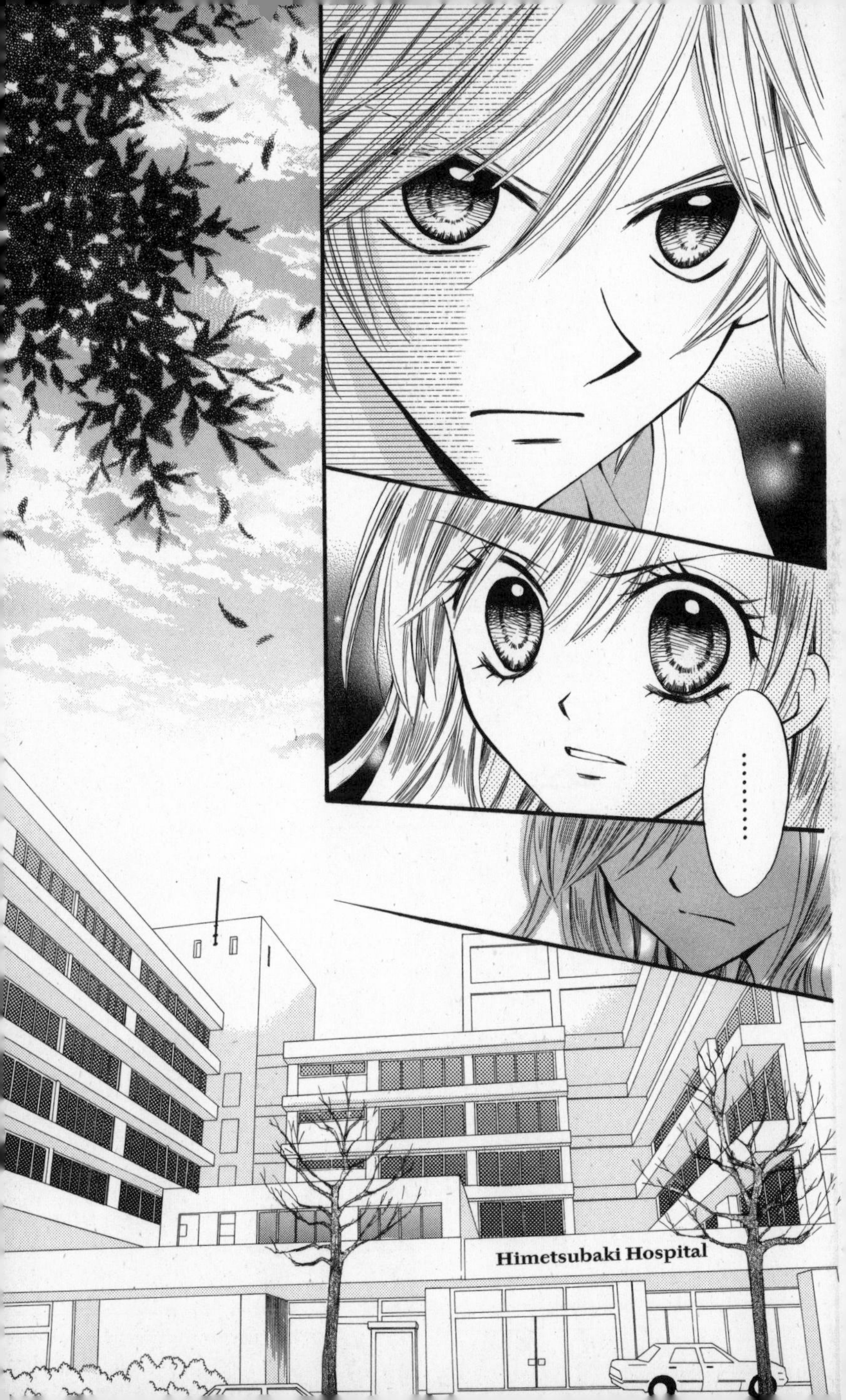
......
Himetsubaki Hospital

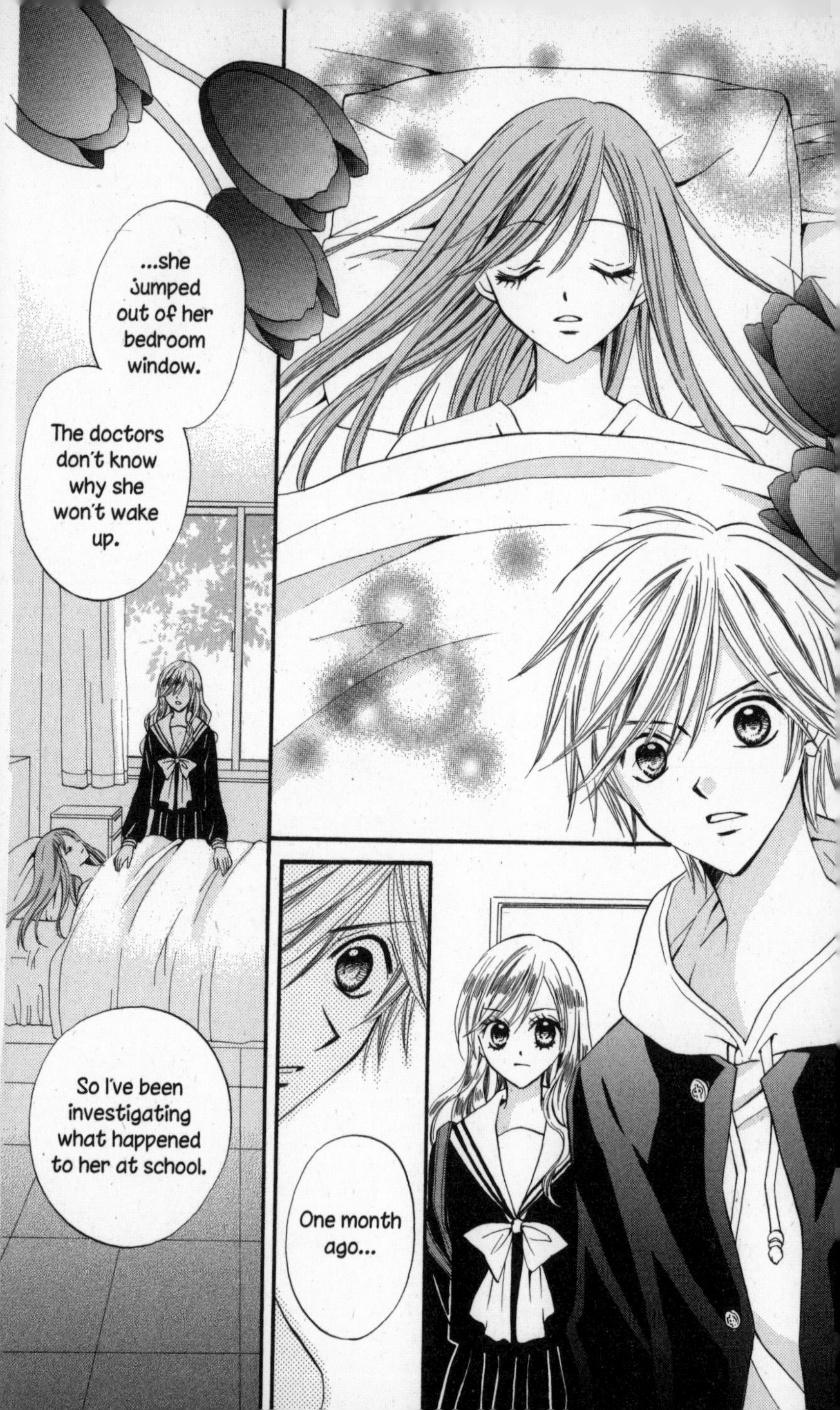
One month ago...
...she jumped out of her bedroom window.
The doctors don't know why she won't wake up.
So I've been investigating what happened to her at school.

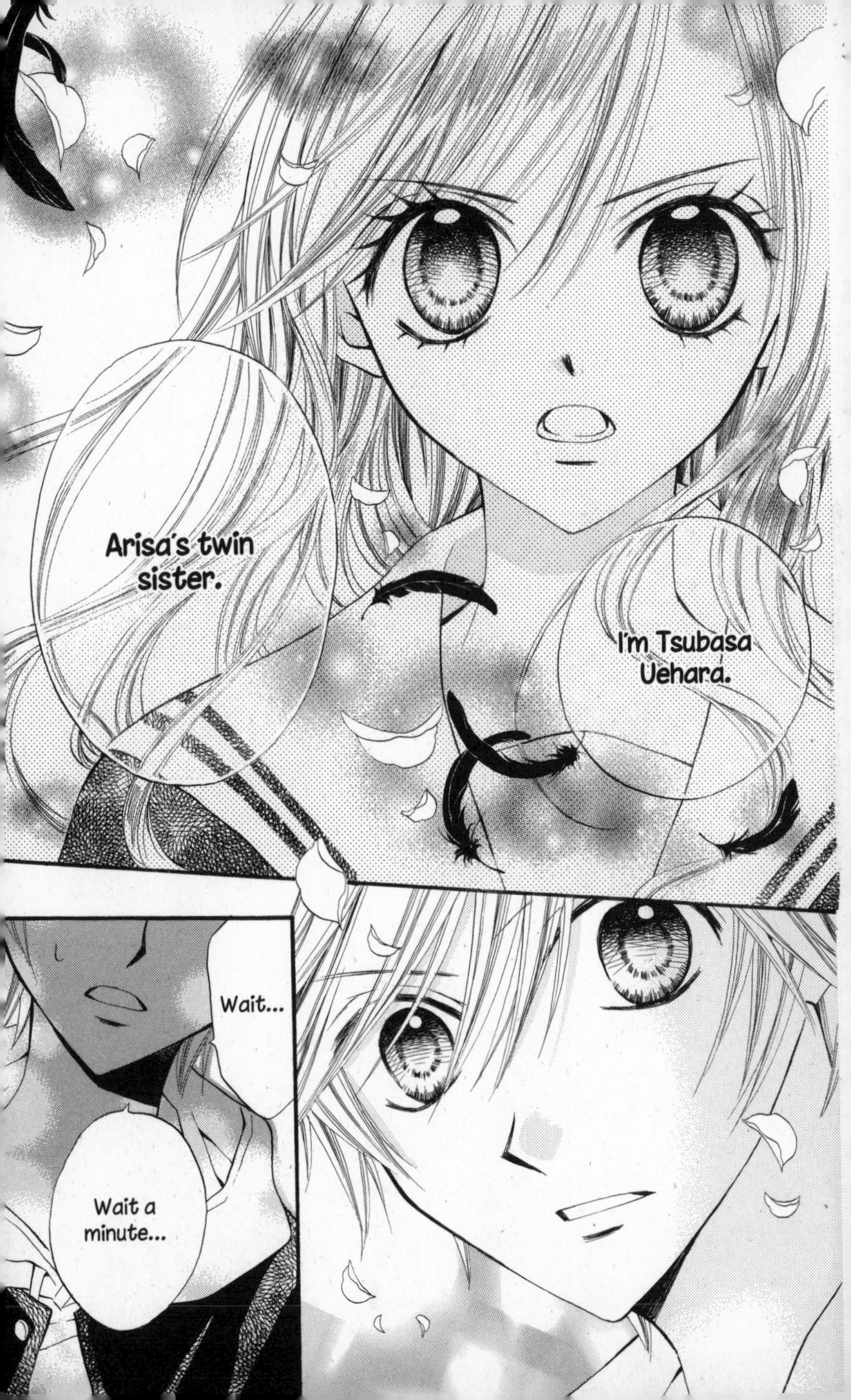
I'm Tsubasa Uehara.
Arisa's twin sister.
Wait...
Wait a minute...

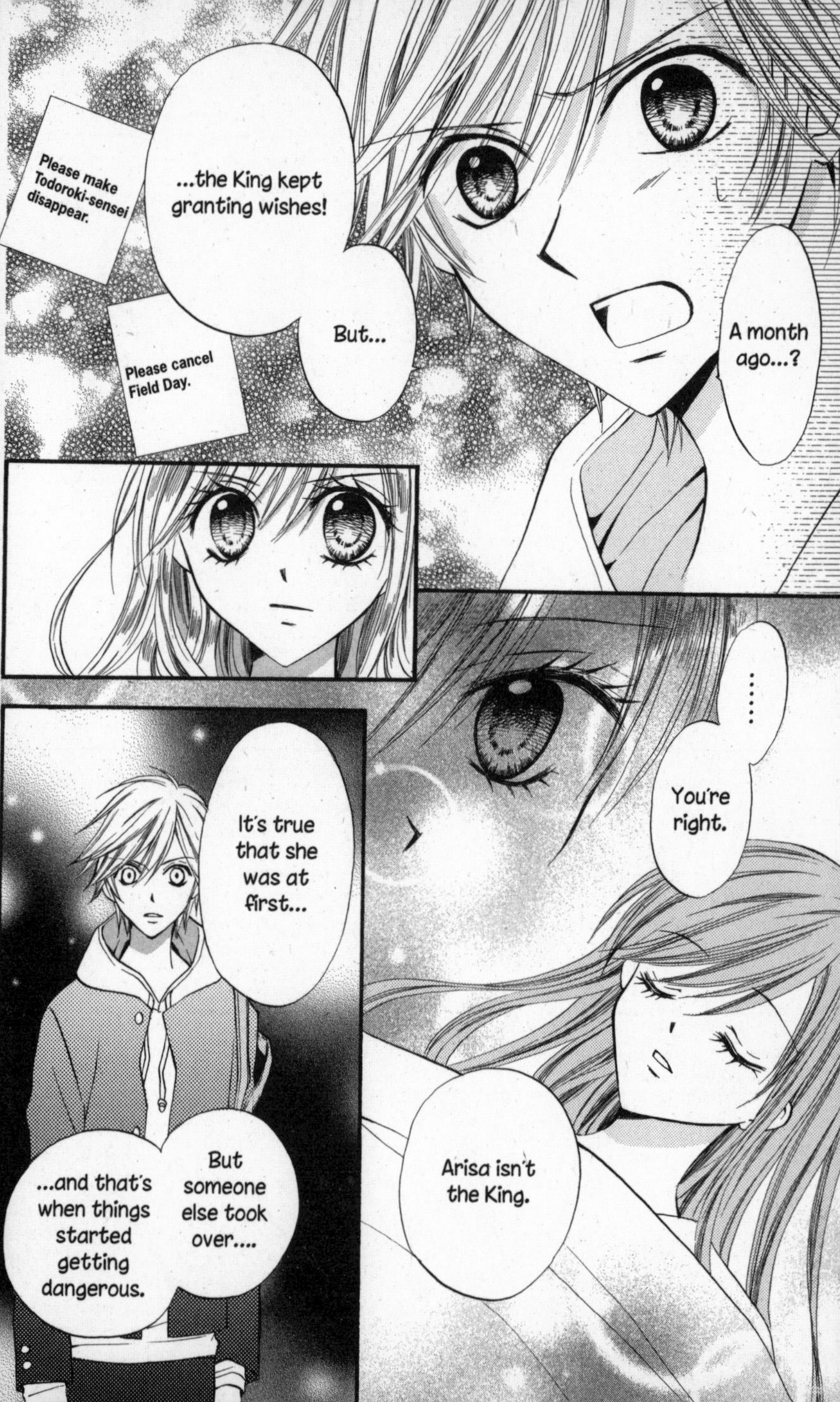
A month ago...?
But...
...the King kept granting wishes!
Please make Todoroki-sensei disappear.
Please cancel Field Day.
......
You're right.
Arisa isn't the King.
It's true that she was at first...
But someone else took over....
...and that's when things started getting dangerous.

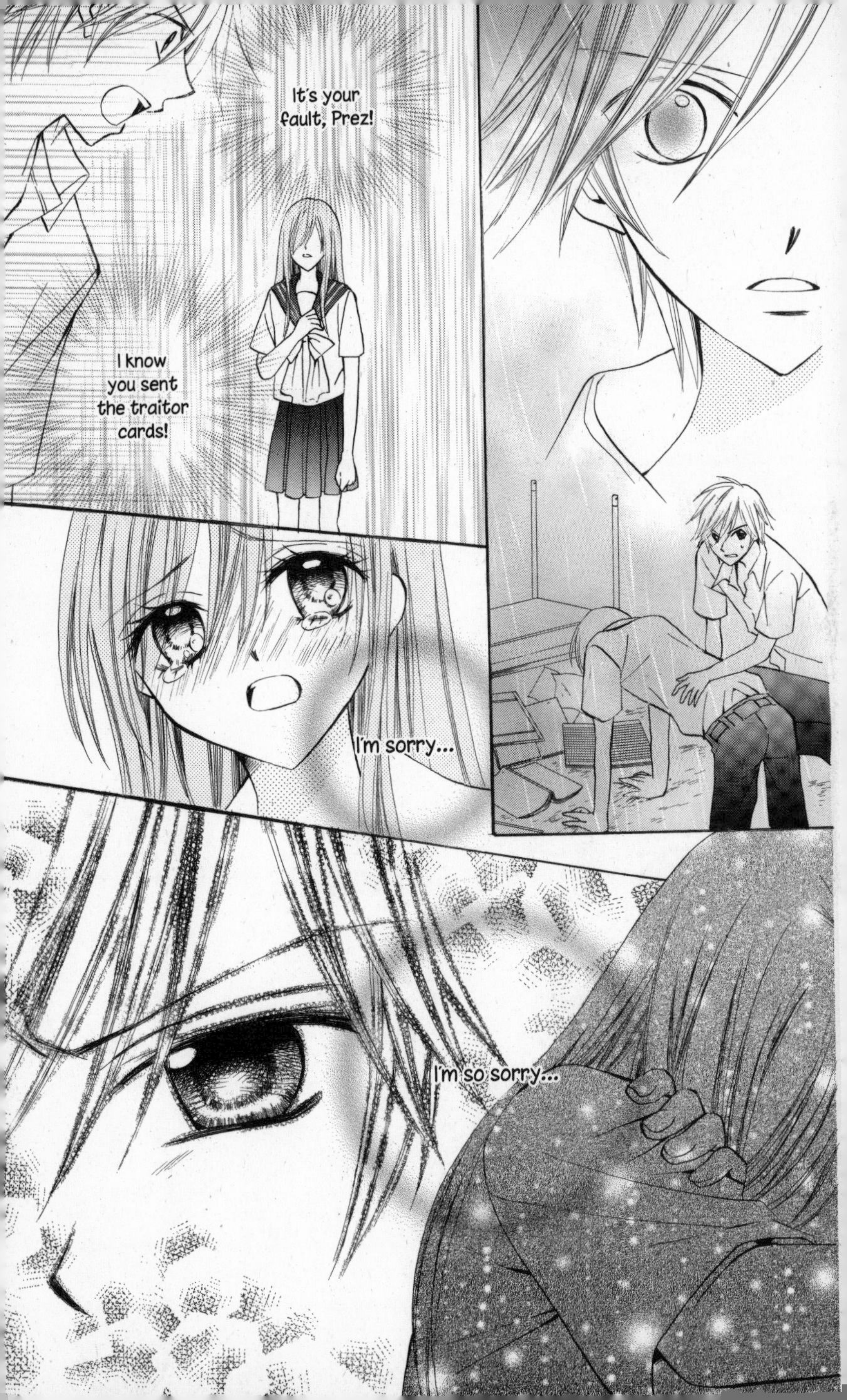
It's your fault, Prez!
I know you sent the traitor cards!
I'm sorry...
I'm so sorry...

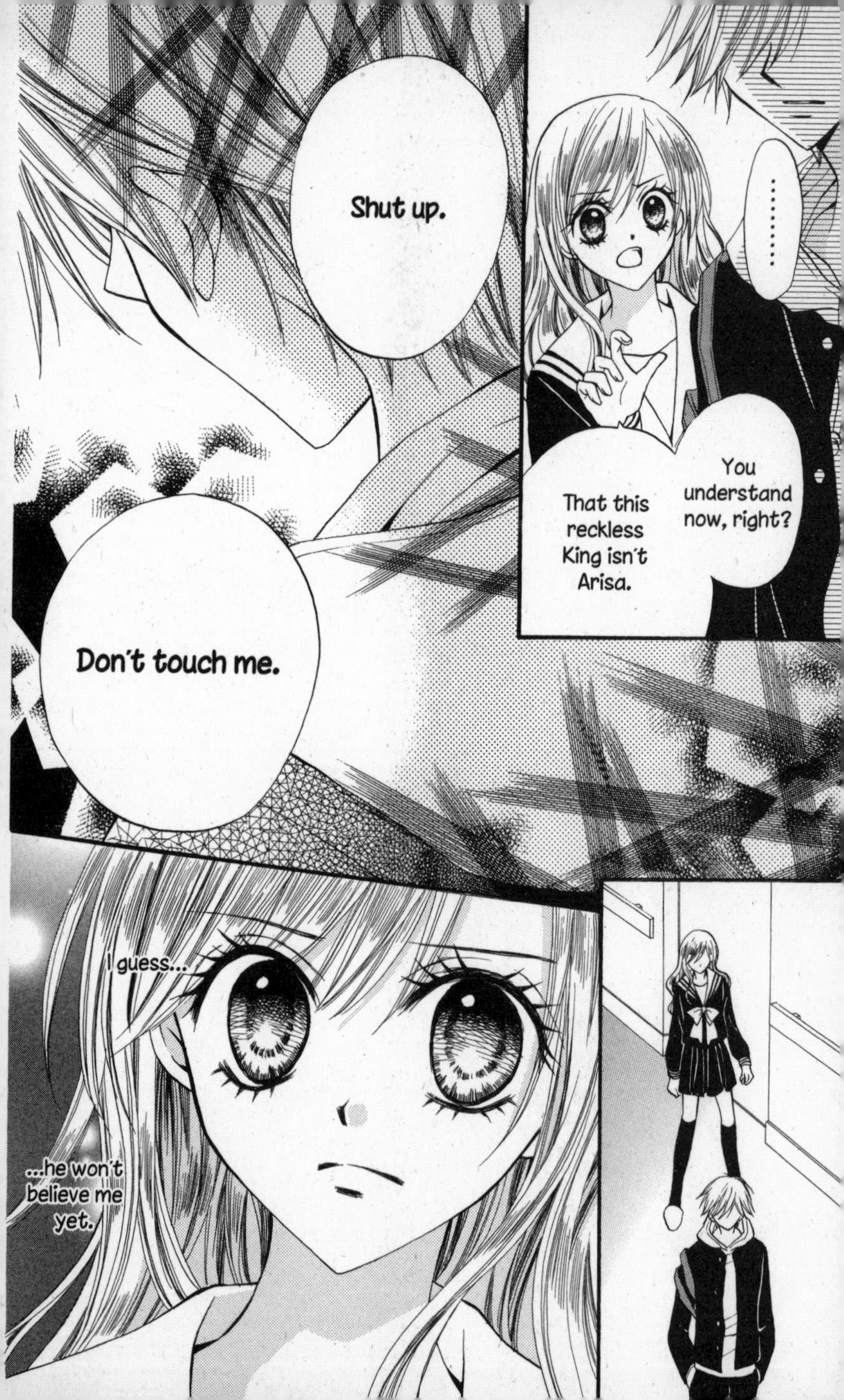
......
You understand now, right?
That this reckless King isn't Arisa.
Shut up.
Don't touch me.
I guess...
...he won't believe me yet.

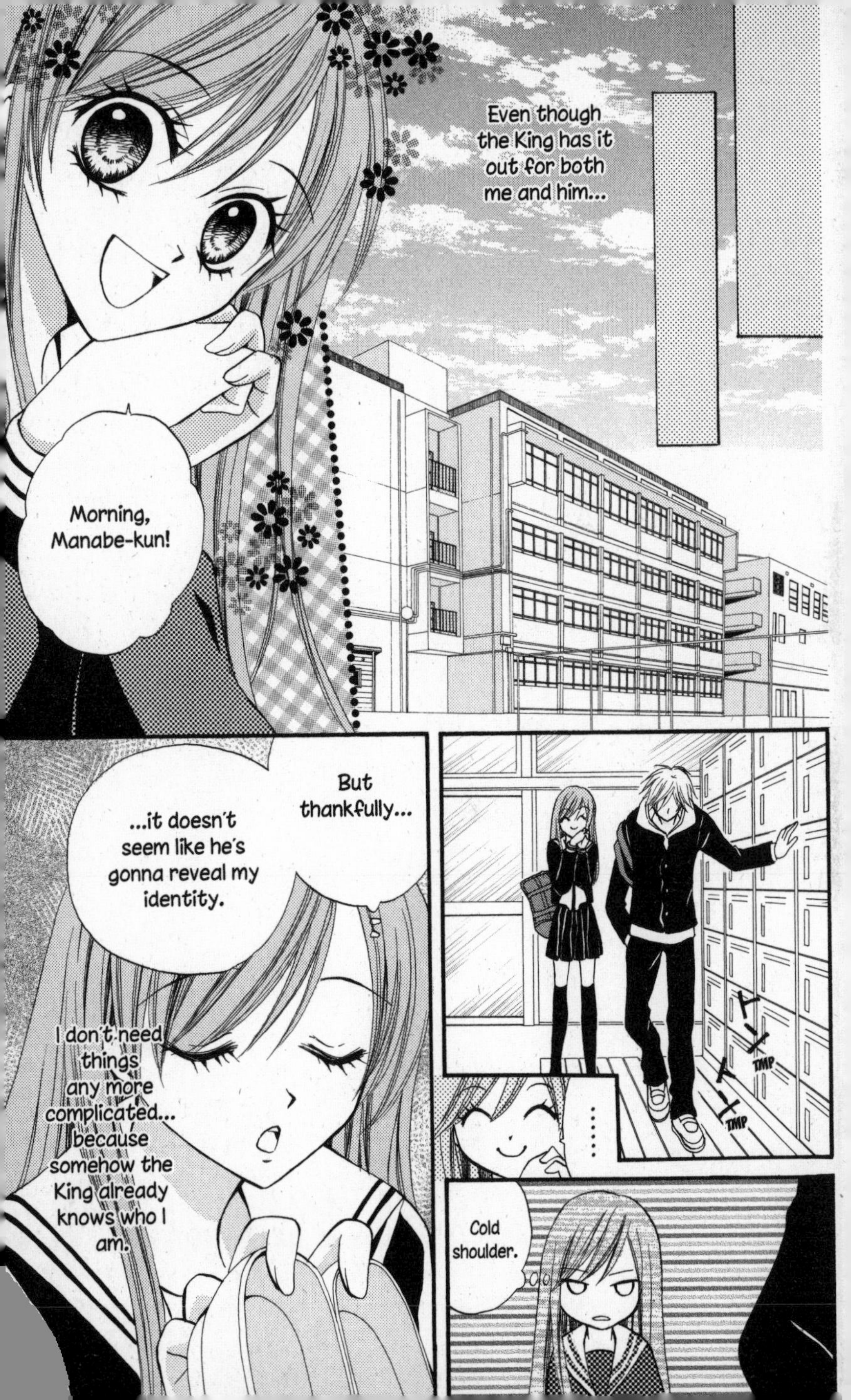
Even though the King has it out for both me and him...
Morning, Manabe-kun!
TMP
TMP
......
Cold shoulder.
But thankfully...
...it doesn't seem like he's gonna reveal my identity.
I don't need things any more complicated... because somehow the King already knows who I am.

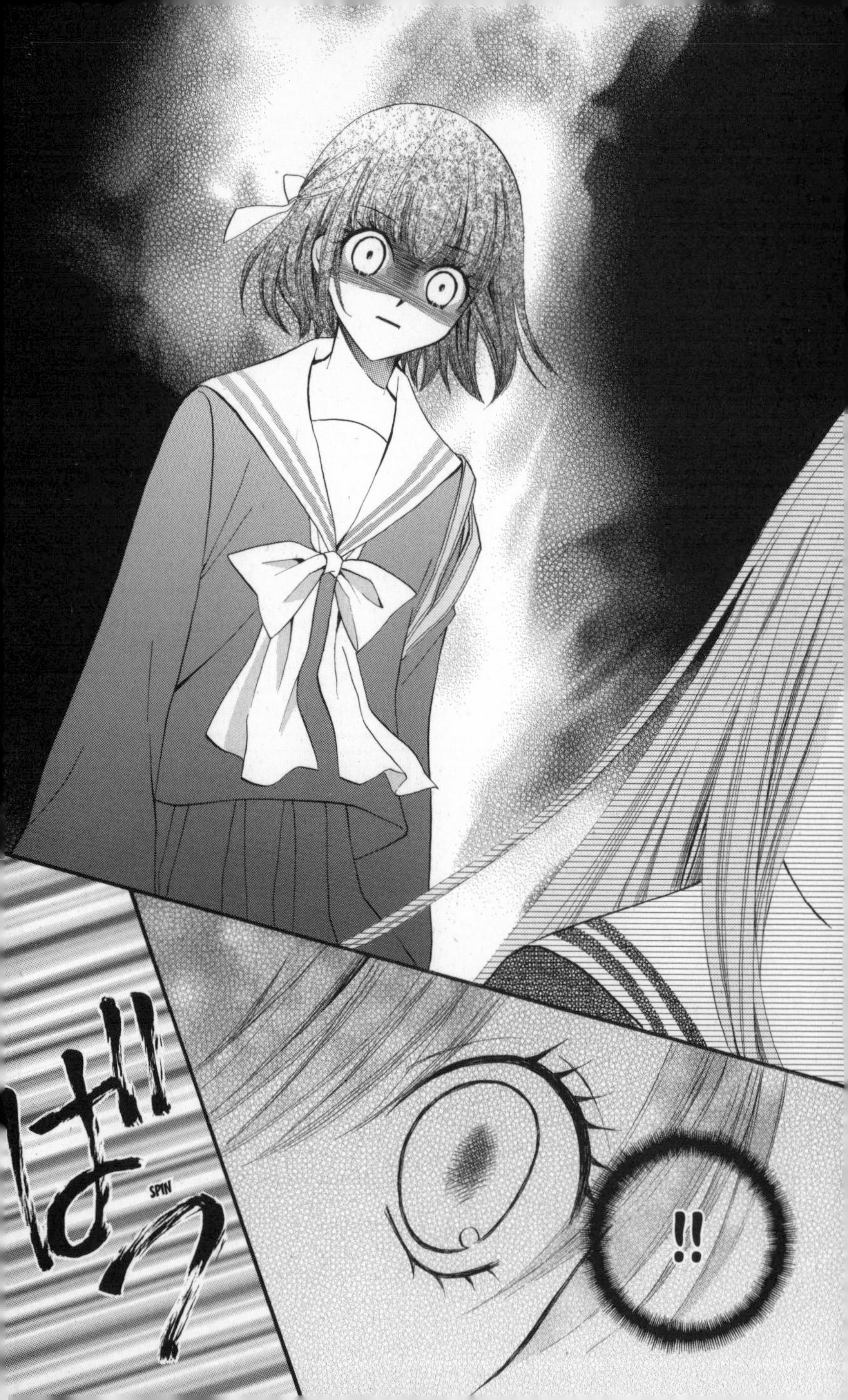
!!
はっ
SPIN

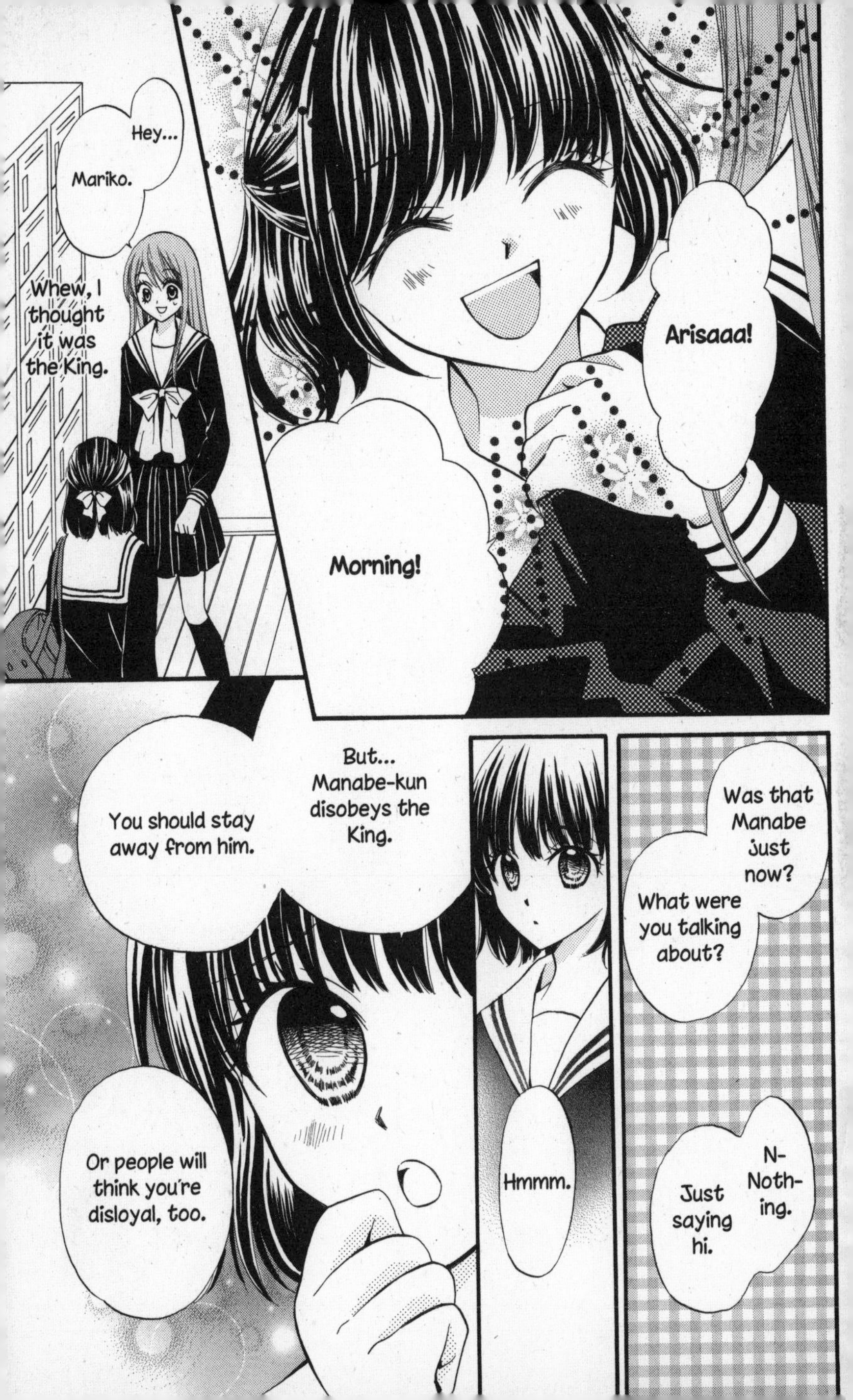
Arisaaa!
Morning!
Hey... Mariko.
Whew, I thought it was the King.
Was that Manabe just now?
What were you talking about?
N-Noth-ing.
Just saying hi.
Hmmm.
But... Manabe-kun disobeys the King.
You should stay away from him.
Or people will think you're disloyal, too.

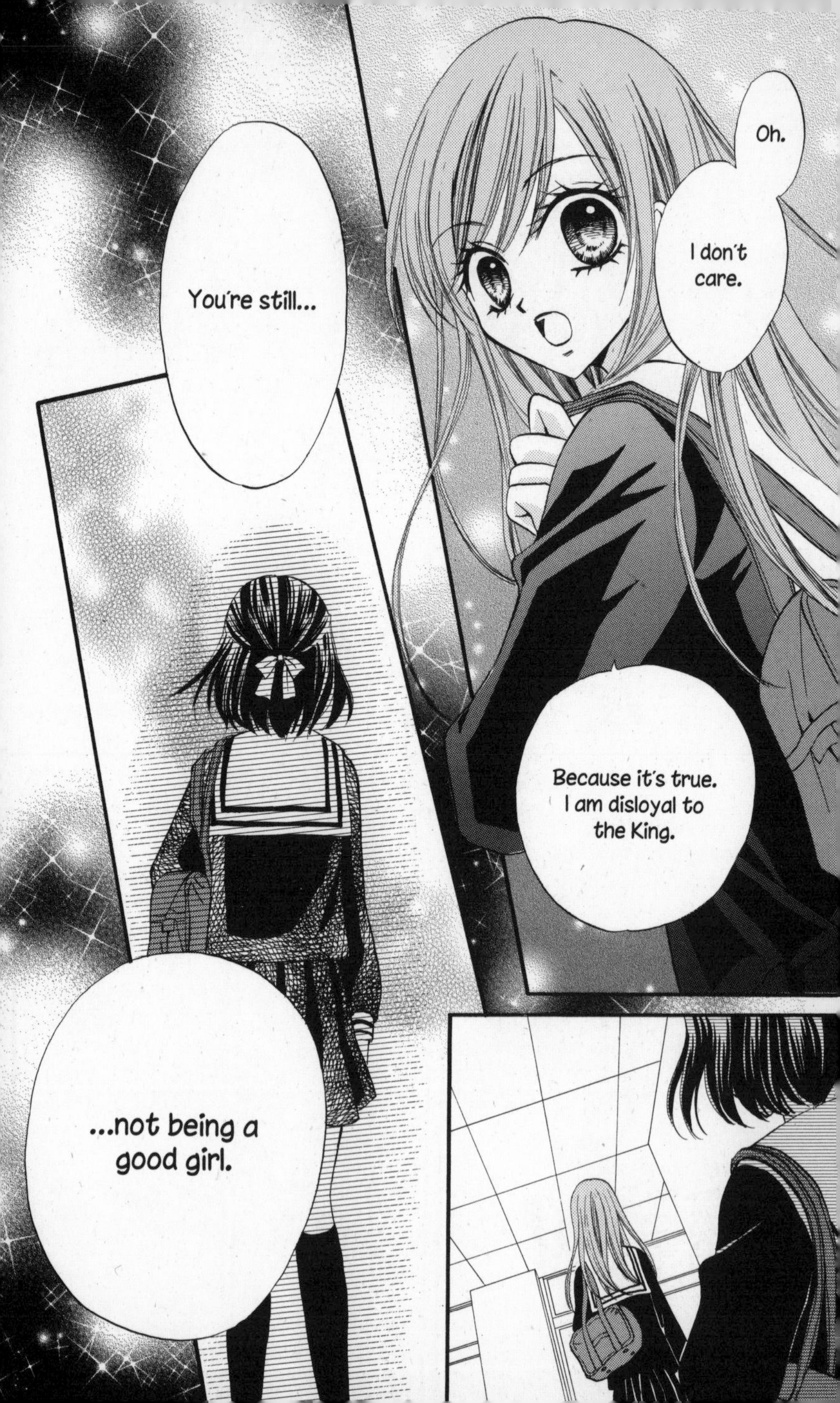
Oh.
I don't care.
Because it's true. I am disloyal to the King.
You're still...
...not being a good girl.

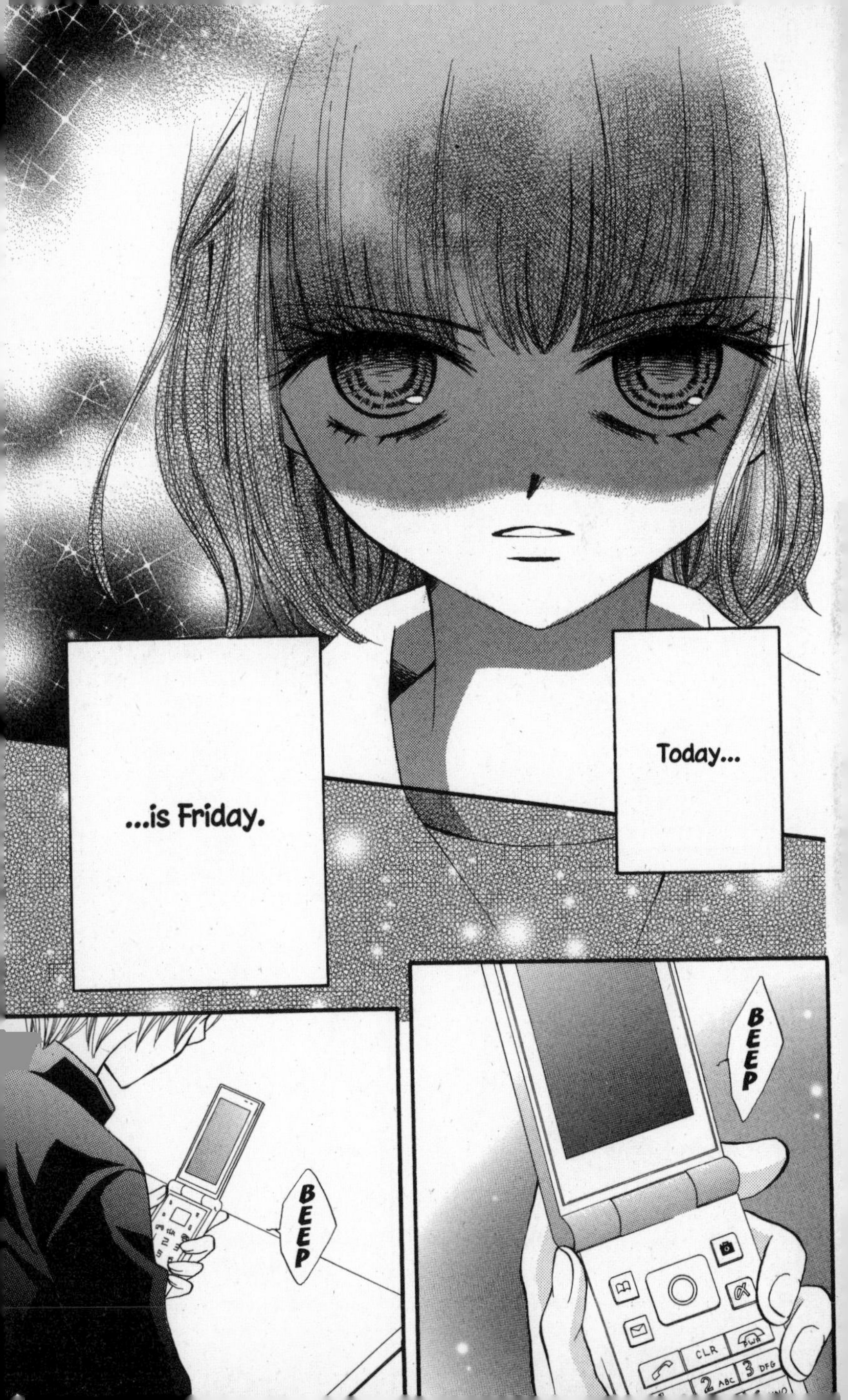
Today...
...is Friday.
BEEEP
CLR
2 ABC
3 DFG
BEEEP

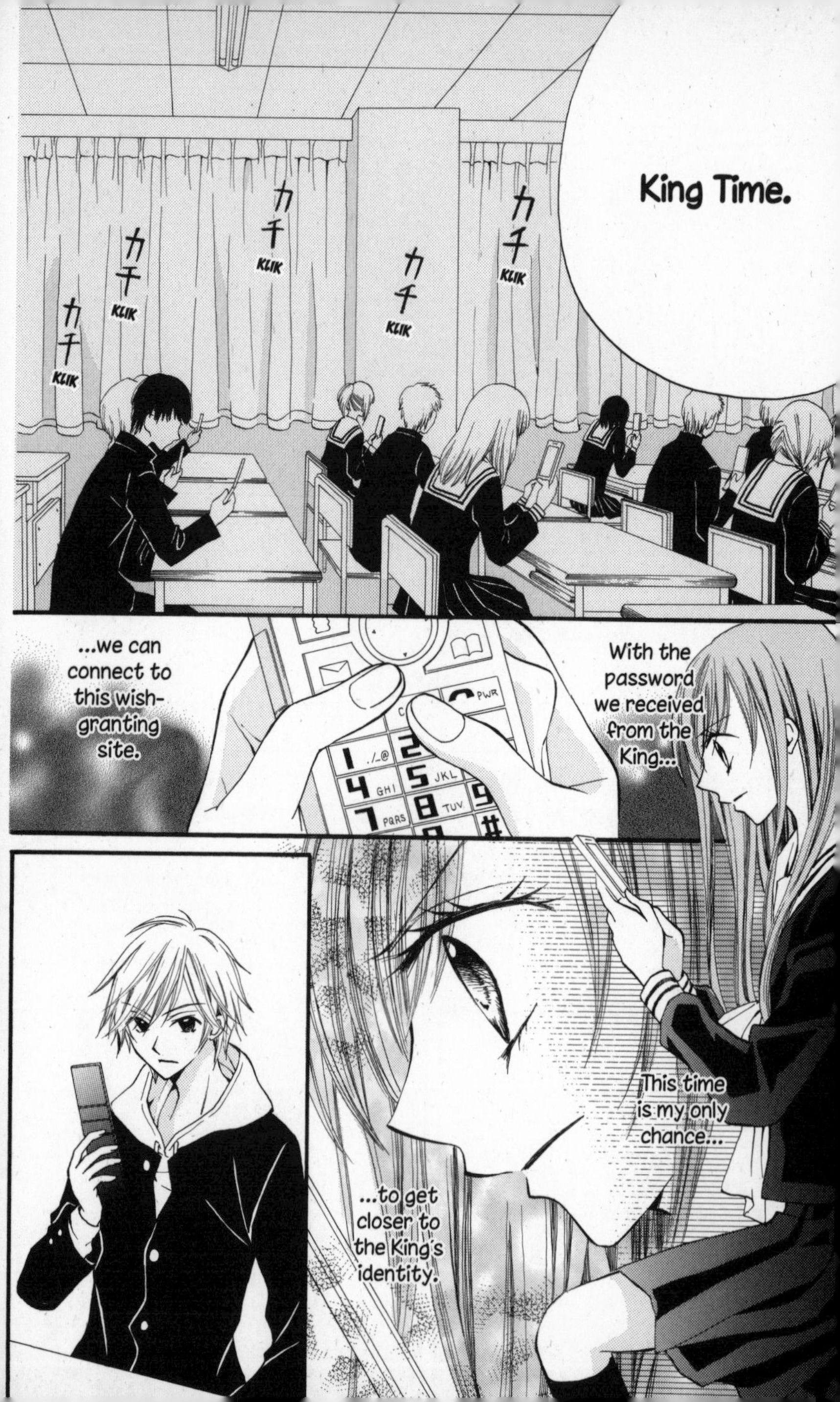
King Time.
カチ KLIK
カチ KLIK
カチ KLIK
カチ KLIK
カチ KLIK
With the password we received from the King...
...we can connect to this wish-granting site.
This time is my only chance...
...to get closer to the King's identity.

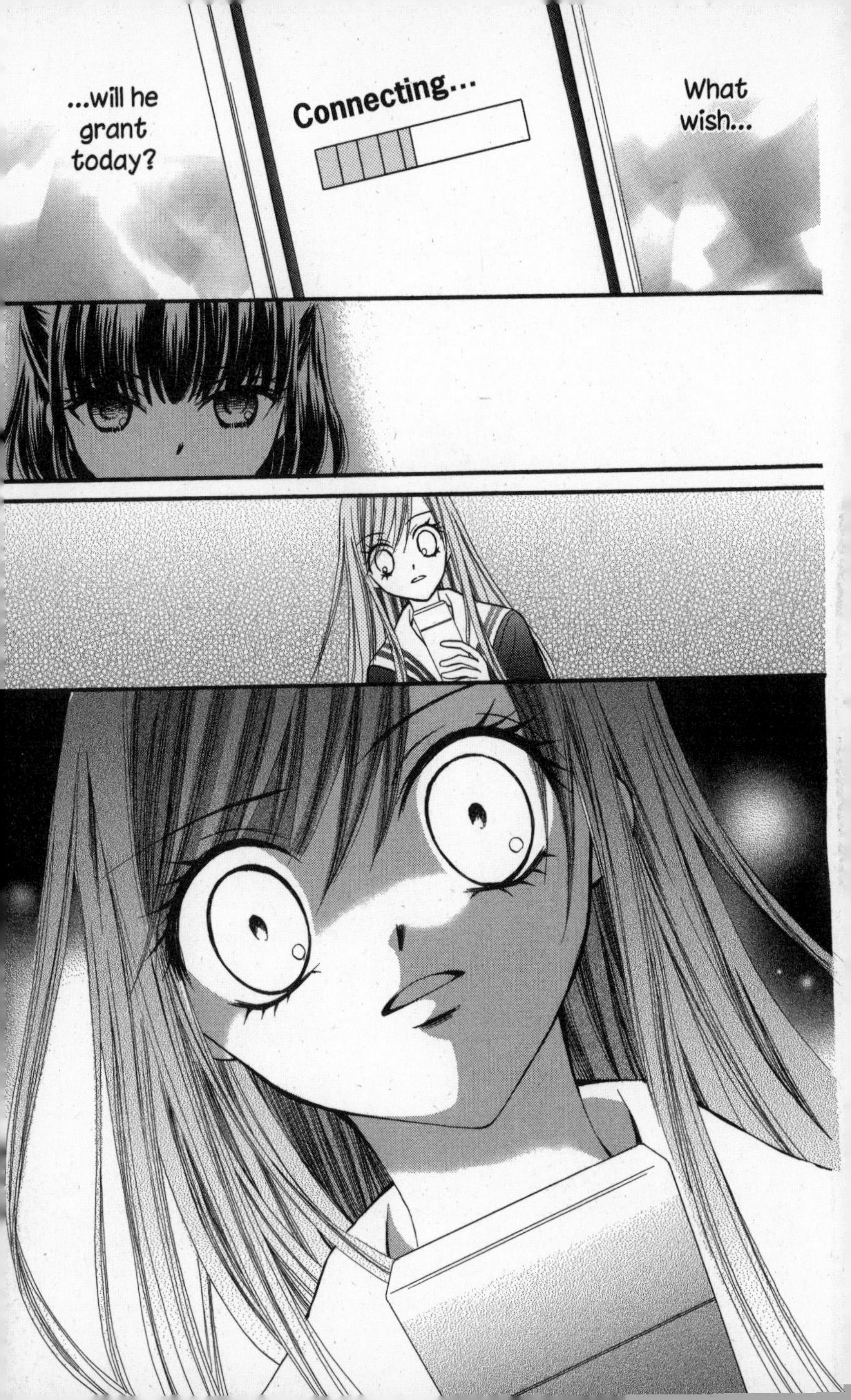
What wish...
Connecting...
...will he grant today?

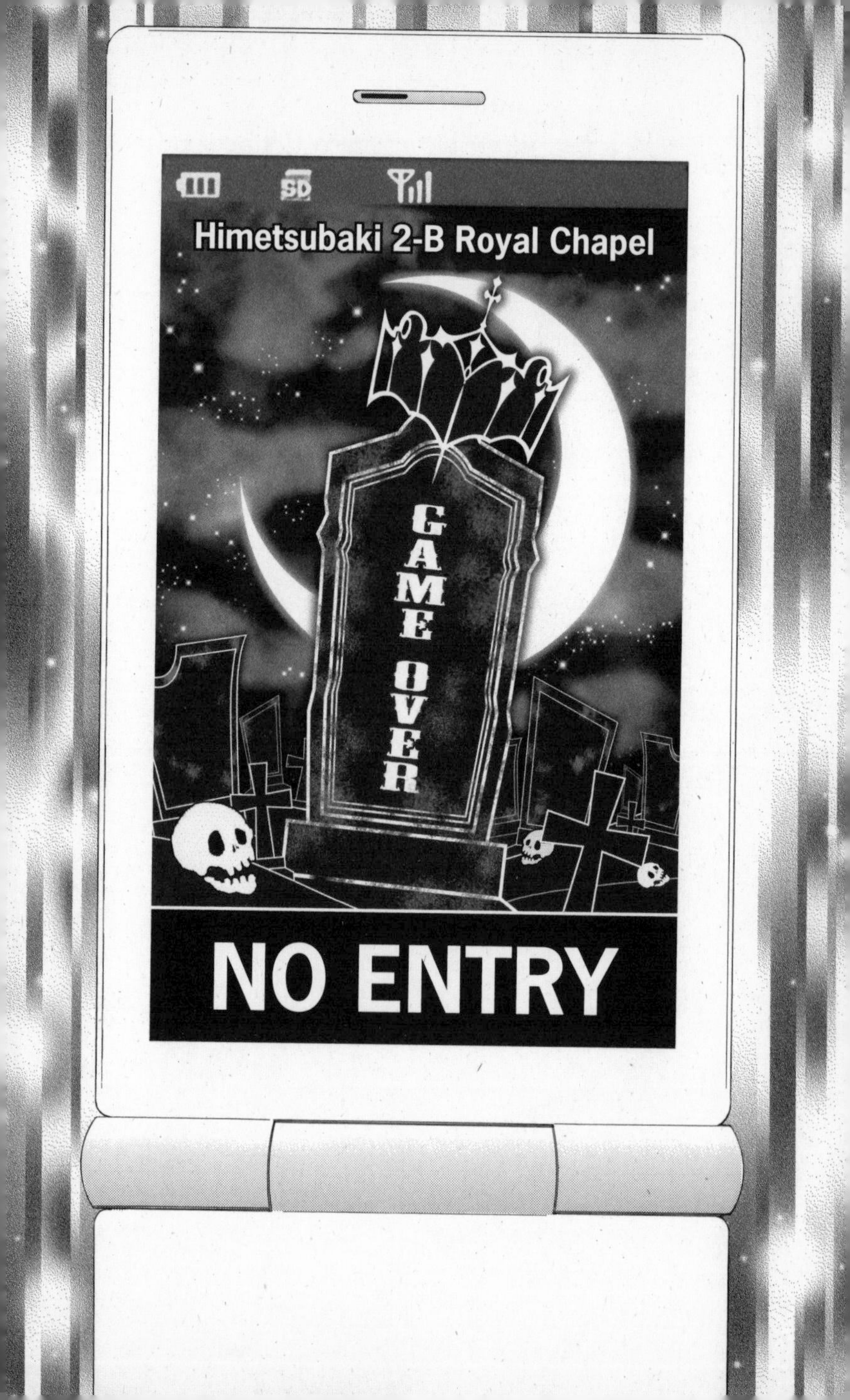
Himetsubaki 2-B Royal Chapel
GAME OVER
NO ENTRY

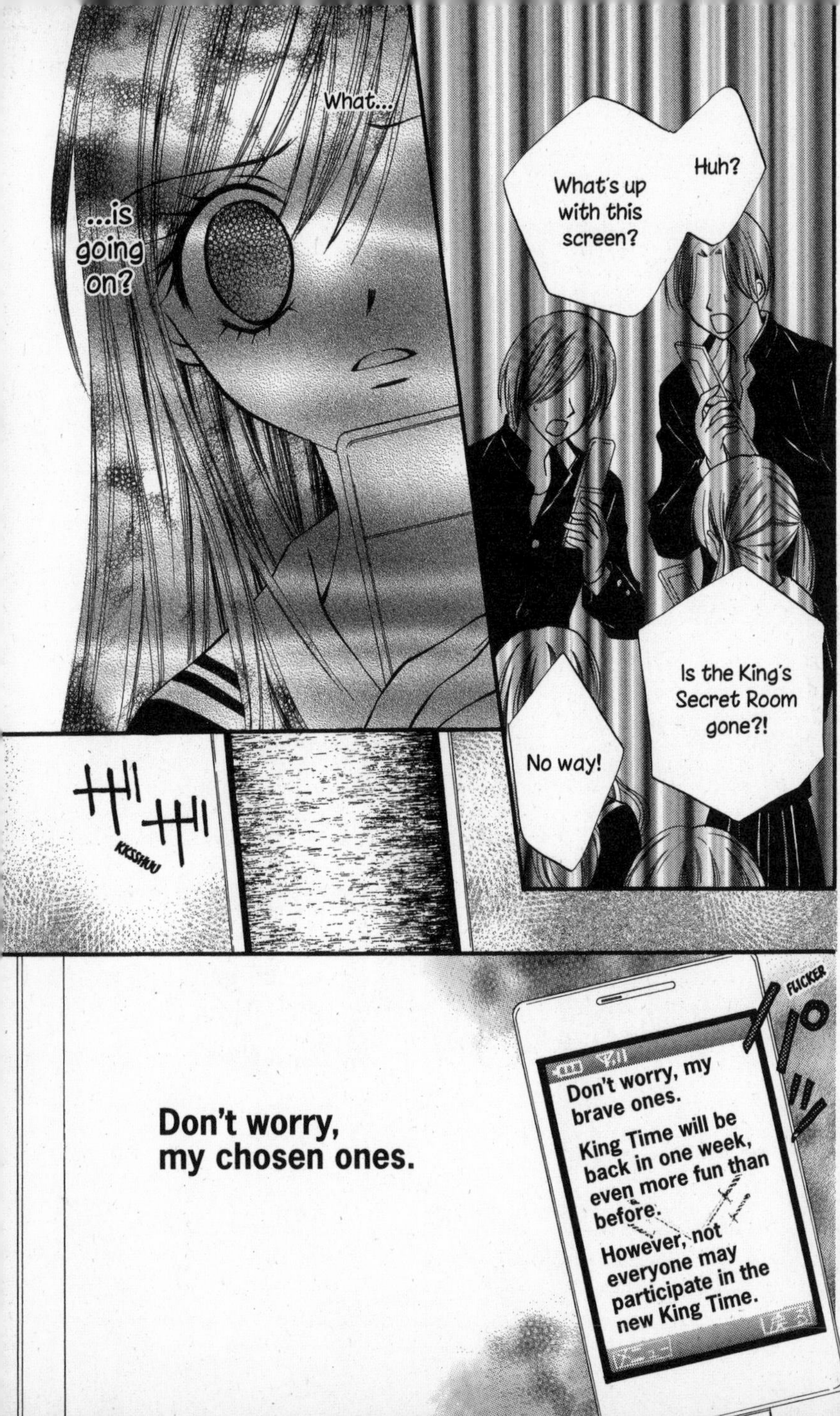
Huh?
What's up with this screen?
Is the King's Secret Room gone?!
No way!
What...
...is going on?
KKSSHUU
FLICKER
Don't worry, my brave ones.
King Time will be back in one week, even more fun than before.
However, not everyone may participate in the new King Time.
Don't worry, my chosen ones.

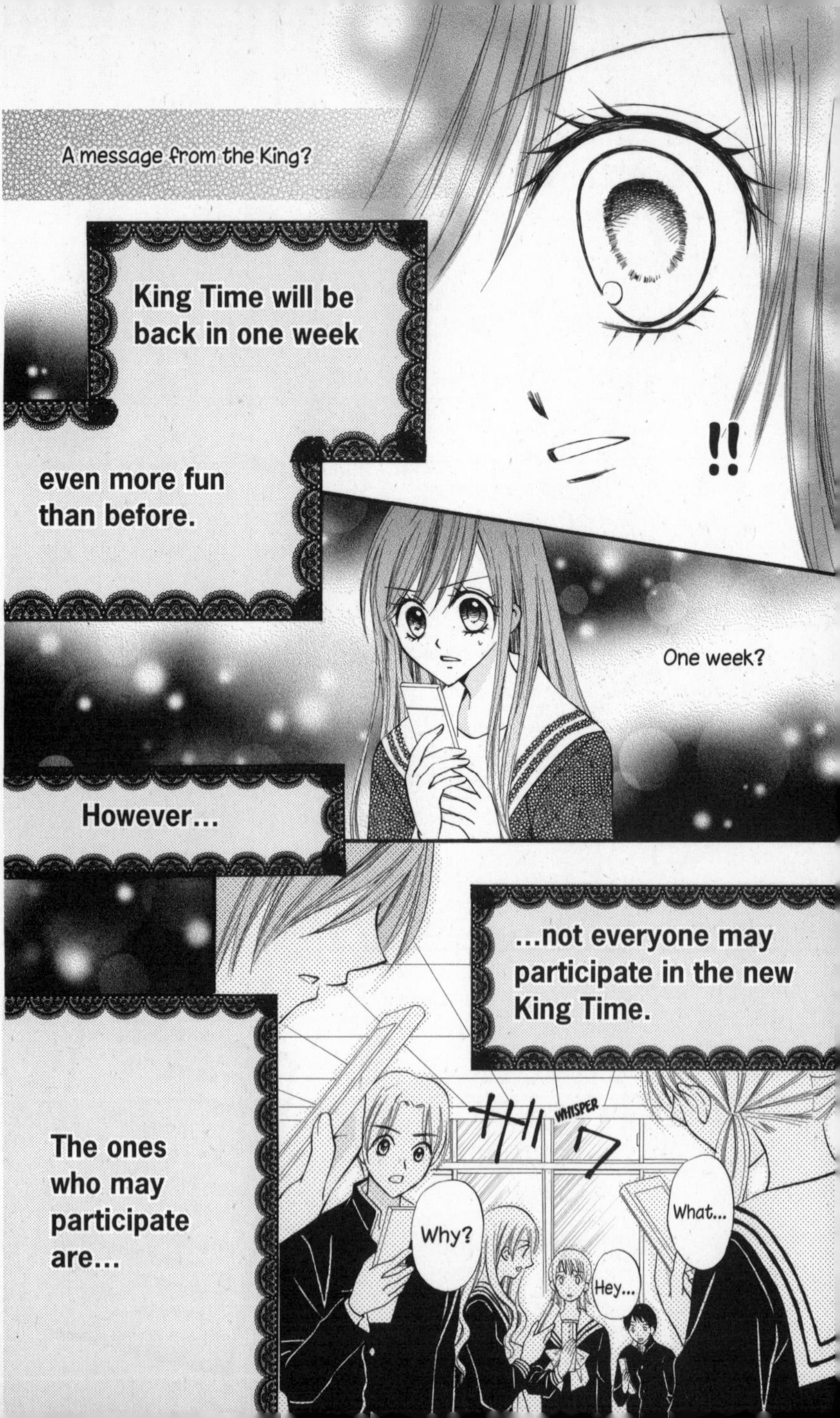
A message from the King?
King Time will be back in one week
!!
even more fun than before.
One week?
However...
...not everyone may participate in the new King Time.
WHISPER
What...
Hey...
Why?
The ones who may participate are...

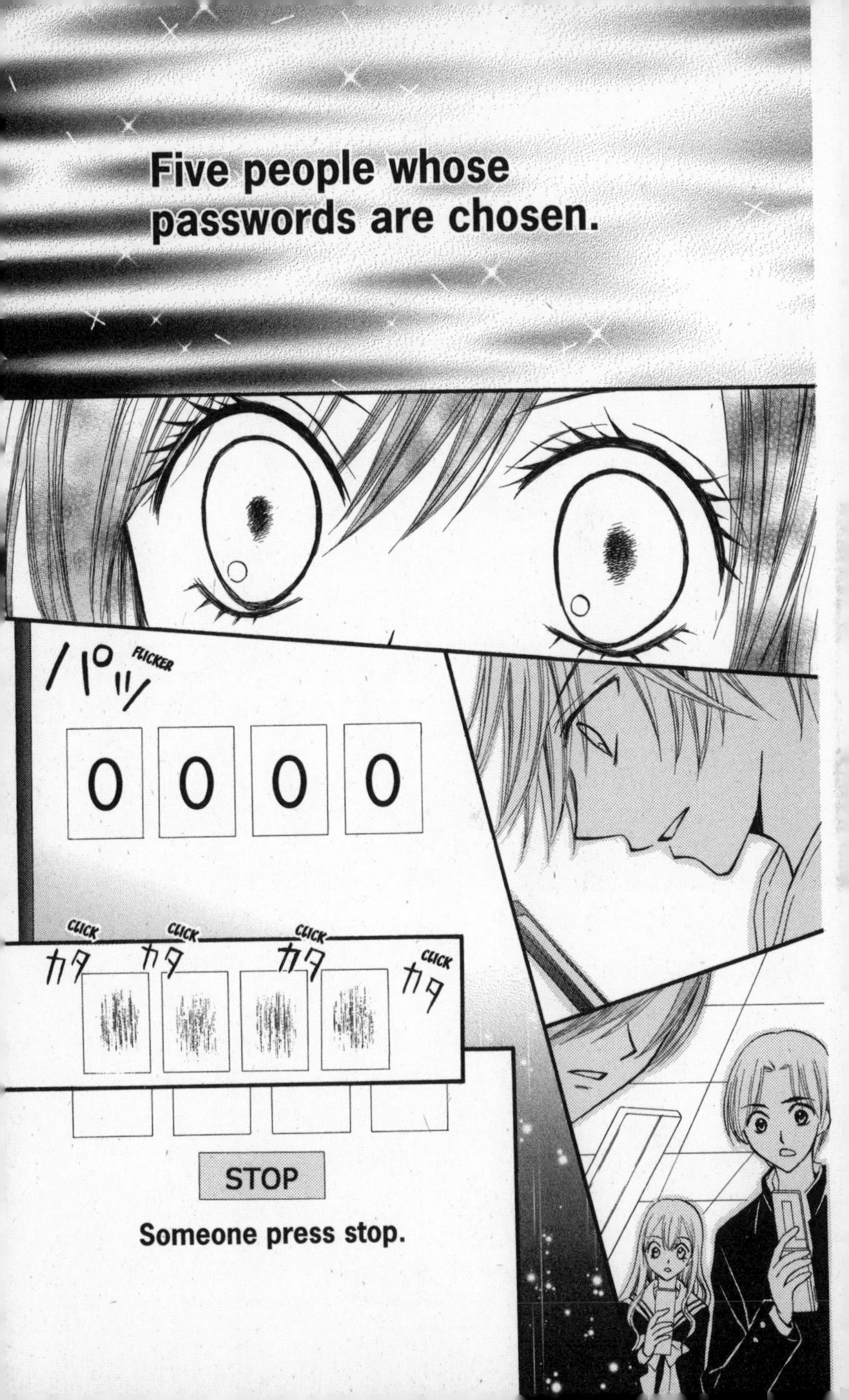

Five people whose passwords are chosen.
パッ
FLICKER
0 0 0 0
カタ
CLICK
カタ
CLICK
カタ
CLICK
カタ
CLICK
STOP
Someone press stop.

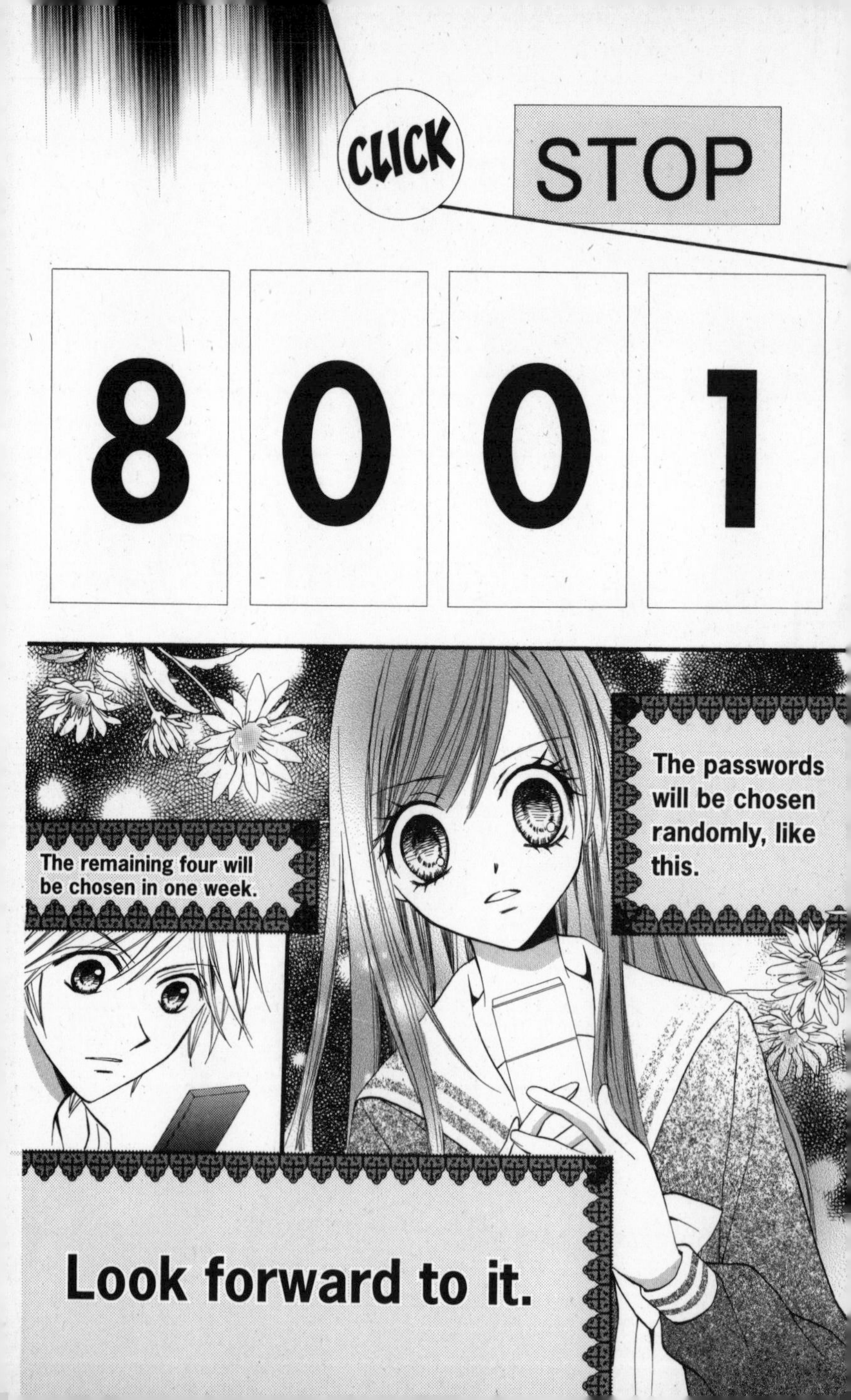
STOP
CLICK
8001
The passwords will be chosen randomly, like this.
The remaining four will be chosen in one week.
Look forward to it.

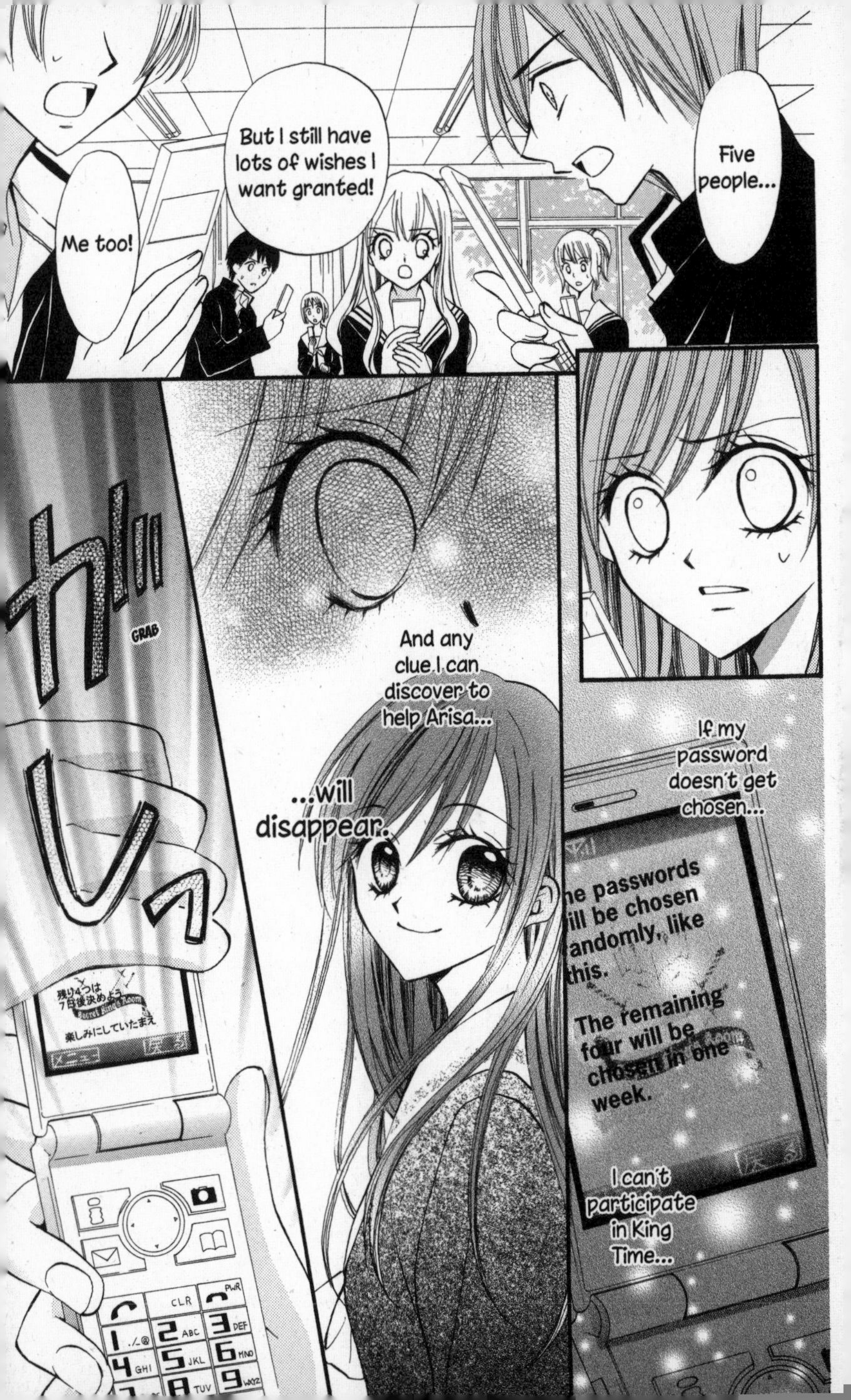
Five people...
But I still have lots of wishes I want granted!
Me too!
If my password doesn't get chosen...
he passwords ill be chosen andomly, like this.
The remaining four will be chosen in one week.
I can't participate in King Time...
And any clue I can discover to help Arisa...
...will disappear.
GRAB
残り4つは7日後決めよう
楽しみにしていたまえ

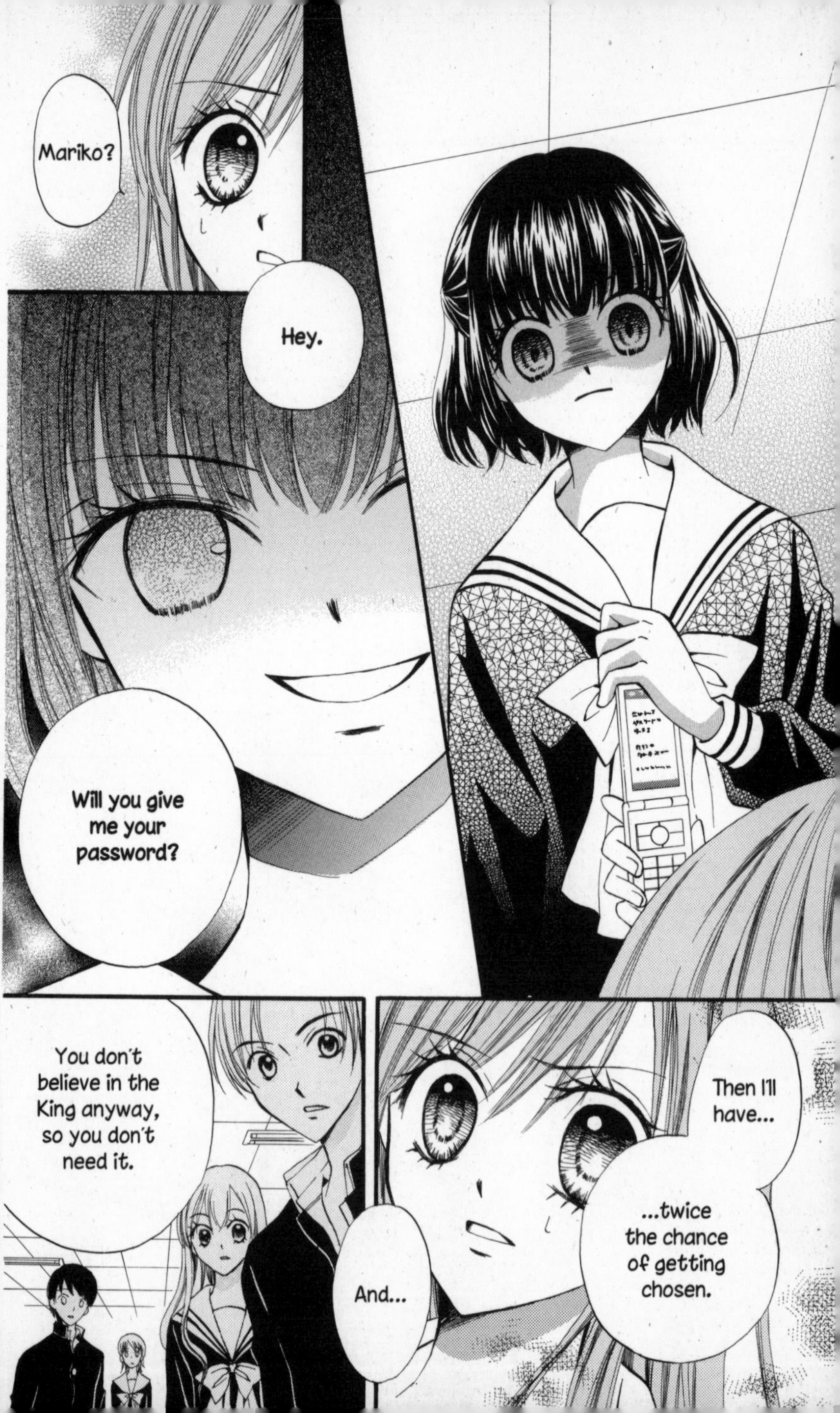
Mariko?
Hey.
Will you give me your password?
Then I'll have...
...twice the chance of getting chosen.
And...
You don't believe in the King anyway, so you don't need it.

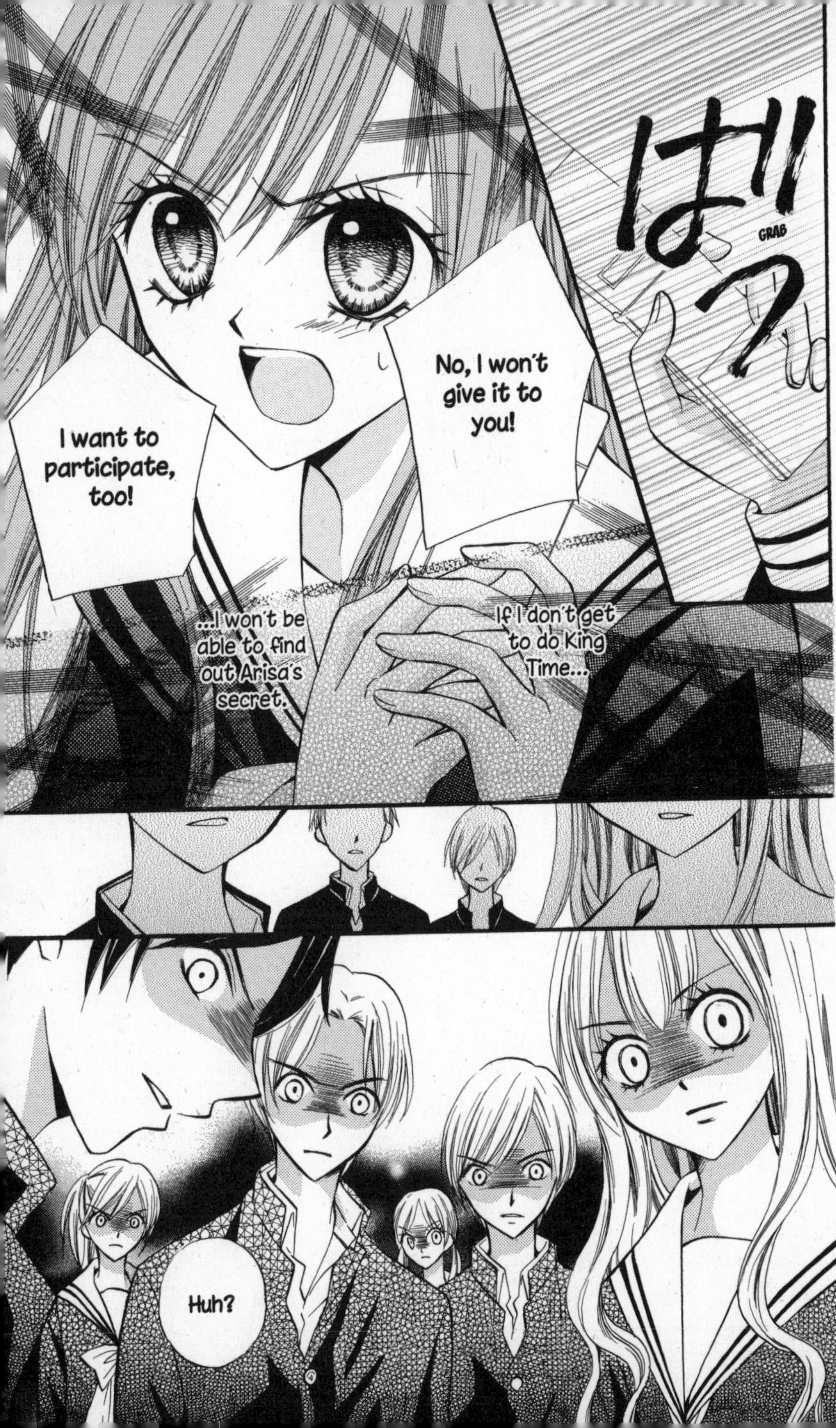
ばっ
GRAB
No, I won't give it to you!
I want to participate, too!
If I don't get to do King Time...
...I won't be able to find out Arisa's secret.
Huh?

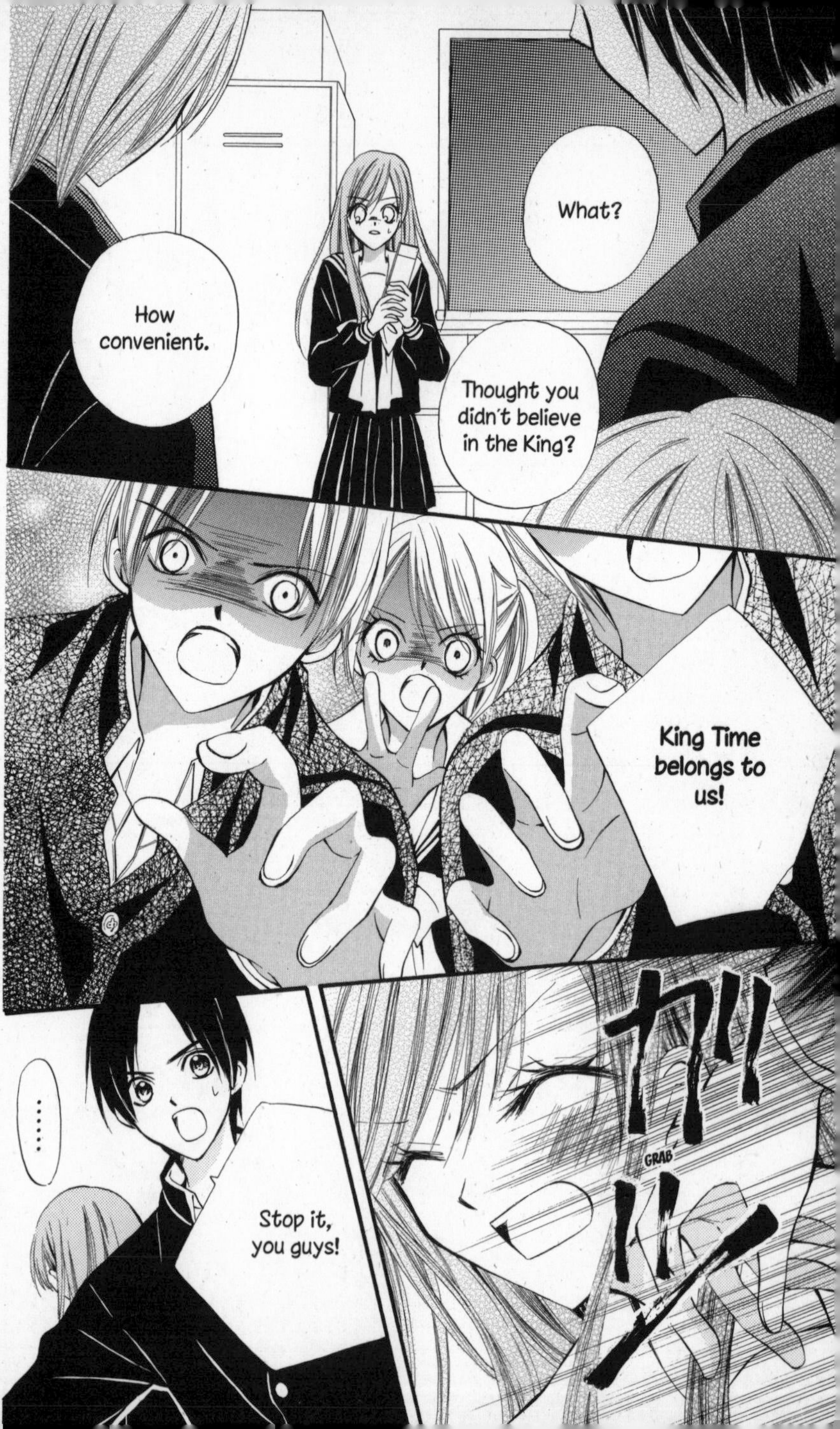
What?
How convenient.
Thought you didn't believe in the King?
King Time belongs to us!
カッ
GRAB
……
Stop it, you guys!

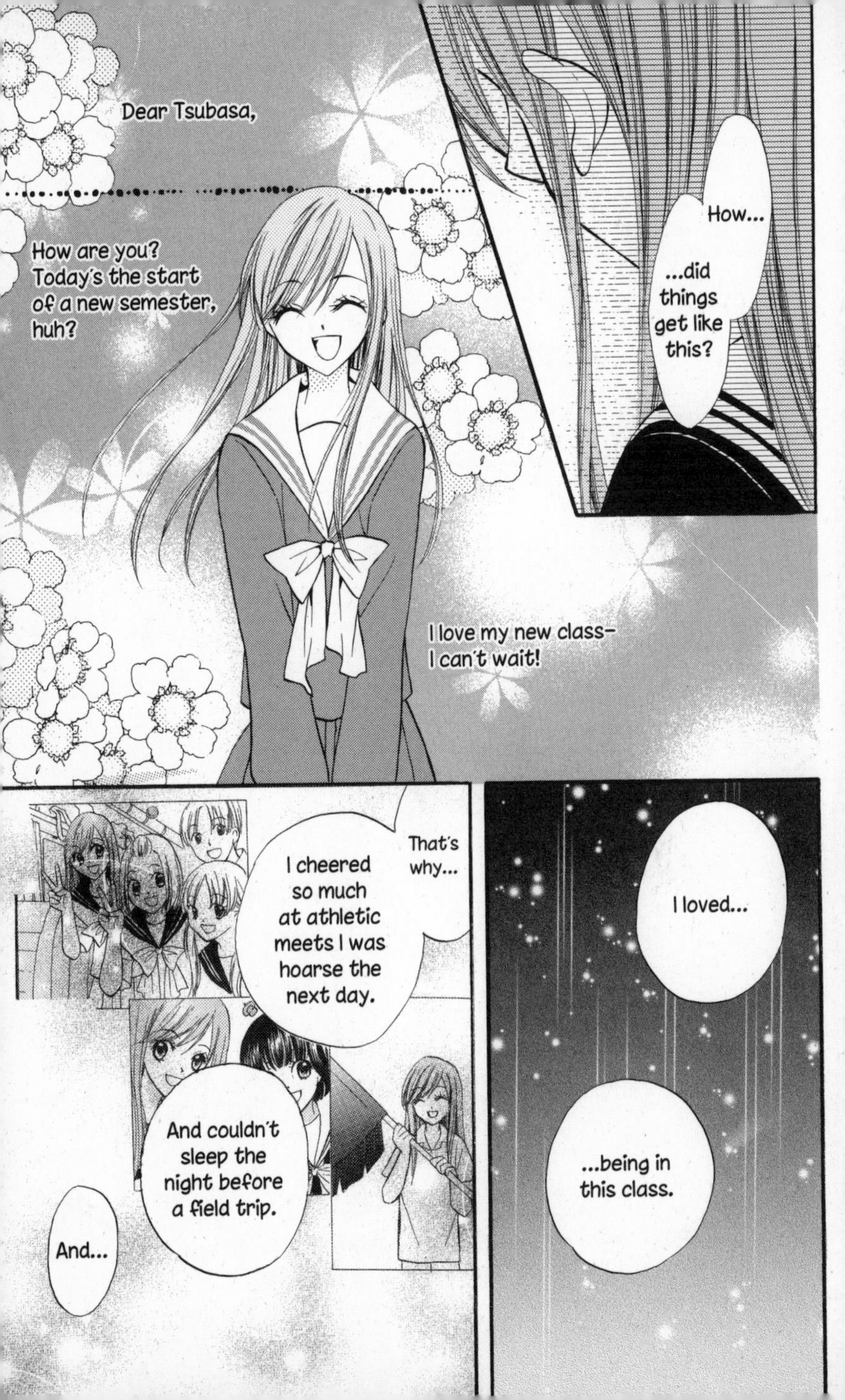
How...
...did things get like this?
Dear Tsubasa,
How are you? Today's the start of a new semester, huh?
I love my new class– I can't wait!
I loved...
...being in this class.
That's why...
I cheered so much at athletic meets I was hoarse the next day.
And couldn't sleep the night before a field trip.
And...

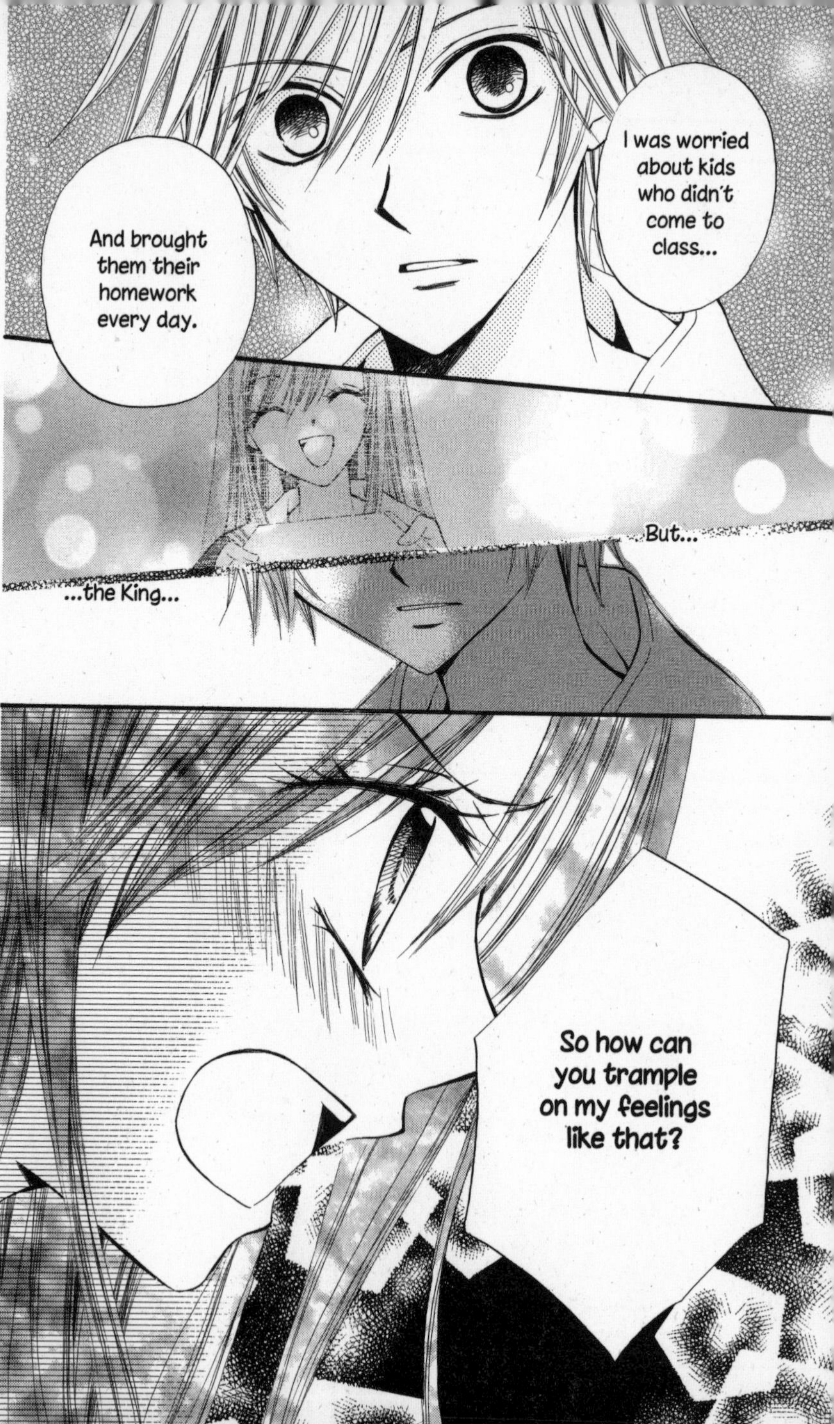
I was worried about kids who didn't come to class...
And brought them their homework every day.
But...
...the King...
So how can you trample on my feelings like that?

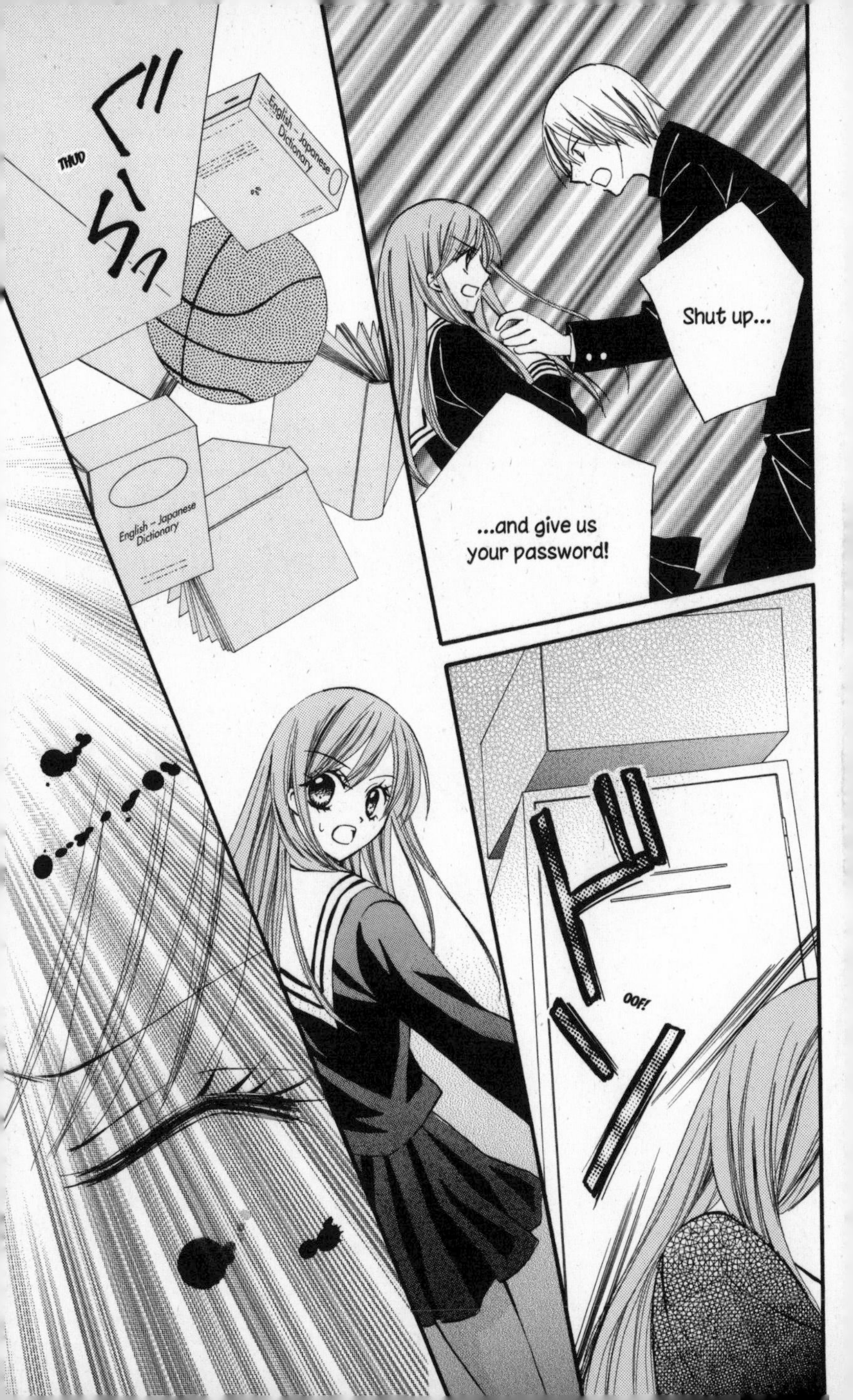

Shut up...
...and give us your password!
THUD
English - Japanese Dictionary
English - Japanese Dictionary
OOF!

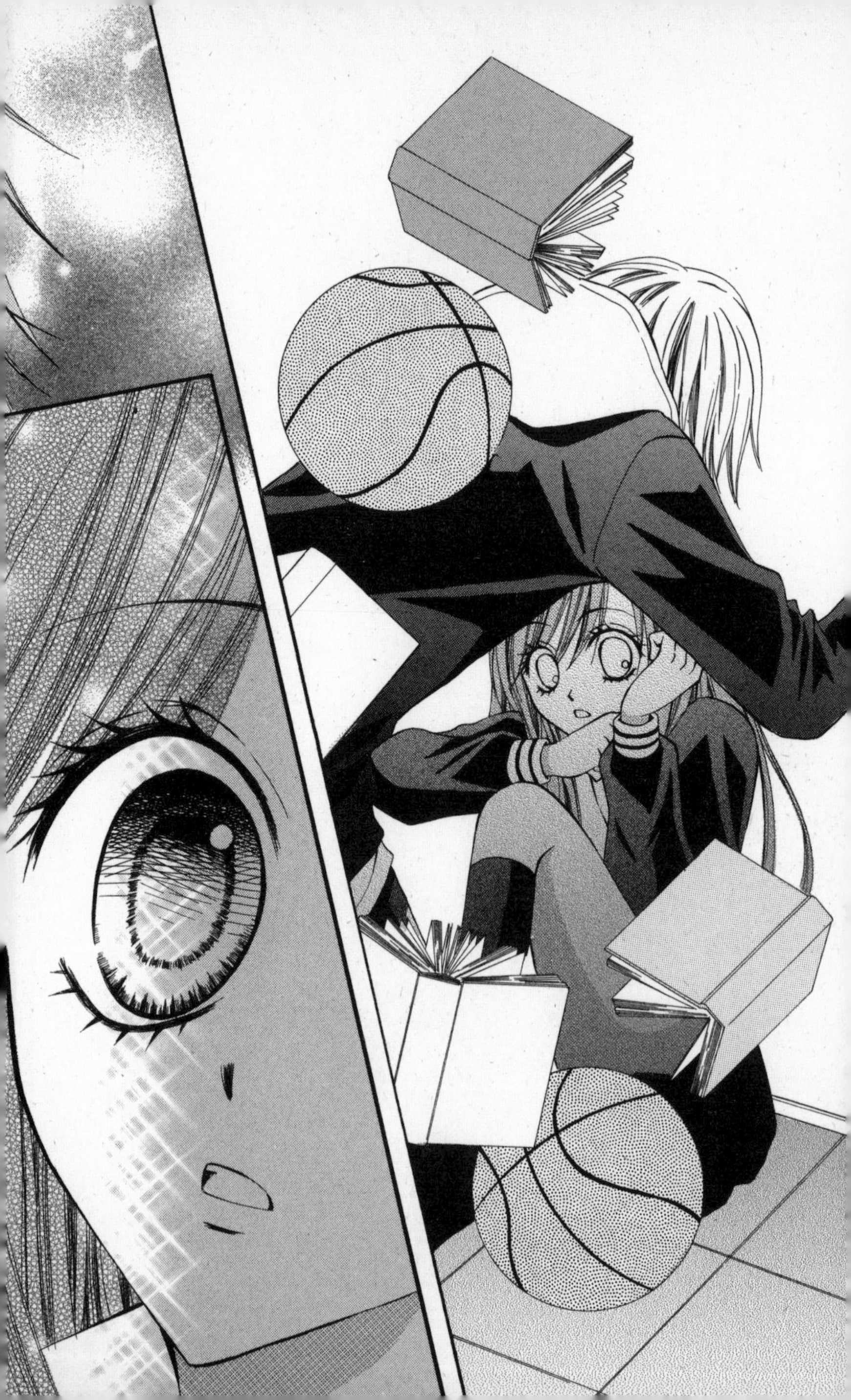

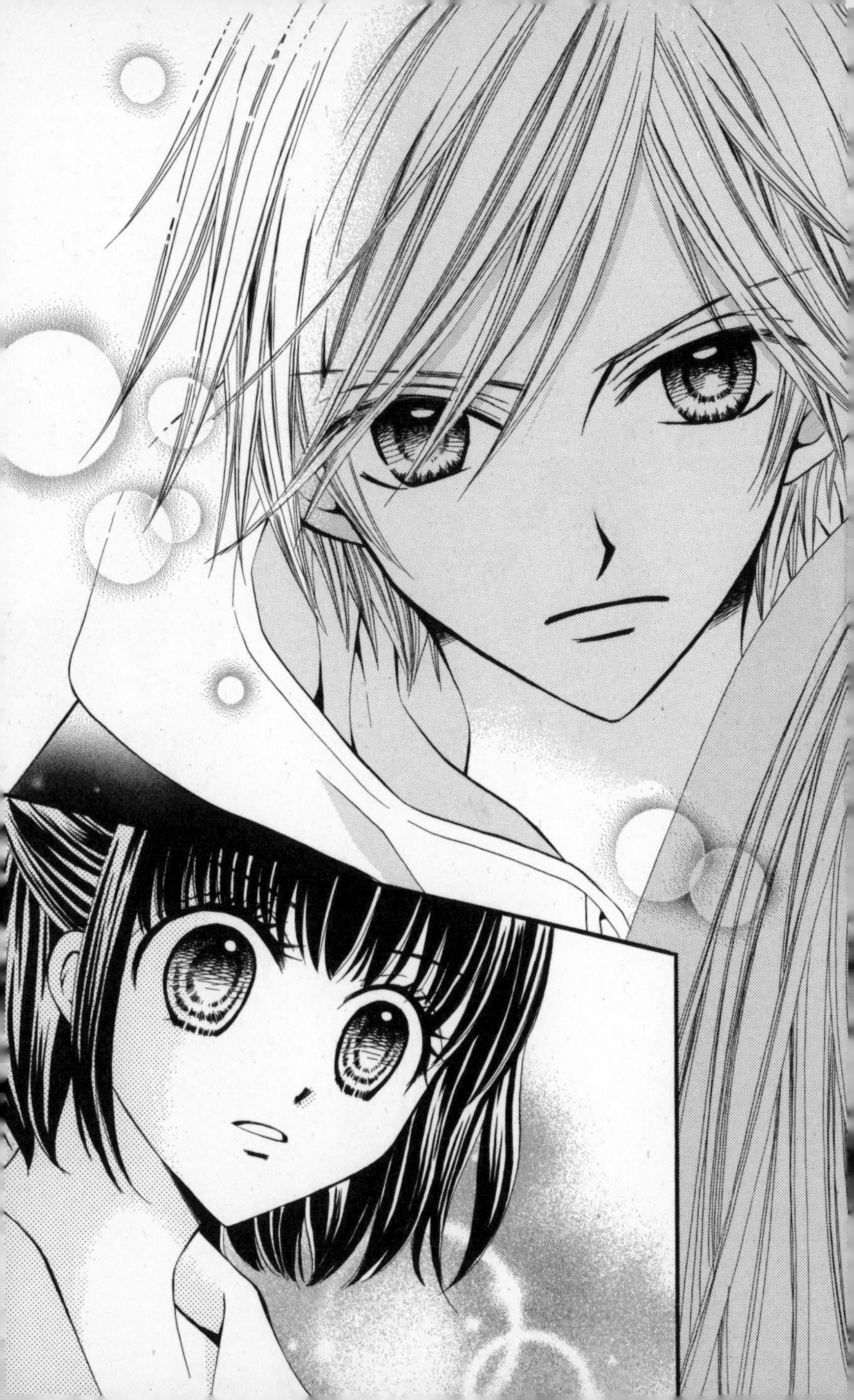

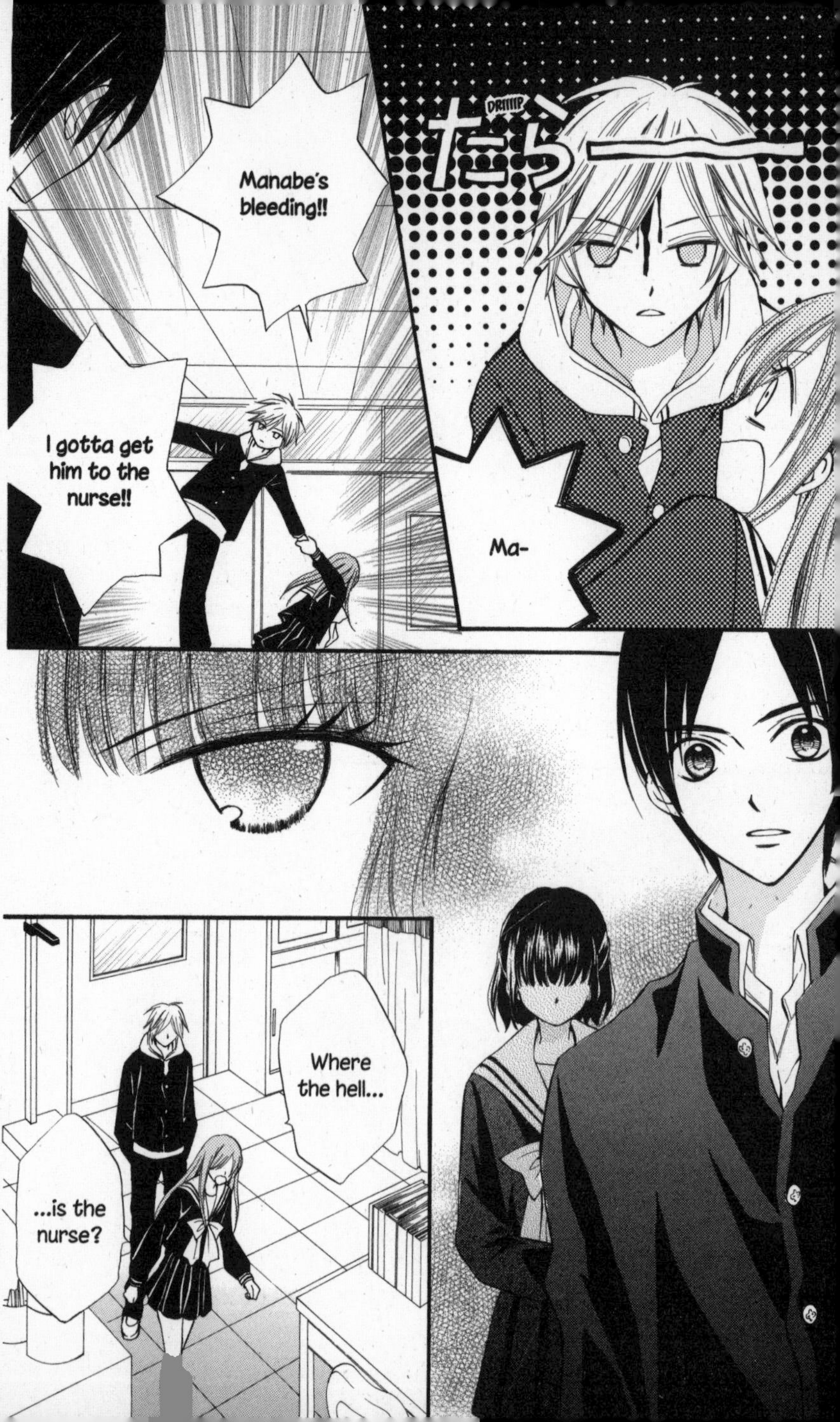
DRIIIP
Ma-
Manabe's bleeding!!
I gotta get him to the nurse!!
Where the hell...
...is the nurse?

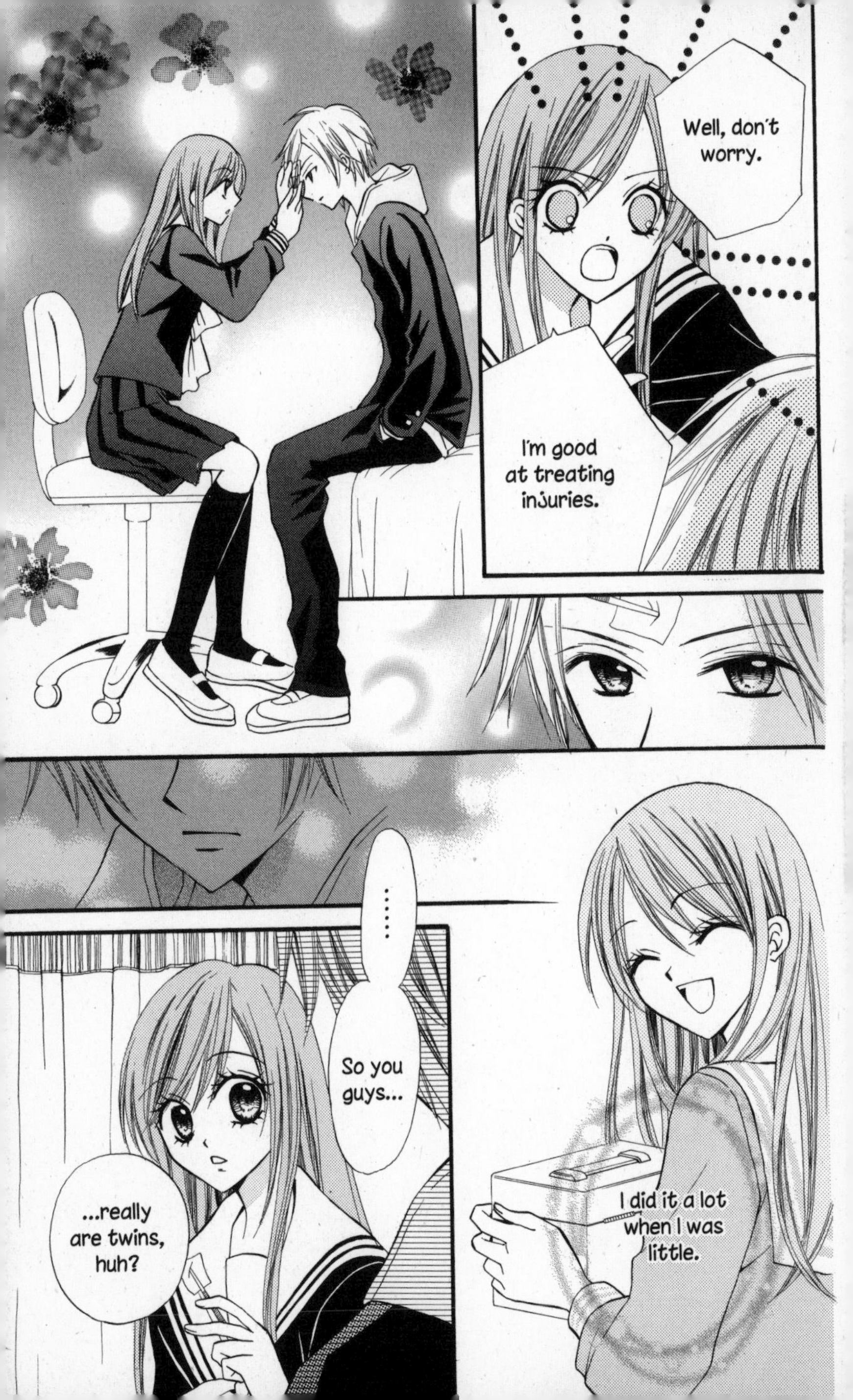
Well, don't worry.
I'm good at treating injuries.
I did it a lot when I was little.
......
So you guys...
...really are twins, huh?

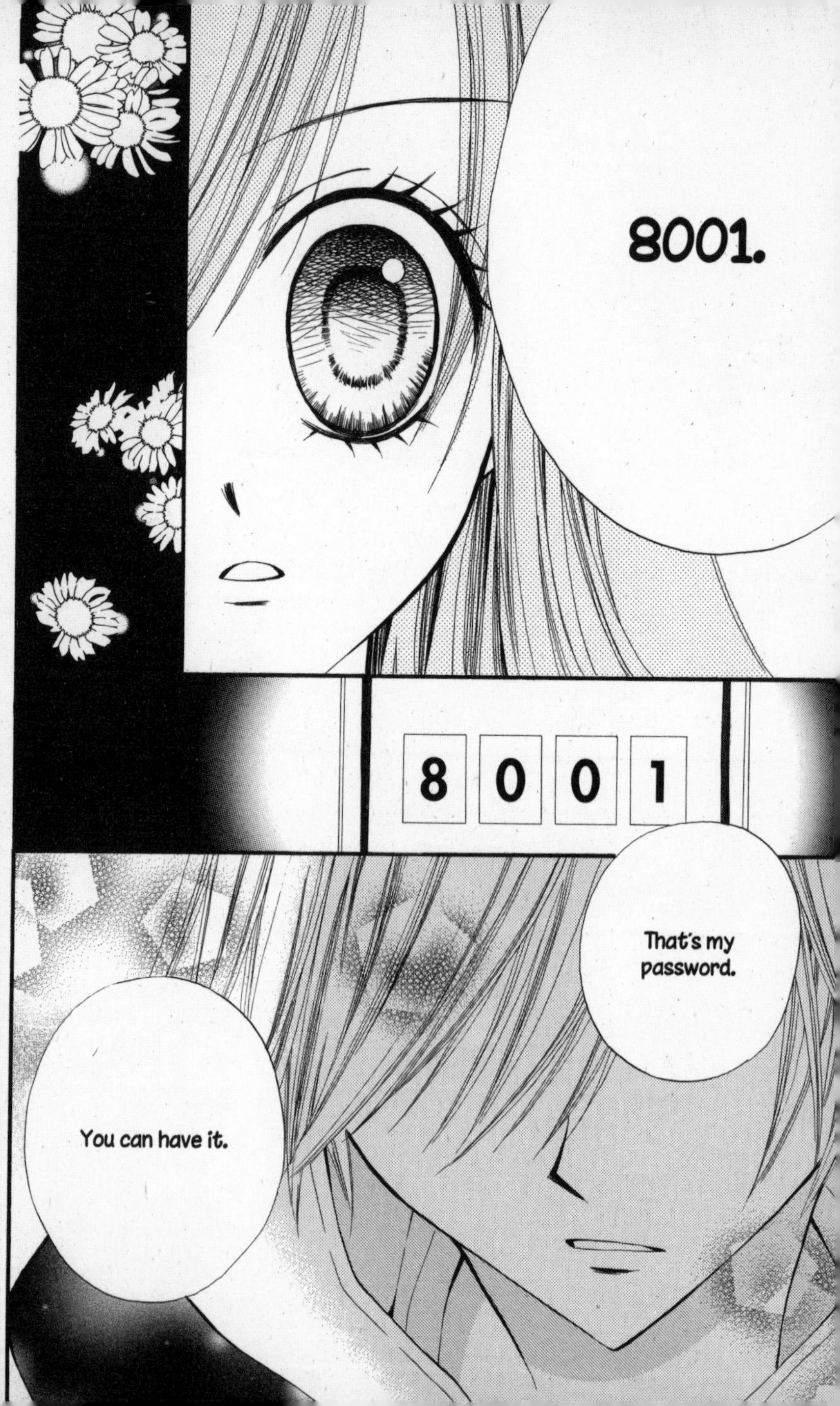
8001.
8 0 0 1
That's my password.
You can have it.

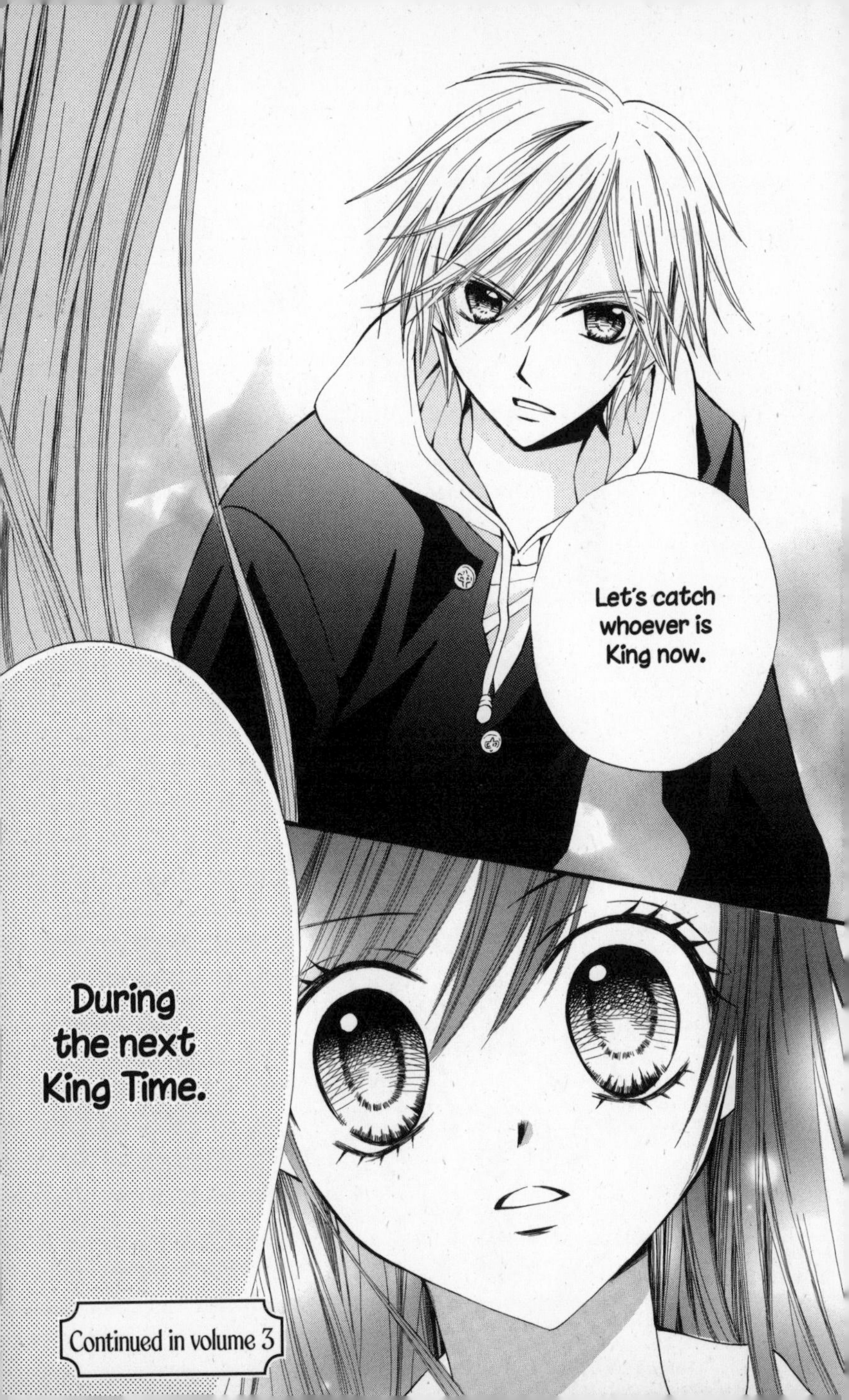
Let's catch whoever is King now.
During the next King Time.
Continued in volume 3

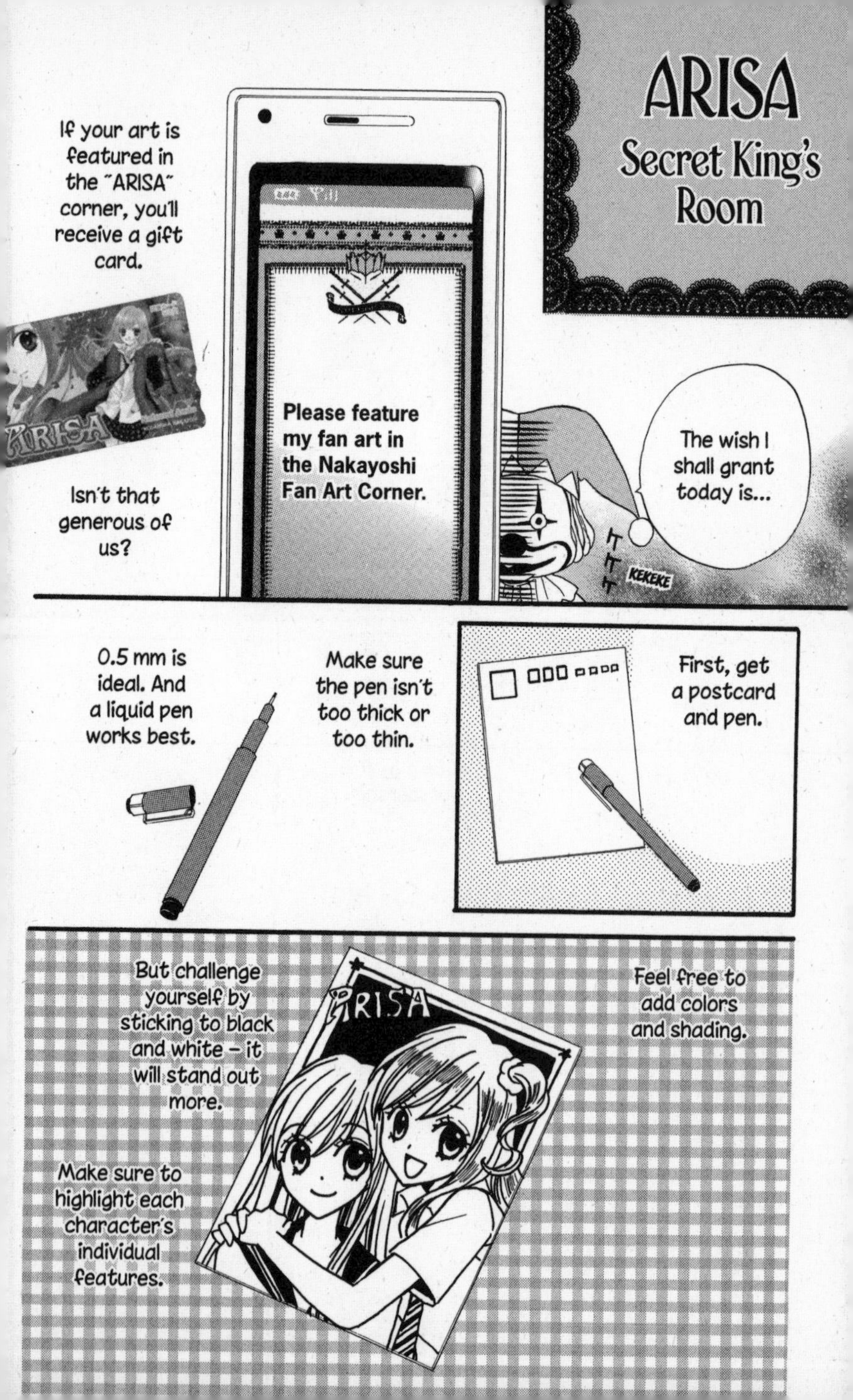
ARISA
Secret King's Room
The wish I shall grant today is...
KEKEKE
Please feature my fan art in the Nakayoshi Fan Art Corner.
If your art is featured in the "ARISA" corner, you'll receive a gift card.
Isn't that generous of us?
First, get a postcard and pen.
Make sure the pen isn't too thick or too thin.
0.5 mm is ideal. And a liquid pen works best.
Feel free to add colors and shading.
ARISA
But challenge yourself by sticking to black and white – it will stand out more.
Make sure to highlight each character's individual features.

Editors from ARISA will choose the winners.

I asked them what they are looking for in the fan art:

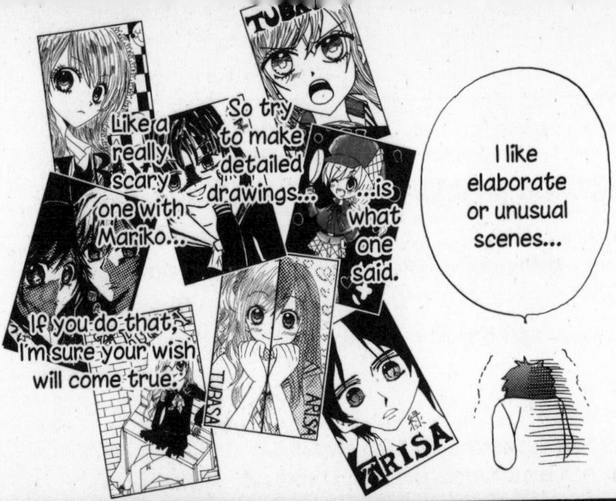

I like elaborate or unusual scenes...
Like a really scary one with Mariko...
...is what one said.
So try to make detailed drawings...
If you do that, I'm sure your wish will come true.
TUBASA
ARISA

We'll be waiting for art worthy of receiving the King's prize.

Address: 107-8652 Tokyo Akasaka Post Office PO Box 91
Nakayoshi Publishing Attn: ARISA Fan Art

Thank you:

T. Nakamura
S. Okada
M. Shirasawa
H. Kishimoto
M. Nakata
A. Nakamura
My assistants and editors at Nakayoshi
Red rooster
Takashi Shimoyama

Please send questions and comments to:
107-8652
Tokyo Akasaka Post Office PO Box 91
Nakayoshi Publishing

Natsumi Andō

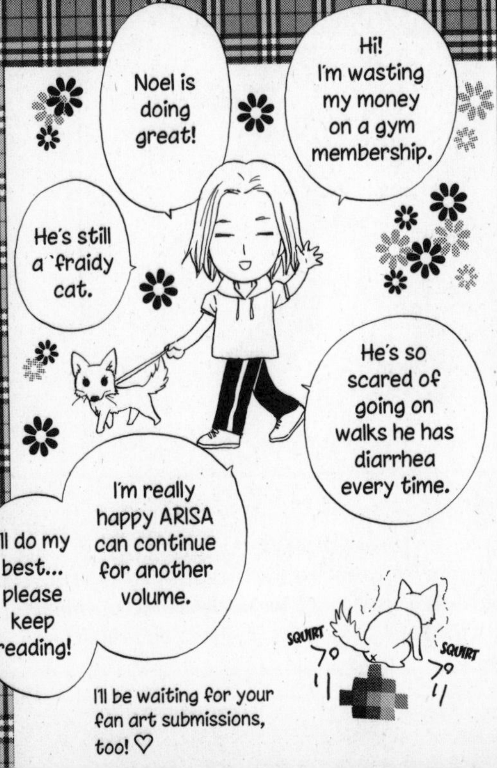

Hi! I'm wasting my money on a gym membership.
Noel is doing great!
He's still a `fraidy cat.
He's so scared of going on walks he has diarrhea every time.
SQUIRT
SQUIRT
I'm really happy ARISA can continue for another volume.
I'll do my best... please keep reading!
I'll be waiting for your fan art submissions, too! ♡

Translation Notes

Japanese is a tricky language for most Westerners, and translation is often more art than science. For your edification and reading pleasure, here are notes on some of the places where we could have gone in a different direction with our translation of the work, or where a Japanese cultural reference is used.

The King

In Japanese, there is no pronoun used to refer to the King. It is not clear in the Japanese whether the King is male or female. This is more difficult in English, so the King is referred to as "he" in this translation. Keep in mind this does not necessarily mean the identity of the King is a male (or isn't).

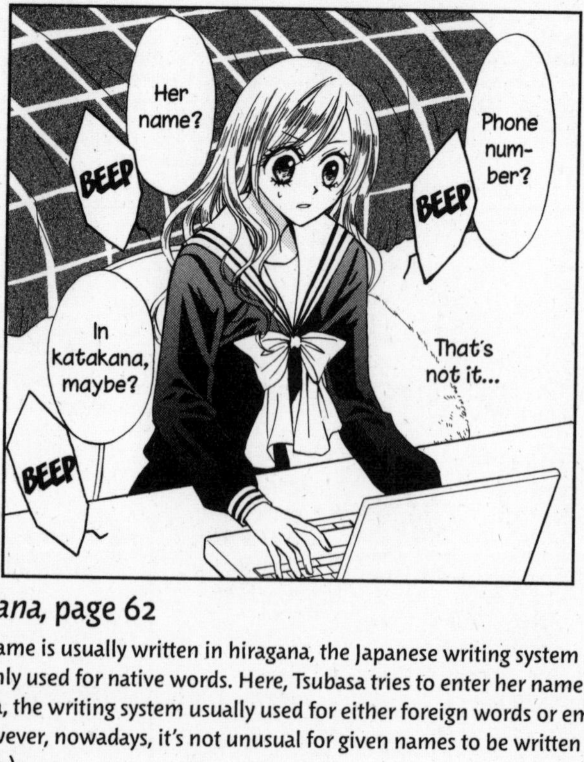
Phone number?
BEEP
Her name?
BEEP
That's not it...
In katakana, maybe?
BEEP

Katakana, page 62

Arisa's name is usually written in hiragana, the Japanese writing system commonly used for native words. Here, Tsubasa tries to enter her name in katakana, the writing system usually used for either foreign words or emphasis. (However, nowadays, it's not unusual for given names to be written in katakana.)

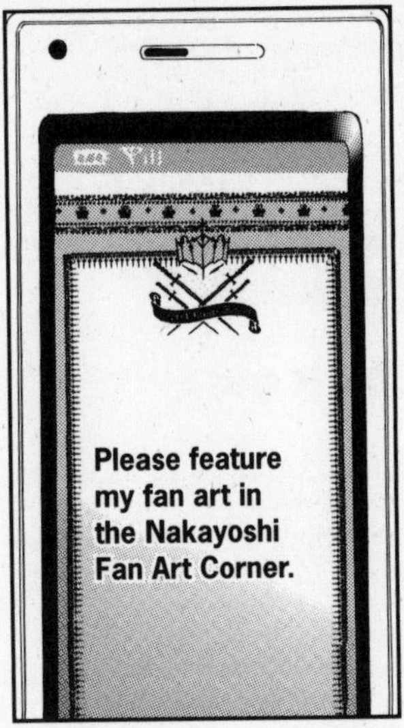
Please feature my fan art in the Nakayoshi Fan Art Corner.

Nakayoshi, page 164

Meaning "good friend," a monthly shōjo manga magazine published by Kodansha which features ARISA, among others.

THE Wallflower
YAMATONADESHIKO SHICHIHENGE

BY TOMOKO HAYAKAWA

It's a beautiful, expansive mansion, and four handsome, fifteen-year-old friends are allowed to live in it for free! But there is one condition—within three years the young men must take the owner's niece and transform her into a proper lady befitting the palace in which they all live! How hard can it be?

Enter Sunako Nakahara, the horror-movie-loving, pock-faced, frizzy-haired, fashion-illiterate hermit who has a tendency to break into explosive nosebleeds whenever she sees anyone attractive. This project is going to take far more than our four heroes ever expected; it needs a miracle!

Ages: 16 +

Special extras in each volume! Read them all!

VISIT WWW.KODANSHACOMICS.COM TO:
- View release date calendars for upcoming volumes
- Find out the latest about new Kodansha Comics series

SHUGO CHARA!

PEACH-PIT
CREATORS OF *DEARS* AND *ROZEN MAIDEN*

Everybody at Seiyo Elementary thinks that stylish and supercool Amu has it all. But nobody knows the real Amu, a shy girl who wishes she had the courage to truly be herself. Changing Amu's life is going to take more than wishes and dreams—it's going to take a little magic! One morning, Amu finds a surprise in her bed: three strange little eggs. Each egg contains a Guardian Character, an angel-like being who can give her the power to be someone new. With the help of her Guardian Characters, Amu is about to discover that her true self is even more amazing than she ever dreamed.

Special extras in each volume! Read them all!

VISIT WWW.KODANSHACOMICS.COM TO:

- View release date calendars for upcoming volumes
- Find out the latest about new Kodansha Comics series

KODANSHA COMICS

TOMARE!

[STOP!]

You're going the wrong way!

Manga is a completely different type of reading experience.

To start at the *beginning*, go to the *end*!

That's right! Authentic manga is read the traditional Japanese way—from right to left. Exactly the *opposite* of how American books are read. It's easy to follow: Just go to the other end of the book, and read each page—and each panel—from the right side to the left side, starting at the top right. Now you're experiencing manga as it was meant to be!